THE C# TYPE SYSTEM

THE C#
TYPE SYSTEM

Build Robust, Performant, and Efficient Programs

by Steve Love

no starch press®

San Francisco

Printed in the United States of America

First printing

27 26 25 24 23   1 2 3 4 5

ISBN-13: 978-1-7185-0158-4 (print)
ISBN-13: 978-1-7185-0159-1 (ebook)

Publisher: William Pollock
Managing Editor: Jill Franklin
Production Manager: Sabrina Plomitallo-González
Production Editor: Sydney Cromwell
Developmental Editor: Rachel Monaghan
Interior Design: Octopod Studios
Cover Illustrator: Gina Redman
Technical Reviewer: Jon Skeet
Copyeditor: Sharon Wilkey
Proofreader: Carl Quesnel
Indexer: BIM Creatives, LLC

For information on distribution, bulk sales, corporate sales, or translations, please contact No Starch Press® directly at info@nostarch.com or:

No Starch Press, Inc.
245 8th Street, San Francisco, CA 94103
phone: 1.415.863.9900
www.nostarch.com

Library of Congress Control Number: 2023012406

For my wife, Fran: best friend, fiercest
critic, and staunchest supporter

About the Author

Steve Love is a professional developer with over 20 years of experience using C# in a wide range of industries, including logistics, public services, and finance. He is the editor of *C Vu*—the members' journal of the ACCU (*https://accu.org*)—as well as a frequent speaker at conferences.

About the Technical Reviewer

Jon Skeet is a staff software engineer for Google, working on the .NET client libraries for Google Cloud Platform. He's a regular contributor to Stack Overflow, the creator of the .NET date/time library Noda Time, and the author of *C# in Depth*, now in its fourth edition. Jon loves diving into all aspects of C# and occasionally twisting it horribly out of shape.

BRIEF CONTENTS

CONTENTS IN DETAIL

4
IMPLICIT AND EXPLICIT COPYING 105

5
TYPES OF EQUALITY 139

6
THE NATURE OF VALUES
175

7
VALUE TYPES AND POLYMORPHISM
211

ACKNOWLEDGMENTS

This book has benefited greatly from the support, encouragement, and criticisms of many people. I'm extremely grateful to Jon Skeet, who provided honest and detailed feedback on all the material. Jon's expert eye caught many of my errors and incorrect assumptions early on, giving me the opportunity to do better! Any errors and inconsistencies that remain are wholly my fault.

Thanks also to the editorial and production teams at No Starch Press, especially Rachel Monaghan, Sharon Wilkey, Jill Franklin, and Sydney Cromwell, for their patience, diligence, and good humor.

The list of people who have in some way contributed to the content of this book is extremely long because the book distills a lot of knowledge I have somehow accumulated over more than two decades of reading books and articles, listening to talks at conferences, and just talking to other programmers. To all the people who are habitually generous with their time and wisdom, you're an inspiration, and I'm very grateful.

More directly, thank you to these busy folks who kindly reviewed chapter drafts and shared their thoughts: Andy Balaam, Tim Barrass, Jack Berry, Fran Buontempo, Liz Chadwick, Pete Goodliffe, Richard Harris, Kevlin Henney, Jez Higgins, Jon Jagger, Burkhard Kloss, Will Mainwaring, Chris Oldwood, Daniel Pludowski, Richard Poulton, Jackie Ungerer, Emyr Williams, and Matthew Wilson.

I'd also like to acknowledge the folks at JetBrains for their excellent .NET tools, without which writing this book would have been a great deal more difficult.

Special thanks to Francis Glassborow, whose help and encouragement led to my first published writing and, from there, to this book. His knowledge, wisdom, experience, and insight touch each one of these chapters.

INTRODUCTION

According to the C# Language Specification, "C# is intended to be a simple, modern, general-purpose, object-oriented programming language." C# may look simple on the surface, but it has hidden depths even in its most fundamental features. The type system is a central element of C# and is the foundation upon which all C# programs are built. This has been true from the earliest versions of C#, and will continue to be relevant as the language evolves. *The C# Type System* isn't a gallery of the latest language features, and we won't delve into every detail of the latest edition, because C# is constantly advancing; instead we'll focus on the language's rich support for creating your own types and examine how best to employ the type system to improve your designs and write clearer, simpler, more efficient programs.

Many languages allow users to define their own types, but C# is different in that it makes a clear distinction between classes, which are reference types, and value types. *Classes* are the default choice for implementing a design in C# and the general-purpose mechanism for custom types, as they support all the object-oriented features that C# has to offer. In contrast, *value types* are much more specialized, which is why they're often misunderstood and dismissed as an advanced feature that's irrelevant for most applications. It's true that value types aren't suitable for many custom types in an application, and they may not be necessary in every design, but they have several advantages that are frequently underappreciated.

Using typical real-world examples, this book will walk you through defining and implementing value types effectively and efficiently so that they work successfully with all the other types in your applications. Specifically, we'll explore the following:

- Why C# distinguishes between value types and reference types, and what that means in practice

- What makes value types different, both syntactically and semantically, from other types

- How incorporating value types can improve your code and help you express designs more clearly

- Which characteristics of value types, beyond those defined by the language, are most important to their role in an application

- Where you can use value types to enhance an application's performance

Who Should Read This Book

If you've learned the basics of C# and wish to expand your understanding of the language to become a better programmer, this book is for you. Nothing in the chapters that follow is particularly advanced, but the content is intended to help you understand some of the underlying features, principles, and concepts of C# programming. My hope is that this book will allow you to move beyond simply writing runnable programs using correct C# syntax to writing idiomatic and efficient C# programs that your colleagues can easily understand.

To follow the examples, you'll need experience with creating your own classes; familiarity with constructors, methods, and properties; and a basic understanding of how virtual methods can be overridden by derived classes. Some practice with exceptions, both in employing them and handling them to manage errors, will also be useful. An appreciation of the mechanics of defining generic types and methods, although not essential, will also be helpful; in particular, some experience using the generic collection classes provided by the Standard Library will give you insight into how generics work in C#. *The C# Type System* isn't a beginner's guide and doesn't discuss how to compile and run your code, but you aren't expected to know the dark corners of the language. That said, I hope that some parts of this book will amuse and perhaps even surprise more advanced users.

When features are fundamental, we sometimes become complacent about them. With that in mind, many chapters in this book cover details that experienced C# programmers might consider introductory. Those topics are intended to set the scene for some less widely understood concepts that depend on them.

If you have more than just a passing familiarity with C# code or experience with another object-based language such as Java or C++, I hope that the examples and commentary here will help you better understand C# syntax and semantics and better appreciate why C# is the language it has become.

The book doesn't cover all aspects of C# programming; the focus is intentionally on the interactions between value types and reference types. In that discussion, we'll venture into C# generics, collections, Language Integrated Query (LINQ), and threading, but only superficially. We *won't* be discussing unsafe code or C# pointers. (Actually, there's one mention of *managed* pointers. Otherwise, we're solid.)

We won't cover how to create web services, interact with databases, or write distributed programs intended for deployment as cloud or microservice applications, but the techniques and underlying principles of C# presented will help improve the applications you create for those domains and others.

If you've asked or been asked when a value type would be a better choice than a reference type in a C# program and found yourself unable to give a satisfactory response, you should find this book useful.

Organization and Requirements

The book is organized into eight chapters, each presenting a different aspect of value types in action:

Chapter 1: Making the Most of the Type System   Examines the importance of user-defined value types and how introducing even simple types in an application can make the code easier to read and understand. It covers the importance of accurate names, the benefits of encapsulating application-specific behavior, and ways to make your own types intuitive and simple to use.

Chapter 2: Value and Reference Types   Looks at why C# has both reference types and value types and compares them in detail. We consider how different kinds of objects use memory, what that means for their lifetimes, and how the differences between types affect construction, equality, and copying. We review nullable value types and compare them with the newer nullable reference type feature.

Chapter 3: Reference and Value Parameters Examines the four types of method parameters and how to pass arguments to them, as well as how passing behavior differs between value types and reference types. We distinguish between passing a reference type variable and passing an argument *by reference* and explore how that relates to mutability and side effects. We also consider how to pass value type instances by immutable reference to optimize performance.

Chapter 4: Implicit and Explicit Copying Discusses how values are copied in a program and how the differences in copy behavior between value types and reference types can have unintended consequences in our code. In particular, we distinguish between variables and values and explore how making value types immutable can help prevent some common copying-related errors. We also look at ways to mitigate the potential inefficiencies that copying can introduce.

Chapter 5: Types of Equality Covers the various ways that values can be compared for equality and what happens under the hood during these comparisons. Implementing value-based equality comparisons is a common source of error, so we'll walk through how to do so safely and correctly, as well as how to take advantage of facilities provided by the compiler for this purpose.

Chapter 6: The Nature of Values Outlines the characteristics and roles of different types in an application and how a value type's role is more than just being a convenient way to store data. We examine what *value semantics* means and what makes an object a good candidate to be a value type. We also consider the importance of ordering objects and distinguish between equality and equivalence.

Chapter 7: Value Types and Polymorphism Explores why inheritance isn't an appropriate form of polymorphism for value types, working through an example to demonstrate the problems that can arise. We look in detail at the difference between subclassing and subtyping, and we discuss how other kinds of polymorphism are more suitable for working with values.

Chapter 8: Performance and Efficiency Considers how different types affect an application's performance and how to precisely measure performance to make evidence-based decisions. The chapter covers how accepting default behavior can adversely affect our code's performance, while also addressing common myths regarding compiler-generated code and efficiency.

Many of the code snippets use a simple test to demonstrate a behavior or language characteristic. The examples use NUnit fluent-style assertions, which provide a commonly understood and compact way to represent the concepts being discussed. Several other unit-testing frameworks are available for C#, and you should be able to easily translate the NUnit test snippets to other styles.

It won't take long for you to discover that the code examples, on their own, usually don't compile in the form in which they're presented. For the sake of brevity, some details, such as importing namespaces or defining Main, are omitted. The code examples are intended to focus your attention on a concept rather than to show a legal program.

Modern Features

In recent years the language designers have put a great deal of effort into enhancing C#'s support for creating efficient, high-performance applications. While the central ideas of the language have remained unchanged, new facilities have been added, particularly with respect to simple value types, and new features incorporated to enable C# programmers to take advantage of value types to maximize application performance. This book explores some of those features but in the context of *classic* C# programming, not just high-performance computing. Some of those features can make your programs clearer for human readers, as well as more efficient at run time.

Most of the code examples throughout the book demonstrate concepts that have been widely used in C# over several versions, some using features that have been part of C# since version 1.0. For more recently introduced features, the minimum compiler version is indicated.

Using value types effectively in your applications requires some additional thought on your part, not just about how those types are designed, but also about how they're used. *The C# Type System* describes in detail how value types behave in a wide variety of scenarios, allowing you to write C# in a modern, idiomatic, and effective manner. Having a deeper understanding of how value types fit into the C# type system will help you enrich your designs and write better programs.

Why Value Types?

Whereas the *class* is the poster child of object-oriented programming and design, the humble *value type* is often overlooked. However, judicious use of value types can bring many benefits, including better performance. Value type instances aren't individually allocated on the heap or subject to garbage collection. Allocating objects on the heap carries a small performance penalty since the garbage collector must inspect every object in memory, whether or not it's in use, to ascertain whether it's eligible for collection.

Reducing the heap-based memory of a program is likely to mean the garbage collector runs less often and has to do less work when it does run. Reducing heap memory pressure is likely to improve the speed of the code you write. Although the garbage-collection algorithm has been carefully tuned to minimize its impact on a running program, avoiding garbage collection altogether is even more efficient.

Making all your objects into value types almost certainly won't magically improve your programs' performance, but there's much more to the value type story than simply performance, just as there's more to source code than a program, and more to programming than typing. Understanding value semantics can help you determine where you might employ value types in a design and how to implement them to best achieve your goal. Equally importantly, understanding value semantics will help you determine where a value type would *not* be appropriate.

Over the course of this book, you'll learn what value semantics means for C# programs, and how to use value types successfully and efficiently. Along the way, we'll look in detail at both how and why value types behave as they do. First, though, we'll explore using simple value types to make our code easier for humans to understand. Let's get started.

1

MAKING THE MOST OF THE TYPE SYSTEM

Clear and readable source code matters much more to humans than it does to computers. Whether we're trying to debug existing code or learning to use a new feature, we inevitably find ourselves reading through source code. It's important to ensure that our code is as readable as possible so that its meaning is clear to other readers. Code that's hard to follow or easily misunderstood is a breeding ground for errors.

One way to improve the clarity of our code is to use the type system to our advantage by creating our own types and giving them names that clearly describe their purpose. Good names are important for all the types in a system, but it's easy to neglect the simple value types that represent an application's most granular information.

In this chapter, we'll examine a short but unclear piece of code and improve it over several iterations through a series of techniques that will help you learn how to use the type system effectively. By the end of the chapter, you'll have a better understanding of how custom value types contribute to easy-to-understand code and how to incorporate a rich set of types into your designs.

We'll explore the following:

- How custom types can help express meaning and make code more self-documenting
- How to encapsulate domain-specific behavior to reduce errors
- Where to use some syntax features from C# v9.0 and v10.0 for compact and readable code
- How to make using custom types easy and natural in commonplace code

To begin, let's look at a simple example of value types in action and why they're such an important feature of our designs

The Value of Good Names

Choosing good names for identifiers can be difficult but has a major impact on the clarity of our code. Consider the Displacement method in Listing 1-1.

```
public static (double, double)
Displacement(double t, double v, double s)
{
    var x = v * s * Math.Cos(t);
    var y = v * s * Math.Sin(t) - 0.5 * 9.81 * Math.Pow(s, 2);
    return (x, y);
}
```

Listing 1-1: An example of bad variable naming

The method's three parameters—t, v, and s—are poorly named, and their purpose isn't immediately clear. We'll use this code throughout the chapter to explore a variety of ways to improve it and better define its intent.

The purpose of the Displacement method is to calculate the position of a projectile on its ballistic arc, given an initial angle and velocity, and the time elapsed since the projectile was launched. If you're familiar with the equations for projectile motion, you may recognize the algorithm, but the variable names provide no clue whatsoever to their purpose. When called, the Displacement method calculates the coordinate value of the projectile relative to its launch point, as illustrated in Figure 1-1.

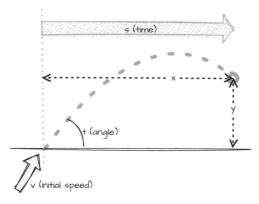

Figure 1-1: Projectile displacement

The angle, initial speed, and time labels in Figure 1-1 correspond to the t, v, and s parameters for Displacement, respectively. The x and y values correspond to the components of the tuple returned by that method. The projectile is launched with an initial speed, at a particular angle, and follows a well-defined ballistic arc. The Displacement method calculates the projectile's position on that arc after a given amount of time has passed.

We won't go into the algorithm being used here, as our focus is merely on making the purpose of this method more immediately clear. The first barrier to our understanding of the Displacement method is the meaning of its parameters and return value.

I have deliberately exaggerated the issue with single-letter names, but I've seen similar examples in the real world and thought, *What on earth do those parameters represent?* Even if we carefully inspect how the parameters have been used, determining their meaning requires being familiar with the equations. That is just poor code craft. Not all of us have kept up with our ballistics studies.

We want to make it as easy as possible for the reader to determine the purpose of the method, whether they're familiar with the topic or not. The quickest way to accomplish this is to ensure that the parameter names better reflect what they represent. In particular, code should avoid relying on specialist jargon. The t here stands for *theta*, which is typically used in physics to represent the magnitude of an angle, but even if we replaced t with the full word theta, readers unfamiliar with this mathematical convention would be unlikely to make that connection.

Instead of using potentially obscure single-letter names, let's give the parameters names that properly signify their meaning:

```
public static (double, double)
Displacement(double angle, double speed, double elapsedTime)
{
--snip--
```

By renaming t as **angle**, v as **speed**, and s as **elapsedTime**, we've made their purpose clearer. Changing velocity to speed might seem a minor change, but the names we use *matter*. While the use of v for *velocity* is common, speed is a more accurate description of this value's purpose. *Velocity* is a technical term with a specific meaning in physics; it represents *both* magnitude (speed) and direction. If we name code elements as accurately and properly as we can, we reduce the risk of those names being misunderstood.

Selecting good names is a first step toward making code clearer and easier to read. However, we can do much more to improve our code's clarity and remove ambiguity about what those identifiers represent. We might reasonably ask, for example, in what units the angle, speed, and elapsedTime parameters are measured. We'll address that later in the chapter, but first we need a more sophisticated mechanism than the double type allows.

Adding Clarity Through Types

All the Displacement method's parameters are of the same type: double. This makes it easy for anyone, including ourselves, to accidentally mix up argument values when calling the method—without any warning from the compiler.

The double type itself is not the specific culprit here; we'd have the same problem if the parameters were all string or all bool types. Even if each parameter were of a different built-in numeric type, plenty of potential for problems would still remain because of the presence of the implicit promotion rules between them. Moreover, clarifying the parameter names doesn't necessarily help the calling code, especially if the method is called with plain constant values like so:

```
var result = Displacement(.523, 65, 4);
```

Hard-coded values such as those used in this example are called *magic numbers* because there's no explanation of their meaning or purpose. We could replace the magic numbers with better-named variables to make their purpose clearer, but the caller of the method might still supply the arguments in the wrong order.

One common way for the calling code to address such out-of-order errors is to specify the parameter name for each argument. Let's see that in practice before looking at how to use different types to distinguish between the argument values.

Named Arguments

Embedding the parameter name for each argument being passed to a method makes the purpose of those arguments much more visible in the calling code, as shown here:

```
var result = Displacement(angle: .523, speed: 65, elapsedTime: 4);
```

This call to the `Displacement` method specifies which parameter receives each value being supplied. The caller must match the parameter names of the method but can order them in any way they like:

```
var result = Displacement(elapsedTime: 4, speed: 65, angle: .523);
```

Naming the arguments makes the order in which they're passed irrelevant. The compiler will ensure that each argument value gets passed to the right parameter according to its name, not its position.

This technique puts the responsibility of clarity onto the *caller* of the method. If the caller forgets or doesn't bother to name the arguments, the compiler won't warn them. The compiler will also give no warning if the caller mixes up the value for `angle` with `speed`. The code will compile, and the program will run, but it will almost certainly give incorrect results. Worse, the code might give a result that is almost correct for one specific set of arguments and then fail at the worst possible moment when different values are passed. The causes of errors like this can be difficult to track down.

Custom Types

The problems we're seeing with the `Displacement` method stem from using the double type to represent several distinct concepts. This is a variation of the *Primitive Obsession* code smell, which describes any code that has an overreliance on primitive types—that is, those types that are built into the language, such as `int`, `double`, and `string`.

Measurements and quantities such as speed commonly have numerical representations, but the double type is too general; it can be used to represent a wide variety of values, including `angle` and `speed` in our example, making it possible for the caller of the code to provide the wrong values. The `angle` and `speed` quantities are measured in different ways to mean different things. Using a raw double does not express the distinctions between them clearly enough. An angle of 45 degrees is a very different value from a speed of 45 meters per second.

The well-known solution to primitive obsession is to provide our own types with distinct purposes and to ensure that no implicit conversions exist between them. This enables the compiler to identify any arguments that are used inappropriately. Instead of using double to store quantities of `angle` and `speed`, Listing 1-2 defines two types that more positively convey their differences.

```
public struct Angle
{
    public double Size { get; set; }
}

public struct Speed
{
    public double Amount { get; set; }
}
```

Listing 1-2: Defining our own types

Our user-defined structs `Angle` and `Speed` are still quite primitive; they're merely wrappers around a public property (`Size` and `Amount`, respectively) that allows us to read or write the value being represented in each case. We'll improve this design, but for now it meets the immediate need: to distinguish values of angle from values of speed by their type rather than just by the parameter names.

Listing 1-3 demonstrates how we use these new types for the parameters to the `Displacement` method.

```
public static (double, double)
Displacement(Angle angle, Speed speed, TimeSpan elapsedTime)
{
--snip--
```

Listing 1-3: Using custom types as parameters

The C# Standard Library does not provide any abstractions for angles or speeds, but it does have the `TimeSpan` type, which is ideal for the `elapsedTime` parameter. Now the *type* of each parameter describes its value, so the parameter names have less responsibility. Any attempt to provide the arguments in the incorrect order, like substituting speed for angle, will cause the compiler to complain with a fairly obvious error message about not being able to convert `Speed` to `Angle`.

Encapsulation

Using distinct types for the values in a design emphasizes each value's role rather than its representation, making the code more self-documenting for human readers and allowing better error checking by the compiler. We've achieved our stated goal of preventing arguments to `Displacement` from being positioned incorrectly, but right now `Speed` and `Angle` are simple types that just *have* a value, rather than *being* a particular kind of value.

These types do not encapsulate their values in any way because their values are exposed as the publicly mutable `Size` and `Amount` properties. Those properties are currently the only way to create instances of those types, as we do in Listing 1-4, where we use object initialization to set the property values.

```
var result = Displacement(angle: new Angle { Size = .523 },
                          speed: new Speed { Amount = 65 },
                          elapsedTime: seconds);
```

Listing 1-4: Using object initialization to create inline argument instances

Using the public properties to set the values here is unnecessarily verbose. Listing 1-5 simplifies the syntax by adding constructors so we can create new instances directly with a value instead of having to set a public property.

```
public struct Speed
{
    public Speed(double amount)
        => Amount = amount;

    public double Amount { get; set; }
}

public struct Angle
{
    public Angle(double size)
        => Size = size;

    public double Size { get; set; }
}
❶ var result = Displacement(new Angle(.523), new Speed(65), seconds);
```

Listing 1-5: Adding constructors for Speed and Angle

Here, when we call `Displacement`, we construct the `Angle` and `Speed` instances with their values instead of setting their properties ❶. Now that the type names are more descriptive, the order of the arguments is not ambiguous, so naming the arguments is no longer so important.

These constructors use the *expression body syntax*, introduced for methods in C# v6.0 and available since C# v7.0 for constructors. With this syntax, instead of a block enclosed by braces {...}, the expression is a single assignment separated from the constructor's signature by the => symbol. Since `Speed` and `Angle` each have only a single property to initialize, the expression-bodied constructors are concise and convenient.

Compare the final line with Listing 1-4. The changes to `Angle` and `Speed` in Listing 1-5 allow us to construct the values we want instead of using the object initializer in each case. This reduces the amount of typing the caller has to do but, more importantly, expresses more directly that a `Speed` or `Angle` *is* a value instead of just *having* a value.

Immutability

Currently, our values are all mutable, but once we've given an `Angle` or `Speed` a value in its constructor, we don't need to allow that value to change. If we require an `Angle` with a different value, we can create a new instance with that value.

We achieve this immutability by removing the set accessor for the `Size` property of `Angle` to make it a read-only property. Then the only way to provide a value is via the constructor, and that value is permanent and immutable. We'll do the same for the `Amount` property of `Speed`, as shown in Listing 1-6.

```
public readonly struct Speed
{
    public Speed(double amount)
        => Amount = amount;

    public double Amount { get; }
}
```

Listing 1-6: Making Speed immutable

To ensure that the Speed instance can't change, we also make it readonly. The compiler will then ensure that no members of Speed can modify the state and will fail to compile any attempt to change an instance.

Designing our types to be immutable makes our code easier to reason about during code inspection because we don't need to consider the various ways that instances of our type might change. This is especially important in multithreaded programs, but making value types read-only can also improve performance in some circumstances by enabling the compiler to use certain optimizations.

Value Validation

Having introduced constructors for our types, we can use those constructors to check for invalid arguments and raise exceptions if the user passes illegal values. For example, sensible values for a speed must be nonnegative. In Listing 1-7, we check that the value given the constructor is not less than 0 and throw an exception if it is.

```
public Speed(double amount)
{
    if(amount < 0)
        throw new ArgumentOutOfRangeException(
            paramName: nameof(amount),
                message: "Speed must be positive");
    Amount = amount;
}
```

Listing 1-7: Prohibiting out-of-range values

The constructor of Speed validates the value provided, and since the constructor is the only way to provide a value for Speed, we ensure that only legal Speed values can be created. We should use the constructor to prohibit other illegal argument values, such as double.NaN, and perhaps even add an upper limit of the speed of light. If we attempt to create a Speed with an illegal value, we get a run-time exception.

The ArgumentOutOfRangeException type is defined in the Standard Library and is a good example of a descriptively named type. Note that in Listing 1-7, we name the arguments for the ArgumentOutOfRangeException constructor, *which takes two plain string parameters* (paramName: and message:). Otherwise, the order of those arguments is easily muddled, especially since the similarly named ArgumentException takes the same parameters in the reverse order!

Validating the parameter value in Speed's constructor is one example of encapsulation: we've put the validation logic in one place instead of scattering it among any methods that use it. Now, any methods that use a Speed instance automatically benefit from the range check performed by Speed's constructor.

NOTE *A major benefit of creating our own types is that we encapsulate their responsibilities, thereby reducing the responsibilities of the methods that use them. Minimizing duplicated code is yet another way we make our code clearer, easier to use, and much less difficult to maintain.*

The constructor for Speed establishes a *class invariant*—a condition that must hold for the lifetime of any instance of the type—specifying that a Speed value is never less than 0. The invariant can never be broken because we made Speed immutable. Once a valid Speed instance is created, its value never changes, and it's impossible to create a Speed instance with an invalid value.

Testing

By encapsulating the validation within the Speed type, we can also test the class invariant independently of any algorithms that depend on it. In Listing 1-8, we attempt to create a Speed instance with a negative value to test that the constructor throws an exception.

```
[Test]
public void Speed_cannot_be_negative()
{
    Assert.That(
        () => new Speed(-1),
        Throws.TypeOf<ArgumentOutOfRangeException>());
}
```

Listing 1-8: Testing constraints on Speed

Because the validation code is encapsulated within the Speed type, we need only this one test for it. We don't need to separately test that Displacement, or any other method using Speed, rejects invalid speed values. All the testing for Displacement can focus on ensuring that the algorithm is correct, without being concerned about parameter validation.

Using types for domain concepts, then, has several advantages. Code using our types is clearer because of the self-describing characteristics of the type. We separate concerns, making the program easier to understand and the testing more focused and specific. This makes the tests simpler, and easier to maintain when the code being tested needs to change.

Refactoring

Now that we've addressed the issues with the Displacement method's parameters, let's look at its method body to see if we can make further improvements by refactoring the implementation. Listing 1-9 shows our current code for Displacement.

```
public static (double, double)
Displacement(Angle angle, Speed speed, TimeSpan elapsedTime)
{
    var x = speed.Amount * elapsedTime.TotalSeconds * Math.Cos(angle.Size);
    var y = speed.Amount * elapsedTime.TotalSeconds * Math.Sin(angle.Size)
            - 0.5 * 9.81 * Math.Pow(elapsedTime.TotalSeconds, 2);

    return (x, y);
}
```

Listing 1-9: The current Displacement implementation

This code works correctly, but we have some issues to take care of. We've made the code more verbose by using the Speed, Angle, and TimeSpan types as parameters, requiring us to access properties of those parameters to obtain their values. Note that we use the TotalSeconds property here; one common error is to use the Seconds property of a TimeSpan object when the intention is to obtain the total number of seconds being represented, but Seconds returns only the seconds component of the TimeSpan. Given a TimeSpan representing 1 minute precisely, the Seconds property would return 0, while the value for TotalSeconds would be 60.

The Displacement method would be clearer if we could use the variables *directly* in the algorithm, like this:

```
    var x = speed * elapsedTime * Math.Cos(angle);
    var y = speed * elapsedTime * Math.Sin(angle)
            - 0.5 * 9.81 * Math.Pow(elapsedTime, 2);
```

The algorithm also relies on three hard-coded values. Magic numbers like this often indicate that we need to provide names to clarify their purpose. It's common to find the same magic number used in more than one place, so if the value changed for any reason, we'd need to hunt for every use and make sure we updated them all.

While we can see that multiplying by 0.5 is the same as dividing by 2, the meaning of 9.81 is much less obvious. The value 0.5 and the 2 used in the call to Math.Pow are simply arithmetic values; giving them names might obscure their purpose rather than clarifying it. The value 9.81, on the other hand, stands out as having a more significant purpose. Once again, to understand the meaning of this number, we need prior knowledge that 9.81 is an approximation of the effects of Earth's gravity on an object. We'll address this issue first with the simple fix of naming this value.

Replacing Magic Numbers with Named Constants

Replacing magic numbers in code with a descriptive name clarifies their meaning to readers unfamiliar with the algorithm's details. One way to do this is to create a new value type, similar to Speed, to represent the measurement. However, when we need only a few well-known values, using named constants to represent them is often simpler. For now, we need only a single value (for Earth's gravity). Listing 1-10 shows one way we could indicate that value's purpose by giving it a meaningful name.

```
public static class Gravity
{
    public const double Earth = 9.81;
}
```

Listing 1-10: Simple encoding of magic numbers

While the named constant for gravity is the simplest replacement for the magic number, we're passing up an opportunity to benefit from a more general type named Acceleration or something similar. Doing so would give us the greatest flexibility but would also increase complexity and maintenance. Keeping code simple has its own benefits.

We should, however, keep in mind that const values like this are baked into our code by the compiler, so if we change the value of Gravity.Earth but compile against a prebuilt assembly that uses the same constant, the overall program could use two different values for the same constant. In the interests of brevity and simplicity, we'll keep the const value and replace the hard-coded number in Displacement with the Gravity.Earth constant so human readers know immediately what it means:

```
--snip-- - 0.5 * Gravity.Earth * Math.Pow(elapsedTime.TotalSeconds, 2);
```

Now if we want to use a more precise approximation of gravity, we only need to change the constant's value instead of searching for all uses of the magic number 9.81, with the caveat that we must remember to recompile any other modules that use that constant.

Simplifying Properties and Values

Our Displacement method is now much more explicit about the meanings of the variables it uses. Listing 1-11 shows its current implementation.

```
public static (double, double)
Displacement(Angle angle, Speed speed, TimeSpan elapsedTime)
{
  ❶ var x = speed.Amount * elapsedTime.TotalSeconds
         ❷ * Math.Cos(angle.Size);
  ❸ var y = speed.Amount * elapsedTime.TotalSeconds * Math.Sin(angle.Size)
          - 0.5 * Gravity.Earth * Math.Pow(elapsedTime.TotalSeconds, 2);

    return (x, y);
}
```

Listing 1-11: Displacement using explicit property access

As noted earlier, accessing the properties of angle, speed, and elapsedTime makes the implementation quite verbose. The Displacement method would be tidier and easier still to read if we could access these properties directly in the operations where they were used. The speed variable's `Amount` property is being multiplied by `elapsedTime.TotalSeconds` ❶, and `angle.Size` is used to call both `Math.Cos` ❷ and `Math.Sin` ❸. Each use of our types requires us to explicitly obtain the corresponding property value in order to multiply two values together, and to pass them as arguments to the `Sin` and `Cos` methods.

We can't change the behavior of a `TimeSpan` variable to allow it to be multiplied by a `Speed`, but a `TimeSpan` can be multiplied by a `double` value. If we could use `Speed` instances as if they were `double` values, we would avoid having to explicitly use their properties in `Displacement`, making the method less cluttered; that is, we would be able to multiply `speed` and `elapsedTime` without using the `speed.Amount` property. Likewise, with the `Angle` type, we could call methods such as `Math.Cos` and `Math.Sin`, which both expect a `double` argument, with the `angle` variable directly if we could treat `Angle` instances as `double` values.

The result of the whole expression would be a `TimeSpan`, which is the result type from multiplying a `TimeSpan` by a number, so we'd need to access the `TotalSeconds` property at some point. Still, removing the need to access the `Amount` and `Size` properties of `Speed` and `Angle` would simplify and shorten the method's implementation.

One way to achieve that outcome is by defining our own implicit conversion operators. This approach is superficially appealing because it is simple to implement, but it has several drawbacks. Let's examine some of those potential problems.

Implicit Conversions

We define an implicit conversion for our own types by implementing an implicit conversion operator method and specifying the target type we need, as shown for `Speed` in Listing 1-12.

```
public readonly struct Speed
{
    --snip--
    public static implicit operator double(Speed speed)
        => speed.Amount;
}
```

Listing 1-12: Defining an implicit conversion for Speed

The target type here is `double`, and we simply return the value of the `Amount` property. We also add a similar conversion operator for `Angle` (not shown here) that returns its `Size` property. Now we no longer need to explicitly use `angle.Size` when calling `Math.Cos` and `Math.Sin`, and we can multiply `speed` by the `elapsedTime.TotalSeconds` value without needing to get the `speed.Amount` property. Compare Listing 1-13 with the earlier version in Listing 1-11.

```
var x = speed * elapsedTime.TotalSeconds * Math.Cos(angle);
var y = speed * elapsedTime.TotalSeconds * Math.Sin(angle)
        - 0.5 * Gravity.Earth * Math.Pow(elapsedTime.TotalSeconds, 2);
```

Listing 1-13: Using implicit conversions

Our implementation of Displacement is now much more compact—but we've introduced some hidden problems.

Unexpected Interactions

Implicit conversions weaken the interface to Speed and Angle by allowing them to participate everywhere that a double might be used, which means they can be used in expressions where it's not appropriate. For example, dividing a speed by an angle would be a legal expression, as demonstrated in Listing 1-14.

```
var angle = new Angle(.523);
var speed = new Speed(65);

var unknown = speed / angle;
```

Listing 1-14: Unplanned behavior resulting from an implicit conversion

This expression is valid owing to the implicit conversions from both Speed and Angle to double, but the result is meaningless, and we get no warning from the compiler. In addition, implicit conversions are usually invisible in our code. If we pass a Speed value to Math.Cos instead of an Angle, the resulting calculation errors could be hard to find.

Discarded Invariants

One of the benefits we realized by introducing a custom type for Speed was that we could encapsulate validation logic in Speed's constructor.

Allowing the implicit conversion from Speed to double means that code using the double result can breach the constraints on the allowable range of a Speed. In Listing 1-15, we subtract one Speed from another smaller value, leaving us with a result that's less than 0.

```
var verySlow = new Speed(10);
var reduceBy = new Speed(30);

var outOfRange = verySlow - reduceBy;
```

Listing 1-15: Unchecked constraints resulting from an implicit conversion

This subtraction expression, which is between two double values as a result of the implicit conversion from Speed to double, will run just fine. The result is negative and thus out of range for a Speed, but it's a perfectly legal double value.

To address this out-of-range value, we need to restrict the permitted operations on Speed and Angle so they make sense for those measurements. This was the whole purpose of introducing a class invariant for Speed to ensure that instances of it always have a valid value. Furthermore, we want to prohibit operations that make no sense, ideally in a way that would allow the compiler to tell us when something is wrong.

We introduced Speed and Angle as specific types so that we could tell them apart, and because using a plain double was simply too general to represent those measurements. However, the implicit conversions make Speed and Angle indistinguishable from double.

We can still achieve our objective of making our types easy to use in arithmetic expressions, but we need to keep control over which operations those types can perform. We'll allow specific operations on Speed and Angle without sacrificing their natural usage or compromising the encapsulation of the types.

Overloading Arithmetic Operators

Our initial motivation for introducing implicit conversions for Speed was to support the multiplication operation between a Speed and the TotalSeconds property of a TimeSpan value. Currently, we must use the Amount property of a Speed to make that calculation, as shown here:

```
var x = speed.Amount * elapsedTime.TotalSeconds *

--snip--
```

Arithmetic operations such as * for multiplication are predefined for the built-in numeric types like double. We can define the meaning of these symbols for our own types by providing arithmetic operator overloads.

Listing 1-16 shows the multiplication operator overload for Speed.

```
public readonly struct Speed
{
    public static Speed operator*(Speed left, double right)
        => new (left.Amount * right);

    --snip--
}
```

Listing 1-16: Supporting multiplication in Speed

We use a target-typed new expression, introduced in C# v9.0, to create the value for operator* to return. The compiler knows that the expected type is a Speed, as it's being directly returned, so we don't need to explicitly specify the type as new Speed(...). The compiler will infer the type according to the value expected by the left side of the expression.

Being able to multiply a speed value by a number makes intuitive sense; something might be traveling at double the speed of something else, for example. We implement the operator by creating a new Speed from the product of the Amount property and the value passed to the operator's parameter. The constructor for Speed will check that the result is within the allowed range of a Speed and will throw an exception if the result is out of range. We can demonstrate that this works with a simple test, such as Listing 1-17, where we attempt to multiply a Speed by a negative number.

```
var speed = new Speed(4);

Assert.That(
    () => speed * -1,
    Throws.TypeOf<ArgumentOutOfRangeException>());

var expect = new Speed(2);

Assert.That(speed * 0.5, Is.EqualTo(expect));
```

Listing 1-17: Testing the multiplication operator

We create a Speed and then verify that when we try multiplying it by -1, the constructor throws an exception. We also ensure that when we halve the value, the operation succeeds with the expected result.

We can define operator overloads for other arithmetic operations and specify precisely the expressions in which Speed is permitted to take part. Values commonly overload arithmetic operators, where it is appropriate to do so.

Not all values are arithmetic in nature, so we need to carefully consider whether to support those operations for a type. For example, creating our own value type to represent a UK postal code would be perfectly natural, but multiplying a postal code by a number or by another postal code makes no sense whatsoever, because postal codes are not arithmetic values. Examples of other nonarithmetic values include US ZIP codes and colors.

By contrast, Speed values should naturally take part in some, but not all, arithmetic expressions. It makes sense to be able to double a Speed, but not to multiply two Speed values together. We can use custom arithmetic operator overloads to control which expressions should be permitted, and by adding explicit support for them, we make Speed easier to use.

Determining a Need for New Types

Whenever we refactor a piece of code, we may discover a requirement or opportunity to introduce a new type. The need for the Speed and Angle types was fairly plain because we introduced them to replace primitive parameter variables. Not all missing abstractions are so obvious.

If we multiply a Speed by a number, the result is a new Speed, but our Displacement method multiplies a Speed by the elapsedTime value, which is not simply a number. Here we split that calculation into separate parts to make it clearer:

```
var tmp = speed * elapsedTime.TotalSeconds; // a Speed value
var x = tmp * Math.Cos(angle.Size);
```

As noted earlier, multiplying a Speed by a number intuitively produces a new Speed. Both tmp and x here are therefore instances of Speed, because of our implementation of the multiplication operator, but note that the elapsedTime.TotalSeconds value is not just any number but rather a TimeSpan instance representing a *time*. Mathematically, the result of this expression is not a speed at all: multiplying a speed by a time produces a *distance*, which we can represent directly in our code by introducing a new Distance type, as shown in Listing 1-18.

```
public readonly struct Distance
{
    public Distance(double amount)
        => Amount = amount;

    public double Amount { get; }
}
```

Listing 1-18: The Distance *type*

We can now create a new overload of operator* for Speed that multiplies a Speed directly by a TimeSpan and produces a Distance. Even better, we can define this overload in addition to the multiplication operator we've already defined that takes a plain double and returns a new Speed. Listing 1-19 shows both operator overloads.

```
public readonly struct Speed
{
    public static Speed operator*(Speed left, double right)
        => new (left.Amount * right);

    public static Distance operator*(Speed left, TimeSpan right)
        => new (left.Amount * right.TotalSeconds);

    --snip--
}
```

Listing 1-19: Overloading operator*

Overloading is versatile. We can overload a method with different types of parameters, and each overload can return a different type. The rules for overloading consider only the method signature—that is, the number and types of the parameters. We can therefore return a Speed from the overload taking a double and return a Distance from the method taking a TimeSpan instance.

Refining the New Type

Next, we need to add behavior to the new Distance type so that it will work correctly in our Displacement implementation. Multiplying a Speed by a TimeSpan gives us a Distance value, which we use in further arithmetic expressions of its own, shown in Listing 1-20.

```
var distance = speed * elapsedTime;     // a Distance

var x = distance * Math.Cos(angle.Size);
var y = distance * Math.Sin(angle.Size)
        - 0.5 * Gravity.Earth * Math.Pow(elapsedTime.TotalSeconds, 2);
```

Listing 1-20: The Distance *type in use*

The expressions for x and y are both now multiplying a `Distance` value by the double values returned from `Math.Cos` and `Math.Sin`. This code will fail to compile because `Distance` needs its own overload of operator*.

As with `Speed` values, multiplying a `Distance` by a simple number produces a new `Distance`. The results of `Math.Cos` and `Math.Sin`, apart from being out of our control, are scalar values, so when we multiply them by a `Distance`, the result is another `Distance`.

`Distance` also requires an overload of operator- so that the subtraction operation used in the calculation for the y value will compile. As with the multiplication, the expression on the right of the subtraction gives a scalar value, so we add the multiplication and subtraction operators for `Distance` in Listing 1-21.

```
public static Distance operator*(Distance left, double right)
    => new (left.Amount * right);

public static Distance operator-(Distance left, double right)
    => new (left.Amount - right);
```

Listing 1-21: Arithmetic operations for `Distance` values

With these overloads, we can use the `Speed` and `TimeSpan` values naturally together to produce `Distance` values. Those values, in turn, work seamlessly with the other required expressions.

Dealing with Design Imperfection

Our `Displacement` method returns a tuple of two `double` values. However, with our changes, the x and y values being returned have become instances of `Distance` rather than plain `double` values. This introduces another terminology problem with respect to the return value: in physics, a distance, like a speed, is always either 0 or a positive value. Combining a distance with the result of a trigonometric function like `Cos` is a coordinate position, rather than a distance, and can be negative.

We identified the `Distance` type from the result of multiplying a speed by a time, but there is no straightforward way to distinguish the result of `Math.Cos` or `Math.Sin` from a plain number like 0.5, denying us the opportunity to add an overload of the multiplication operator in `Distance` to return a new type, such as `Position`, rather than another `Distance`. We have reached the limits of exploiting the types we have chosen for modeling real-world concepts.

An obstacle like this may be the symptom of a deeper design smell, an indication that the problem might be resolved by a change in design perspective. In this instance, we may be able to achieve a more complete solution by reworking `Displacement`'s algorithm in terms of a full-fledged `Velocity` type instead of the relatively primitive `Speed` and `Angle` types. Exploring that solution is fairly complex, however, and best left to a text dedicated to modeling physics problems, leaving us with a pragmatic decision to make.

One option is to create a `Position` type, or something similar, to replace `Distance`. This approach suffers from the drawback that the arithmetic operations we defined for `Distance` do not apply so naturally to a `Position`. Moreover, if `Distance` is useful elsewhere in an application, it makes complete sense that when we multiply a `Speed` by a `TimeSpan`, the result is a `Distance`, not a `Position`.

An alternative approach is to do nothing and permit `Distance` to have negative values in the context of our application. While `Distance` would then be an imperfect representation of its counterpart in physics, this approach benefits from simple and natural uses in other areas. In Listing 1-22, we change the return type of `Displacement` to use `Distance` values directly, which further simplifies the implementation.

```
public static (Distance, Distance)
Displacement(Angle angle, Speed speed, TimeSpan elapsedTime)
{
    var x = speed * elapsedTime * Math.Cos(angle.Size);
    var y = speed * elapsedTime * Math.Sin(angle.Size)
            - 0.5 * Gravity.Earth * Math.Pow(elapsedTime.TotalSeconds, 2);

    return (x, y);
}
```

Listing 1-22 The new `Displacement` method

We could have retained the existing return type by returning the `Amount` property of the x and y variables. For example, if `Displacement` is already widely used, altering the type it returns might be intrusive. Nonetheless, introducing the richer `Distance` type more widely in an application has benefits similar to replacing the `double` parameters in `Displacement` with the `Speed`, `Angle`, and `TimeSpan` types.

However we decide to best serve the requirements of the application and its users, we can make more pressing improvements to the types used by `Displacement`. We're still explicitly using `angle.Size` in the `Displacement` method when we call methods in the standard `Math` static class. Before we attempt to address that, we need to think carefully about which units of measurement each type represents.

Encoding Units

Measurements like speeds, angles, and distances can have multiple representations, according to the units we're using for them. As our code stands, our `Speed`, `Angle`, and `Distance` types do not make those units clear. For example, is speed in meters per second or miles per hour? Are the angles measured in degrees or radians? Using the wrong unit of measurement can introduce errors that are particularly hard to diagnose.

All the equations used in `Displacement` assume that speed is measured in meters per second. This is a reasonable default, because meters per second is the universal International System of Units (SI) unit of speed, but it is implied. If we used a value for speed in kilometers per hour, we'd certainly get unexpected results.

Similarly, we don't currently specify the units for the Angle type. Code that deals with trigonometry commonly uses radians as the unit of measurement, and all the trigonometric functions in the Math class, such as Sin, expect angle values in radians. Most people, however, think of angles in degrees, and confusing the two is a common source of error.

This exposes the issue of usability: should our code require units that are more convenient for their implementation or more intuitive for the user? Let's consider this question and investigate whether it's possible to achieve both aims simultaneously.

C# has several features we can use to encode units, and one common approach is to represent the different units by using an enum. At first glance, this might seem the obvious solution, but it can cause issues. We'll explore this option and then investigate an alternative solution using static methods to create our types with the required units.

Itemizing Units with enums

An *enumerated type*, or enum, is a set of related strongly typed constants. Using an enum allows us to specify all the units our type supports. Listing 1-23 modifies our Speed type to use an enum to account for units.

```
public readonly struct Speed
{
    public enum Units
    {
        MetersPerSecond,
        KmPerSecond,
        KmPerHour
    }

    public Speed(double amount, Units unit)
    {
        if(amount < 0)
            throw new ArgumentOutOfRangeException(
                paramName: nameof(amount),
                message: "Speed must be positive");

        Amount = amount;
        In = unit;
    }

    public double Amount { get; }
    public Units In { get; }
}
```

Listing 1-23: Specifying units for Speed by using an enum

In this code, the Units enumeration is a public type nested within Speed, telling us that a speed can be represented in meters per second, kilometers per second, or kilometers per hour.

While it's tempting to abbreviate all the names, shortening MetersPerSecond *to* Ms *might be confused with* milliseconds, *so it's best to spell out the unit in this case.*

The constructor for Speed takes a number for the magnitude, and the user must provide one of the enum values for the required units. The user can use the In property later to discover which units were used when a particular Speed instance was created. By supporting several units of measurement, we make Speed more generally useful in other applications.

Representing supported units with an enum is superficially appealing because it seems simple to implement. However, this approach suffers from drawbacks that become apparent when we need to decide how to handle two values that have different units.

Value Comparisons and Unit Conversions

We need to consider conversions between units in several places in our Speed implementation. For instance, these two Speed values use different units but nevertheless represent the same speed:

```
var limit = new Speed(3.6, Speed.Units.KmPerHour);
var unit  = new Speed(1,   Speed.Units.MetersPerSecond);
```

These two Speed variables do not compare equal by default, because their Amount and In properties have different values. We can address that problem by customizing the behavior of equality comparisons for Speed, perhaps by converting both values to meters per second and comparing those values for equality. However, we have other, more subtle problems to solve too.

Earlier, we added operator overloads to Speed to support multiplying them by a scalar value or a time. Adding support for other arithmetic operations, including adding two Speeds, would be reasonable. We'd have to convert both values to a common unit in order to add them together, but what unit should the result be in?

One option would be to always scale every Speed value to meters per second—as we do in Listing 1-24 by using Speed's constructor to convert the parameter value according to the required units—but this approach introduces different problems.

```
public Speed(double amount, Units unit)
{
    if(amount < 0)
        throw new ArgumentOutOfRangeException(
            paramName: nameof(amount),
            message: "Speed must be positive");

    Amount = unit switch
    {
        Units.KmPerHour       => amount * 1000 / 3600,
        Units.KmPerSecond     => amount * 1000,
        Units.MetersPerSecond => amount,
```

```
                    _                 => throw new ArgumentException(
                                             message: $"Unexpected unit {unit}",
                                             paramName: nameof(unit))
        };
}
```

Listing 1-24: Scaling to a common value

This `Amount` property is assigned the value of a `switch` expression, available as of C# v8.0, which uses the type of the unit parameter value to scale the `amount` value to meters per second. The final _ selector in the `switch` is an example of a discard pattern and is used if the type of unit doesn't match any of the previous types. Here, we throw an exception in these circumstances, which might occur if we updated the `Units` enum with a new element without updating the constructor.

Note that we use the `unit` parameter only to determine how to scale the `amount` parameter. The units are not stored, so there's no `In` property either, because a `Speed` is always reported in meters per second.

Storing all instances of `Speed` using the same units solves the problem of equality comparisons and arithmetic operations, but it has other drawbacks.

Limitations of Using enums for Units

Being able to create `Speed` instances using various units is one thing, but users of the `Speed` type will also likely expect to be able to obtain the value in different units. The necessary conversions are straightforward to implement: Listing 1-25 repurposes `In` as a method to convert from the internal meters per second value to the units required.

```
public Speed In(Units unit)
{
    var scaled = unit switch
    {
        Units.KmPerHour       => Amount / 1000 * 3600,
        Units.KmPerSecond     => Amount / 1000,
        Units.MetersPerSecond => Amount,
        _                     => throw new ArgumentException(
                                         message: $"Unexpected unit {unit}",
                                         paramName: nameof(unit))
    };
    return new Speed(scaled, unit);
}
```

Listing 1-25: Obtaining converted values

The `switch` expressions, like those in Listings 1-24 and 1-25, are a characteristic of code that uses enumerations to distinguish different types. Those conversions can be cumbersome and would be a maintenance headache if we added new units.

Always converting Speed values to meters per second in the constructor presents an additional problem: the amount used to create a Speed is altered when we use units other than MetersPerSecond. To demonstrate the issue, consider Listing 1-26, where we copy a Speed value by using its Amount property and the same units used to create the original.

```
var original = new Speed(3.6, Speed.Units.KmPerHour);

var copy = new Speed(original.Amount, Speed.Units.KmPerHour);

Assert.That(original.Equals(copy), Is.True);
```

Listing 1-26: Testing equality of copied values

Most people would expect this test to pass, but it fails because original.Amount was converted to meters per second by Speed's constructor. The solution is to use the In method to make the copy, like this:

```
copy = original.In(Speed.Units.KmPerHour);
```

Converting all Speed values to the common unit of meters per second simplifies the implementation of Speed, but it's less convenient for users wishing to use Speed values measured in a different unit.

In the same way, although representing Angle values in radians is convenient when we need to use an angle in a trigonometric method, it's much less convenient for users. As mentioned earlier, most humans naturally think of angles in degrees rather than radians, and while the conversion is relatively simple, it's not part of the Standard Library.

We therefore still need to bridge the gap between what's intuitive for a user and what our code uses internally. Next, we look at an alternative approach to enumerations: using static methods that make our types convenient for humans to use and also work seamlessly with standard methods like Math.Sin.

Static Creation Methods

Instead of using a constructor with an enum parameter to represent units, we can employ the *Class Factory Method* pattern, which replaces public constructors with static methods to simplify creating instances. These methods have names that reflect the units they represent instead of requiring a separate enum value to identify those units.

In our Speed type, we use the class factory methods in Listing 1-27 to convert the input value to the units used by Speed internally, and return a new Speed instance with that converted value.

```
public static Speed FromMetersPerSecond(double amount)
    => new (amount);

public static Speed FromKmPerSecond(double amount)
    => new (amount * 1000);
```

```
public static Speed FromKmPerHour(double amount)
    => new (amount * 1000 / 3600);
```

Listing 1-27: Using class factory methods to encode units

Here, we have three separate ways to create a new Speed, each returning a Speed value converted from the units indicated by the name of the
method. When we require a new Speed instance, we use the method representing the units we want, as demonstrated in Listing 1-28.

```
var limit =  Speed.FromKmh(88);
var sound =  Speed.FromMetersPerSecond(343);
var escape = Speed.FromKmPerSecond(11.2);
```

Listing 1-28: Creating Speed values with our new class factory methods

Now there's no need for Speed's constructor to be public. If we allow
our users to create Speed instances directly with new, they'll bypass the class
factory methods and lose the benefits of the conversions. To avoid that, in
Listing 1-29 we make the constructor private.

```
private Speed(double amount)
{
    if(amount < 0)
    {
        throw new ArgumentOutOfRangeException(
            paramName: nameof(amount),
            message: "Speed must be positive");
    }
    Amount = amount;
}
```

Listing 1-29: Making our Speed constructor private

The constructor still contains the validation logic, but now it can be
called only by our class factory methods, with the argument suitably scaled
to meters per second. We can't prevent instances of Speed from being default-
initialized, but that results in the value being 0, a value that is the same
regardless of the units. Note that this is not always true, so we need to be
alert for cases where this does *not* hold. For example, 0 degrees Celsius is
not the same as 0 degrees Fahrenheit for temperature.

Symmetry in Design

While our class factory methods allow us to create Speed values from values
measured in different units, the internal representation of a Speed value is
in meters per second. To improve usability, we need to provide corresponding conversions in the other direction, so users of Speed can choose the units
they want when they obtain the value. In Listing 1-30, we add properties to
convert a Speed from its internal value to the unit encoded in the name of
the property.

```
public readonly struct Speed
{
    --snip--
    public double InMetersPerSecond => amount;
    public double InKmPerSecond     => amount / 1000.0;
    public double InKmPerHour        => amount / 1000 * 3600;

    private readonly double amount;
}
```

Listing 1-30: Viewing Speed in different units

We introduce a private data member that can be used from each of these properties. Doing so avoids *property forwarding* (one property invoking another to obtain the needed value) but also allows us to use an expression body for all three properties. This is largely an aesthetic choice; the most obvious alternative employing property forwarding is shown here:

```
public double InMetersPerSecond { get; }
public double InKmPerSecond     => InMetersPerSecond / 1000.0;
public double InKmPerHour        => InMetersPerSecond / 1000 * 3600;
```

Whichever approach we choose, we have, in effect, renamed the vague Amount property as InMetersPerSecond, whose purpose is to return the internal value of a Speed. The new name better expresses the property's meaning, matches the naming convention used for the other properties, and mirrors the class factory method FromMetersPerSecond.

By using similar naming conventions for the From... methods and the In... properties, we improve the clarity of Speed's interface. When we see a method such as FromKmPerHour, we naturally expect a corresponding method or property that provides the reverse conversion.

The class factory methods and corresponding properties provide a compact way of expressing units in either direction, and they force us to consciously make clear what we mean when we use a Speed.

Making Units Explicit

The Displacement method does not directly use the units of a Speed, because they are encapsulated in the multiplication operator we created for Speed and TimeSpan. Displacement *does* use the units of an angle, although those units are currently implied in the Angle.Size property, as shown in Listing 1-31.

```
var x = speed * elapsedTime * Math.Cos(angle.Size);
--snip--
```

Listing 1-31: Angles in Displacement

Both Math.Cos and Math.Sin require a measurement of an angle in radians, the SI unit for measuring angles. In Listing 1-32, we rename the Size property as InRadians to make the units explicit, and add the conversions to and from degrees as well.

```
public readonly struct Angle
{
    private Angle(double size)
        => radians = size;

    public static Angle FromRadians(double size)
        => new (size);

    public static Angle FromDegrees(double size)
        => new (size * Math.PI / 180);

    public double InRadians => radians;
    public double InDegrees => radians * 180 / Math.PI;

    private readonly double radians;
}
```

Listing 1-32: Adding unit conversions to Angle

Just as we did for Speed, we've added class factory methods to create an Angle in either degrees or radians, with corresponding properties to obtain the value in either unit. Now we can use an Angle easily with methods that require a value in radians, and using Angle is also much more convenient for users, who tend to think in degrees.

Choosing the Most Natural Usage

The Math.Cos and Math.Sin methods take a double argument, so we need to explicitly access the Angle.InRadians property to call those methods. We can't change the parameter type of those methods because they're part of the Standard Library, but we can add similarly named methods to the interface of Angle, which would allow us to encapsulate the explicit need to express the units. We can take three main approaches, each with its advantages and drawbacks, and each implemented by forwarding an Angle value in radians to its counterpart static Sin and Cos methods in the Math static class.

The most direct approach is to introduce Sin and Cos instance methods for Angle, passing the size field value to the corresponding Math method, like this:

```
public readonly struct Angle
{
    --snip--

    public double Sin() => Math.Sin(size);
    public double Cos() => Math.Cos(size);

    private readonly double size;
}
```

This approach works because we've chosen radians as the underlying unit for an Angle and we provide methods to convert to and from degrees.

Listing 1-33 shows how we would use these instance methods in the Displacement method. Compare this with Listing 1-31, where we called Math.Cos directly.

```
var x = speed * elapsedTime * angle.Cos();
var y = speed * elapsedTime * angle.Sin()
        - 0.5 * Gravity.Earth * Math.Pow(elapsedTime .TotalSeconds, 2);
```

Listing 1-33: Invoking our new instance trigonometric methods

Our second option is to provide our own static class mirroring the Math class with static Sin and Cos methods that take an Angle rather than a plain double for their parameters. Each method would need to access the InRadians property because it would not have access to the private size field. While this approach follows a common convention established by the static Math class, we lose the more compact usage of calling a member method.

The third alternative is to define *extension methods*, which are used as if they're instance methods but are defined in a separate static class. Listing 1-34 defines Sin and Cos extension methods to extend Angle's interface.

```
public static class AngleExtensions
{
    public static double Cos(this Angle angle)
        => Math.Cos(angle.InRadians);

    public static double Sin(this Angle angle)
        => Math.Sin(angle.InRadians);
}
```

Listing 1-34: Defining extension methods for Angle

The Cos and Sin methods in the static AngleExtensions class use the special syntax this Angle for their parameter, which tells the compiler that the method is an extension for an Angle. Each method simply forwards the InRadians property of the angle to its counterpart method in the Math namespace. We use the extension methods in exactly the same way we called the instance method versions in Listing 1-33.

One benefit of both the static and extension method implementations that is sometimes overlooked is that neither version depends on the internal representation of Angle. The instance member methods could also be implemented in terms of the InRadians property, but by extracting methods into separate types if they don't rely on the private implementation of Angle, we make the definition of Angle smaller and easier to comprehend. Chapter 6 explores this topic in more detail.

Whichever approach we choose, we'll encapsulate the explicit need to access the angle.InRadians property in order to call the Math trigonometric methods, making it easy for anyone to use our Angle type.

Returning Types Implied by Units

Class factory methods such as those we've introduced for `Speed` and `Angle` are a common way of simplifying the creation of value types. This technique is used by the Standard Library in the `TimeSpan` type, which has methods such as `FromSeconds` paired with a `TotalSeconds` property. The methods encode the units in their names, so creating value instances is very direct:

```
var speed = Speed.FromKmPerHour(234.0);
var angle = Angle.FromDegrees(30.0);
var seconds = TimeSpan.FromSeconds(4.0);
```

When we initialize these variables, we're being explicit about the expected type as well as the units, but a value of 234.0kmh must be a speed. We can't express this directly, but we can get close by using extension methods.

The value 234.0 is a double, and while we can't change its built-in definition, we can create extension methods for the `double` type, as Listing 1-35 shows.

```
public static class DoubleExtensions
{

    public static Speed Kmh(this double amount)
        => Speed.FromKmPerHour(amount);

    public static Angle Degrees(this double amount)
        => Angle.FromDegrees(amount);

    public static TimeSpan Seconds(this double amount)
        => TimeSpan.FromSeconds(amount);

    --snip--
}
```

Listing 1-35: Extending the interface of double

Each extension method returns a new instance of the type implied by the units in the method's name, so the `Kmh` method returns a `Speed` created using the `Speed.FromKmPerHour` class factory method. We use the new extension methods for `double` like this:

```
var speed = 234.0.Kmh();
var angle = 30.0.Degrees();
var seconds = 4.0.Seconds();
```

To avoid having to explicitly add the decimal point for the whole numbers, we could add overloads that extend `int` too. While this technique can be useful to allow a compact syntax for *literal* values, it works less well with variables like this:

```
double value = 234.0;

--snip--

var speed = value.Kmh();
```

However we choose to represent the units of measurement, they are a fundamental and intrinsic part of those types. Without units, a number is merely a number, even if the name of the type is descriptive. If we make the units of our value types easy to define and, just as importantly, make it easy to convert between common units, our custom value types will be easier to use and understand.

A Fully Formed Encapsulated Value

Long parameter lists are a hallmark of unclear code. They often indicate that a method doesn't have one clear responsibility and so would benefit from being refactored. Some or all of the parameters may be related in some way, indicating a missing abstraction. In either case, reducing method parameter lists is another way to improve the clarity of our code.

The Displacement method used throughout this chapter does have a single, clear responsibility and has only three parameters. However, two of those parameters are related: a velocity is a combination of a speed and a direction. We've defined rich types to represent speeds and angles that we can now combine to represent velocity with its own type. Listing 1-36 shows our new Velocity struct.

```
public readonly struct Velocity
{
    public Velocity(Speed speed, Angle angle)
        => (Speed, Direction) = (speed, angle);

    public Speed Speed { get; }
    public Angle Direction { get; }
}
```

Listing 1-36: Defining an encapsulated Velocity type

The Displacement method no longer needs separate speed and angle values, because they're now handled by the Velocity type:

```
public static (Distance, Distance)
Displacement(Velocity v0, TimeSpan elapsedTime)
{
    --snip--
```

Wrapping Speed and Angle into Velocity has two related benefits. First, methods like Displacement that required two parameters to represent a velocity now need only one. Second, `Velocity` is a new abstraction to represent a distinct concept. We can give `Velocity` its own specific set of behaviors and semantics and test the semantics independently of anything else.

Deciding Whether to Abstract Types

Introducing a new type like `Velocity` is not always the most appropriate approach. For example, consider the return value from the `Displacement` method:

```
public static (Distance, Distance) Displacement(
--snip--
```

With our discussion of using types to represent concepts, abstracting the tuple of `Distance` values as a new type may seem attractive. But we should consider several factors, including how the values will be used, whether there's any domain-specific behavior we want to associate with an independent type, and whether adding a new type will increase clarity or obscure it.

If a value is used in only a few places, creating a custom type to represent it may not be worthwhile, unless doing so will also reduce code duplication. If there's behavior that we want to encapsulate, we'll benefit from locating that behavior in one place and being able to test it in one place too.

Whether we can give a useful name to the new type is another important consideration. For example, the tuple of two `Distance` values is similar to a coordinate point, with the x and y values representing distance traveled in two dimensions from a point of origin. However, the name `Coordinate` would be misleading, because the elements of a coordinate are positions or points rather than distances. Now that we've created a `Velocity` type, however, we might consider revisiting the implementation of `Displacement` to try to resolve the design problems noted earlier when we introduced the `Distance` type. Our example doesn't warrant the extra complexity that would involve, so instead, we'll take a simpler approach.

In the value returned from `Displacement`, the names of the tuple components are more important than giving a name to a new type. Rather than defining a completely new type to return from `Displacement`, we can take advantage of rich tuple support in C# v7.0 and onward to directly "unpack" the return value into named variables, as shown in Listing 1-37.

```
var (range, elevation) = Displacement(velocity, TimeSpan.FromSeconds(0.9));

Assert.That(range.InMeters, Is.EqualTo(19.09).Within(.01));
Assert.That(elevation.InMeters, Is.EqualTo(18.78).Within(.01));
```

Listing 1-37: Unpacking tuple values

In this example we use *tuple deconstruction*, giving each member of the returned tuple value its own name. The compiler deduces the type of the range and elevation variables from the values in the tuple, so in this example they're both instances of the `Distance` type. This has the advantages of being both compact and descriptive enough for many purposes.

Summary

We define abstraction as selective ignorance—concentrating on the ideas that are relevant to the task at hand, and ignoring everything else. [. . .] If abstractions are well designed and well chosen, we believe that we can use them even if we don't understand all the details of how they work. We do not need to be automotive engineers to drive a car.
—Andrew Koenig and Barbara Moo, *Accelerated C++*

C# provides a few primitive types, especially for numerical values, and it can be tempting to use them as they are. However, a method that just takes a long list of double parameters can be difficult to decipher. This problem is not restricted to double; methods with a long list of string or bool parameters suffer from the same pitfalls, but the cure is broadly the same.

The built-in types are intended to be applicable to a wide range of problems and to be used as the building blocks for more sophisticated types. C# is, after all, an object-oriented language, and it allows us to model our problems with domain-specific types.

Replacing primitive values with our own types has several practical benefits. It can reduce accidental misuse and defects in the code by ensuring that arguments to methods are explicit. This allows us to take advantage of the compiler's type checking. If we mistakenly transpose arguments, our code will fail to compile. This kind of early failure prevents those mistakes from causing problems at run time or, worse, making it into a live production system and causing us considerable embarrassment.

Creating even simple types also allows us to provide descriptive names that make our code more self-describing. In turn, this spares us from having to produce a lot of separate explanatory documentation, which has a tendency to become stale.

By separating the behavior of a type from the algorithms that use it, and encapsulating that behavior in the type itself, we can test it independently of those algorithms. The type is more cohesive, and the algorithms are clearer and often simpler. Those algorithms themselves become easier for us to test, without having to also test the assumptions and implementations captured by the domain type abstractions.

2

VALUE AND REFERENCE TYPES

We can create new types in C# in several ways, and we need to consider the individual characteristics of each approach to determine which best suits our goals. In particular, knowing how value types differ from reference types helps us choose the right way forward, because these differences have significant and sometimes unconsidered implications when we're defining our own types. Certain trade-offs will affect how we design our type and what we can use it for. In this chapter, we'll investigate those differences and what they mean for our programs.

We'll explore the following:

- What choices we have when creating our own types
- Why C# has both reference types and value types

- How choosing one or the other affects construction, null checking, and other type behavior
- Why value type is not the same as value semantics
- Where different types are stored in memory and how that affects an object's lifetime

User-Defined Types

Most modern programming languages allow you to create custom types. The basic principles of user-defined types in C# will be familiar to programmers of many other languages, but some of the details are different. Therefore, in this section we'll examine the four kinds of user-defined types: structs, classes, and the newer records and record structs (introduced in C# v9.0 and v10.0, respectively).

It's important to recognize that the behavior of these types relies heavily on whether they are reference types or value types. Let's look briefly at each kind of user-defined type with these differences in mind.

Structs and Classes

Listing 2-1 defines a simple struct to represent colors.

```
public readonly struct Color
{
    public Color(int r, int g, int b)
        => (Red, Green, Blue) = (r, g, b);

    public int Red { get; }
    public int Green { get; }
    public int Blue { get; }
}
```

Listing 2-1: Defining a simple struct

The Color struct is marked readonly to indicate that instances of Color are immutable—that is, they never change their value. Correspondingly, none of the three properties (Red, Green, and Blue) has a set accessor, so their values can't be changed after they've been given initial values using the constructor.

The constructor in this example uses the expression body syntax (=>), which you saw in Chapter 1, instead of a body enclosed between braces {...}. We make the expression body a single-line statement by using *tuple assignment*, which assigns the tuple of three parameter values r, g, and b to the tuple of three properties. The compiler translates this syntax into an efficient assignment from the parameter values directly to the respective backing fields for the Red, Green, and Blue properties.

The readonly keyword in the struct's definition is not mandatory but reinforces that instances of Color are immutable. Immutable value types make our code easier to comprehend and may allow some optimizations by the compiler.

By contrast, if we define a `Color` class instead of a struct, we can't use the `readonly` keyword in its definition, although we can make it immutable by not providing set accessors for the properties. The only other difference in defining `Color` as a class is the use of the `class` keyword in the definition:

```
public class Color
{
--snip--
```

The definition of `Color` is otherwise identical to that in Listing 2-1.

The principal difference between these two types is that a class is a reference type, and a struct is a value type. Before we analyze the implications of this difference, let's look at record and record struct types.

Records and Record Structs

As of C# v9.0, we can define a record type with the `record` keyword. Records introduce a new syntax for compactly defining a type. Listing 2-2 creates a record type named `Color`.

```
public record Color(int Red, int Green, int Blue);
```

Listing 2-2: Defining a record

This example shows a *positional* record; the `Color` type has no body, but the type definition has its own positional parameters that are used by the compiler to generate a complete type. Behind the scenes, the compiler translates the record into a class definition, meaning that records are reference types. The compiler also translates the parameter names `Red`, `Green`, and `Blue` into public properties of the same name, along with a public constructor with matching parameters to initialize the property values. The positional parameters are also used by the compiler to generate other methods, including `Equals`, `GetHashCode`, and `ToString`, which are overrides of their counterparts in the `object` base class.

Listing 2-3 creates a new instance of the `Color` record and uses its properties exactly as if it were a class or a struct.

```
var tomato = new Color(Red: 255, Green: 99, Blue: 71);

Assert.That(tomato.Red, Is.EqualTo(255));
Assert.That(tomato.Green, Is.EqualTo(99));
Assert.That(tomato.Blue, Is.EqualTo(71));
```

Listing 2-3: Creating an instance of Color

Here, we use named arguments when constructing the `tomato` variable of type `Color` to emphasize the names given by the compiler to the constructor parameters. Note that the property names used in the assertions are identical to the names used in the constructor, and that both match the names used in the record definition.

NOTE *One important difference between records and structs or classes relates to handling equality comparisons between two instances, a topic we'll examine in more detail in "Identity Equality vs. Value Equality" on page 47.*

Very closely related to records are record structs, introduced in C# v10.0. In contrast to records, which are compiled as classes, record structs are translated by the compiler into struct definitions, making them value types. Otherwise, they're the same as records. Record structs are denoted by the `record struct` keywords, as shown here:

```
public readonly record struct Color(int Red, int Green, int Blue);
```

This record struct, much like the struct in Listing 2-1, is marked `readonly`. If we left out the `readonly` keyword, the properties generated by the compiler would be read-write properties, with both `get` and `set` accessors. Using the `readonly` keyword makes `Color` an immutable record struct.

Inheritance

One common way of representing relationships between classes and between records is to use *inheritance*, or deriving one type from another. However, we can't apply inheritance to structs or record structs; it's available only to reference types.

Another restriction of inheritance is that a record can inherit from another record but not explicitly from a class. Similarly, classes can't inherit from records. In every other respect, records follow the same rules and have the same characteristics as classes as far as inheritance is concerned. Classes and records can define virtual methods and properties, allowing a more derived type to provide its own behavior by overriding the method or property, and we can choose to ignore, override, or hide any virtual methods in a derived type.

In contrast, structs and record structs are implicitly *sealed*, meaning that inheriting from them is prohibited. If we attempt to derive from a struct or record struct, we get a compile-time error. Structs and record structs can't inherit from another user-defined type either.

Another restriction for a class or record is that it can inherit from only one base type. Any attempt at multiple inheritance results in a compiler error. If no base type is explicitly specified, `object` becomes the implied base class. As you'll see in "The Common Type System" on page 45, every type ultimately inherits from `object`, either directly or indirectly. For example, the `Command` class in Listing 2-4 implicitly derives from `object`, while the `DummyCommand` class derives explicitly from `Command`, implicitly inheriting from `object` via the `Command` base class.

```
public class Command
{
    public virtual IEnumerable<Result> RunQuery(string query)
    {
        using var transaction = connection.BeginTransaction();
        return connection.Execute(transaction, query);
    }

    private readonly DatabaseConnection connection;
}

public class DummyCommand : Command
{
    public override IEnumerable<Result> RunQuery(string query)
    {
        return new List<Result>();
    }
}
```

Listing 2-4: Inheritance syntax

This `Command` base class defines a virtual `RunQuery` method, which is overridden in the derived `DummyCommand` class to alter the method's behavior. A stub implementation like `DummyCommand` might be used during testing to avoid having the test code depend on the underlying data store's contents.

Any type may *implement* multiple interfaces, but it's important to understand that inheritance is quite different from interface implementation. When we implement an interface, the implementing method is, by default, *not* virtual. A class or record implementing a method from an interface can choose to make its implementation of the method virtual, but a struct or record struct cannot.

We can explicitly designate any member of a class or record as `protected`, as opposed to `public`, `private`, or `internal`. A protected member is accessible within the class declaring it and to any types that inherit from that class, but it's not visible to any other code. Since value types are sealed, it makes no sense for them to have virtual or protected members. If we try to make a method virtual in a value type definition or to define any protected fields, properties, or methods, we're rewarded with a compiler error.

We can choose to declare a class or record type as `sealed` so that it can't be used for further inheritance. Sealing a class does not affect what *it* can inherit, only what can inherit from it. It's common to seal classes that have value-like characteristics, such as `string`, or when we wish to restrict a class's behavior to that defined in our own implementation. If a class is intended to be immutable, whether or not it's intended to have value-like characteristics, sealing it ensures that its immutability can't be subverted by a mutable derived class.

Records are specifically intended to be value-like types and have value-like behavior defined for them by the compiler. This means we should seal record types unless we have a compelling reason not to do so. We'll look in detail at the meaning of *value-like* and why such types should be sealed in Chapters 6 and 7.

ABSTRACT BASE TYPES

An *abstract* type is one that can be used only as a base type for inheritance; it can't be instantiated directly with new. One implication is that while classes and records can be abstract, structs and record structs can't. It would make no sense: we can't inherit from a value type, so it could never be instantiated.

In an abstract type, we can designate methods and properties as abstract, meaning they have no implementation. Their purpose is simply to define the operations that a concrete type must support. An abstract method or property is implicitly virtual, but providing an implementation for one prompts a compiler error. Abstract types don't have to define any abstract members, but only abstract classes or records can have abstract methods and properties. Any abstract methods or properties remain abstract unless they're explicitly overridden in a derived class. Providing an implementation for an abstract method in a derived type makes that method concrete.

We can inherit one abstract type from another and choose to either provide implementations for the base type's abstract methods or leave them as abstract. We can only directly create an instance of a class or record that is fully concrete; that is, any and all abstract methods have been overridden.

If we inherit from an abstract class, we can't then inherit from any other class because that would be a form of multiple inheritance, which is prohibited.

It can be tempting to think of C# interfaces and their members as being abstract (especially for users familiar with C++, where interfaces are commonly implemented as classes with all pure-virtual methods), but that's not the case. An interface contains only signatures of methods and properties; they are neither abstract nor virtual.

Inheritance is a central feature of object-oriented code, but it applies exclusively to reference types. Inheritance—as well as the features that support it, such as virtual methods—is not appropriate for value types, in part because of the way value type instances use memory.

Type Instance Lifetimes

Value types and reference types differ in the way each uses memory and, more specifically, in the lifetime of their instances. Value type instances are short-lived, and their lifetime is bound to the lifetime of the variables that represent them. For value types, the variable *is* the instance; when we create a new instance of a value type, the target variable effectively contains the instance data—that is, the value of each field of the type.

In many cases, the lifetime of a variable is defined by a block, such as a method body or a foreach loop. Any local variables within the block cease to exist when the block ends. Alternatively, a variable might be contained in another object, in which case the variable's lifetime is defined by the lifetime of the enclosing object. Whenever we copy a value type variable by assigning it to another variable or passing it as an argument to a method, the copy is a whole new instance of the type in a *different* variable.

Reference type instances, on the other hand, are generally long-lived and can be referred to by many variables. When we create a new instance of a reference type, we're given a reference to that instance in memory. Whenever we copy that reference, we're not also copying the instance. The original reference and the copy both refer to the same instance. References are stored in *reference variables.*

All reference type instances are allocated on the heap. Their lifetime is managed by automatic garbage collection, which releases their memory when they're no longer needed by the program. An object is considered unused when the garbage collector determines that no other live references to that instance exist. While reference type instances are not subject to their scope, reference variables *are* subject to scope, so when one goes out of scope, it's no longer a live reference to an instance. The lifetime of a reference type instance, then, is determined by the lifetimes of *all* the references to that instance.

A cost is associated with being allocated on the heap, because the garbage collection process takes time while the program is running. Ensuring that unused heap memory is properly cleaned up is a complex operation and may interrupt a program's normal execution for a short time, so an overhead is associated with reference types.

Value types don't require the overhead associated with garbage collection. The memory used by a value type instance can be freed when the lifetime of its variable ends. To understand lifetime a little better, let's look more closely at what we mean by *variable* in different contexts.

Variables

A *variable* is simply a named area of memory. We use this name—or *identifier*—to manipulate a memory location during the variable's lifetime. C# has five main kinds of variables:

Local variables

These are block-scope variables, where a *block* might be a method with a statement body, the body of a loop, or any section of code delimited by matching braces, {}. When control leaves a block at the closing brace, any variables that are local to the block go out of scope. When an exception is thrown in a block, the control flow also leaves that scope and any containing scope until the exception is caught or the program exits.

Instance fields

These are normal data members, known as *fields*, of structs and non-static classes. Each instance of a type has its own copies of any instance fields. The lifetime of an instance field is defined by the lifetime of the object to which it belongs.

Static fields

These fields are associated with a type, rather than individual instances of the type. The lifetime of a static field is normally tied to an application, so the instances associated with static fields are usually released when an application exits.

Array elements

Individual elements in an array are all variables. We can access a particular element by its index and alter the element instance if it is mutable.

Method parameters

The parameters in a method definition are technically called *formal parameters* but are commonly known as just *parameters*. A parameter's scope is the body of the method, exactly as if the parameter were declared as a local variable within the method's body. In code that calls a method, we pass *actual parameters*, better known as *arguments*, that correspond to the method's parameters.

Regardless of its kind, a variable always has an associated type. This might be an explicitly declared type, as in the declaration int size, or, for local variables, the type might be implied with the var keyword. If the variable's type is a reference type, the variable's *value* is a reference. A non-null reference is a handle to an instance somewhere on the heap. If the variable's type is a value type, the variable's value is an instance of the type.

Variables vs. Values

It's not always easy to intuit what counts as a variable and what counts as a value, but the distinction is important:

- *Variables* can be assigned to, although a readonly field variable can be assigned only within a constructor of the type of which it is a member, or using field initialization (which we'll discuss in "Field Initializers" on page 58).

- *Values* are the results of expressions—such as the result of calling new, the return value from a method, or a constant expression such as a literal number or string literal. Values *can't* be assigned to, but we use them to initialize variables by using assignment or passing them as arguments to method parameters.

Variables, for the most part, have names. Strictly speaking, individual array elements don't have their own names, but for an array variable arr, the expression arr[*index*] is essentially the element's identifier. A value can have a name but doesn't require one: the expression 2 + 2 produces a new value, but it is anonymous unless we assign that value to a variable.

The type of a value defines what an *instance* looks like. Among other things, the type might have multiple fields that need space allocated in memory when an instance of the type is created. The type of a variable defines the sort of value it can contain.

A value is just a pattern of bits. The type is a formal specification for interpreting that bit pattern to give it meaning in a program. Two values with identical bit patterns may be interpreted differently if they are different types. A pattern of bits that are all 0 means one thing if the type is `long`, but something else entirely if the type is `DateTime`.

A variable of value type directly contains its data, whereas a variable of reference type contains a reference to its data. More precisely, reference variables have a value that is a reference to an object somewhere on the heap. Put simply, a reference refers to an instance of a reference type; the value of a reference type variable is a reference.

The relationship between variables and values is that all variables *have* a value, although the value can't be accessed until the variable has been definitely assigned.

Definite Assignment

We can't read the value of a variable unless the compiler is satisfied that the variable has definitely been given an initial value. More formally, a variable can be read only after a value has been *definitely assigned* to it. The C# Language Specification precisely defines what constitutes definite assignment, but the essence is that a variable must have been assigned or initialized with a value at least once before its value is read.

If we try to obtain the value of any variable that hasn't been definitely assigned, the compiler raises an error to tell us that this isn't allowed. For example, when we declare a local variable within a method, it is uninitialized unless or until we assign a value to it. Such variables are initially considered *un*assigned. Conceptually, at least, an unassigned variable doesn't have a value.

When we assign something to a variable, we give that variable a new value. When we read from a variable, we obtain its value. Variables and values are both *expressions*, meaning we can evaluate them to produce a value, as long as they have been definitely assigned.

To reiterate, attempting to read a value from any variable that hasn't yet been definitely assigned is an error. When we use a `var` declaration for a local variable, we must provide an initial value where the variable is declared, because the type of the variable is inferred from the type of the value being assigned to it.

Instances and Storage

Now that we've clearly defined variables and values, we can explore how they relate to type instances. Whether an instance is a value type or a reference type affects where it is allocated and managed in memory; as a result, value type variables have some peculiarities that don't apply to references.

Value types do not always live on the stack, despite common misconceptions. Values for local variables are most often tied to the block scope of a method, and so might be associated with a stack frame for the method, but values can also be contained within another object as a member or an element in an array. Let's examine this more closely by looking at some examples of how variables are embedded in objects.

Embedded Values

If a variable is a field embedded within an instance of another type, its value is allocated within the memory for its enclosing object. This is especially important for value type variables that directly contain the instance of their type. Consider the Color struct in Listing 2-5.

```
public readonly struct Color
{
    public Color(int r, int g, int b)
        => (Red, Green, Blue) = (r, g, b);

    public int Red { get; }
    public int Green { get; }
    public int Blue { get; }
}
```

Listing 2-5: Defining a Color struct with multiple fields

The Color struct has three properties representing the components of an RGB color. When a Color value is used as a field or property in a class, an instance of that class will wholly contain a Color value on the heap. Take, for example, the Brush class in Listing 2-6, which has several fields, one of which is a Color type.

```
public class Brush
{
--snip--
    public enum BrushStyle { Solid, Gradient, Texture }

    private readonly int width;
    private readonly Color color;
    private readonly BrushStyle style;
}
```

Listing 2-6: A Color value embedded within the Brush class

The Brush type is a class and therefore a reference type. When we create an instance of any reference type, it's allocated on the heap. The Brush class has three fields, one of which is a Color instance, which itself has three fields (Red, Green, and Blue). An instance of Brush might look roughly like Figure 2-1 in memory.

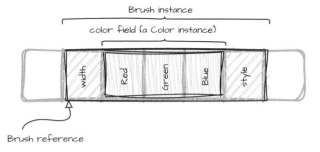

Figure 2-1: A Color value embedded in a Brush instance on the heap

When we create a new `Brush`, the instance is created on the heap and we're given a reference to it. The `color` field occupies memory directly within the memory space for the `Brush` instance. If we implemented `Color` as a record struct instead of a struct, the outcome would be the same. Record structs are value types in exactly the same way as structs and are allocated directly within the memory space of any enclosing object.

Value type instances are not individually garbage collected, but if a value type instance is embedded in another object that has been allocated on the heap, the *memory* used by the value type instance will be reclaimed during garbage collection of the enclosing object.

The lifetime of the `Color` instance represented by the `color` field is tied to the lifetime of the `Brush` instance. When the garbage collector determines that the `Brush` instance is no longer used, it will free up the memory for that instance, including the embedded `Color` value.

Array Elements

When a value type instance is an element in an array, it isn't (strictly speaking) a field of the array object, but the value is still embedded within the memory for the array. Arrays are always allocated on the heap, regardless of the type of their elements. When we create an array, we're given a reference to it. To illustrate, consider this array of `Color` values, where `Color` is a struct:

```
var colors = new Color[3];
```

The `colors` variable here is a reference to an array of three `Color` instances on the heap. The memory layout of the `colors` array might look like Figure 2-2.

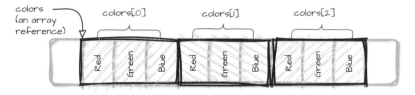

Figure 2-2: An array of Color structs in memory

In the colors array, each element is large enough to store the three int backing fields. If the element type had more fields, each element would require more space on the heap. If the Color type were a record struct rather than a struct, the layout would be identical; recall that the compiler translates record structs into structs.

Reference variables, by contrast, are all the same size, regardless of the number of fields declared in the type definition. The memory required for an array of references is determined only by the number of elements, not the size of each instance.

Whether the elements of an array are references or value type instances, the array is always on the heap, and the array variable refers to its elements. If the garbage collector determines that the array is no longer in use—that is, no live reference variables to it exist—then the memory for all of its elements is freed in one go.

Embedded References

Reference fields are also embedded in their enclosing type, but their instances are not. If we had implemented Color as a reference type in Listing 2-5, rather than a value type, the layout of a Brush instance would be somewhat different. The color field of the Brush class would be a reference, as illustrated in Figure 2-3.

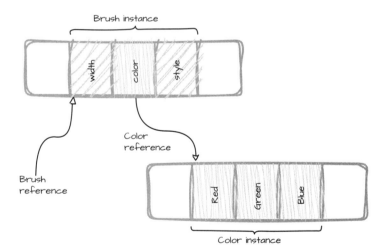

Figure 2-3: A color reference field embedded in a Brush instance

Instead of containing the entire instance of Color within its own memory, the Brush type's color field refers to a separate Color instance somewhere else on the heap. Reference type instances are always allocated on the heap and are independent of one another. This applies to any reference type, so it would be true if we implemented Color as either a class or a record.

The lifetime of the Color instance here is *independent* of the Brush instance. When the Brush instance is no longer used and its memory is released, the

`Color` instance will remain in memory until the garbage collector determines that it's no longer needed.

Field and Property Layout

All user-defined types can contain instance fields and properties. However, structs and record structs have one restriction that does not apply to classes or records: a value type definition can't embed a field of its own type.

You've already seen how value type instances directly contain their fields. If a type has a field that is itself a value type, that field also directly contains *its* data. If the type of that field is the same as its containing type, the compiler is unable to determine how to create it. Consider the simple struct in Listing 2-7 that embeds an instance of *itself* as a field.

```
struct Node
{
    Node p;
}
```

Listing 2-7: A struct containing an instance of itself

This example will not compile. The compiler can't know how to lay out the contained field named p, because p's type isn't fully defined at the point where it is declared. The same is true of properties, because even automatic properties require a backing field, though that field is hidden from us.

The same reasoning applies to an indirect dependency, illustrated in Listing 2-8.

```
struct Tree
{
    Node root;
}
struct Node
{
    Tree leftChild, rightChild;
}
```

Listing 2-8: A struct with a cyclic dependency

Neither the `Tree` type nor the `Node` type can be created here because the layout of each depends on the other. This might sound draconian, but in practice it's rarely a problem, and we have an easy workaround: if we change the definition of either `Tree` or `Node` to make it a reference type, the compiler will accept this code. The rule applies only to value types because, as mentioned previously, references are always the same size regardless of the type to which they refer. This means the compiler doesn't need to know the layout of a class or record to establish a reference to it.

Boxed Values

References can refer only to objects on the heap and can't refer to individual value type instances, even those enclosed within a reference type object. The only way for a reference variable to individually refer to a value type instance is to make a copy of the value, put that copy on the heap, and refer to the copy with a new reference. The process of creating a copy and storing it on the heap, known as *boxing*, is automatic when the type of the variable is a reference type. A boxed value can always be converted back to its original value type, a process called *unboxing*, where the value contained in the box is *copied* into the target variable.

Boxing happens automatically when we refer to a value using a reference variable such as object, or when we pass a value as an argument to a method that takes a reference type parameter. Unboxing is always *explicit*: we need to cast the boxed variable back to its correct value type, as shown in Listing 2-9.

```
public readonly struct Color
{
    public Color(int r, int g, int b)
        => (Red, Green, Blue) = (r, g, b);

    public int Red { get; }
    public int Green { get; }
    public int Blue { get; }
}

var red = new Color(0xFF, 0, 0);
var green = new Color(0, 0xFF, 0);

❶ object copy = green;
Assert.That(object.Equals(❷ red, copy), Is.False);

var copyGreen = ❸ (Color)copy;
```

Listing 2-9: Boxing and unboxing

The type of the copy variable is object, and is therefore a reference, so the value of green gets boxed into copy ❶. Similarly, calling the object.Equals method boxes the value of red, because the method takes two object parameters ❷. We don't need to explicitly cast the value to the object type; it's boxed implicitly. We do require an explicit cast to unbox the value stored in copy into a new variable ❸.

As you'll see shortly when we cover the Common Type System, object is the base class of every type, meaning we can always use object to refer to any other variable, including value type instances. A struct can also implement one or more interfaces. Interfaces are reference types, so if we use either object or an interface type to refer to a value, that value is automatically boxed onto the heap.

A boxed value can be unboxed only to its original type. We can't, for instance, unbox an int value into a double, even though an implicit built-in conversion exists from `int` to `double`. If we attempt to unbox a value to anything other than its original type, we'll get an `InvalidCastException` at run time.

Boxed values are copied to the heap, which means the box is no longer subject to the scope of its variable and may exist beyond the lifespan of its original value. It's up to the garbage collector to clean up boxed values. Chapter 4 discusses boxing in more detail.

Semantics and Type

Value types have semantic implications that go beyond being an instance of a struct or record struct. Choosing a value type instead of a reference type when we define our own types requires much more than a consideration of possible optimizations. Records, in particular, differ from classes, because even though records are compiled into classes and are therefore reference types, they share some important behavioral characteristics with value types.

Before delving into the behavior of record and record struct types, we need to better understand how structs differ from classes.

The Common Type System

C# has a hierarchical type system, known as the *Common Type System*, in which all types derive from `object`, a keyword alias for the `System.Object` type. This is why we can always use `object` to refer to any other variable—although, as you just saw, in the case of value types, the instances are boxed so they can be referred to by `object` references.

Even the built-in types, such as `int` and `float`, inherit from `object`. In fact, all built-in types are aliases for types in the `System` namespace. The `System` types that underlie the numeric types are all structs and therefore value types. For example, `int` is an alias for the `System` type `public readonly struct Int32`.

Enumeration types created with the `enum` keyword are not aliases to `System` types, although they all *derive* from the `System.Enum` class. The individual values of an `enum` declaration have an underlying numeric type, which by default is `int`. We could specify a different numeric type—for example, if we wanted to allow the `enum` elements to have values larger or smaller than is permitted for an `int`.

The non-numeric built-ins `string` and `object` are aliases to classes in the `System` namespace, so they're both reference types.

When we use the `class` or `record` keyword to define our own reference type, our new type derives directly from the `object` base class unless it explicitly inherits from another type. The `object` base class is neither an interface nor `abstract`. It has a mix of virtual, nonvirtual, and static members, which provide the default implementations common to all objects.

All struct types (including record structs) and the `System.Enum` type implicitly derive from `System.ValueType` (for which there's no keyword alias), which in turn derives from the `object` base class, so all struct types derive *indirectly* from object. Value types, unlike reference types, have an interme-diate base class defined by the language.

NOTE *ValueType itself is not a struct, which is sometimes overlooked. All structs implicitly inherit from ValueType, so ValueType itself must be a class. Moreover, ValueType is an abstract class, meaning we can create an instance of object but not of ValueType.*

The ValueType class overrides all the virtual methods defined in the object base class—Equals, GetHashCode, and ToString—and customizes their implementations to provide behavior tailored for value types. The ValueType implementations for Equals and GetHashCode are extremely important because they provide the *value-based* definition of equality that distinguishes value types from reference types. The difference between these implementations has to do with the way values are copied.

Copy Semantics

The difference between where reference types and value types store their instance data has important implications when we copy variables, because copying a reference does not copy the instance. Listing 2-10 shows a simple example to illustrate the difference.

```
   var thing = new Thing { Host = "Palmer" };
❶ var copy = thing;
❷ copy.Host = "Bennings";
   Assert.That(thing.Host, Is.EqualTo("Palmer"));
```

Listing 2-10: Copying a variable

Here we're copying the value of the thing variable into a new variable called copy ❶. Then we assign a new value to the Host property of copy ❷. The test checks that the properties of the original variable haven't changed. The success of the test assertion depends on whether Thing is a value type or a reference type.

As noted earlier, all variables have a value that we may copy to a new variable. If Thing is a value type, any copy we make is a new instance of the type, so if we modify any fields of that copy, those changes have no effect on the fields of the original value. Therefore, if Thing is a struct or a record struct, the test will pass.

If Thing is a reference type, on the other hand, the thing variable's value is a reference. When we copy a reference, only the value of the reference is copied, and it refers to the same instance as the original variable's value. This means if we modify the instance using one reference, that change is reflected in *all* the references to it. Thus, if Thing is a class or a record, the test will fail.

Locks and Reference Semantics

Some situations require the behavior of reference type variables, and using a value type instance would be incorrect or even disallowed. For example, we can't use a value type in a lock statement to prevent a section of code from being executed concurrently by multiple threads. The compiler forbids it because the variable used as a lock needs to be a reference to an object on the heap. The purpose of locking an object is to allow only a single thread to execute the code it protects at any given time. The object instance identifies the lock and can then have multiple references to it from different threads.

The underlying mechanism for the lock statement is the System .Threading.Monitor class. The lock statement translates to the Enter method of Monitor, which takes object as its parameter. Any instance of a value type passed to Monitor.Enter as an argument will automatically be boxed. Each thread calling Monitor.Enter will box the value separately, and the acquisition of the lock would never fail, rendering it pointless.

When we've finished with the lock, we need to call Monitor.Exit and pass the *same* reference used to acquire the lock with Monitor.Enter. The compiler inserts the code to call Monitor.Exit at the closing brace of a lock block. If we use a value type, the call to Exit will result in a new boxed value on the heap, and so will be a different reference to that used in the call to Enter. The result is that releasing the lock will fail with a SynchronizationLockException error.

This is one situation actively requiring reference semantics, because passing a reference to the Enter method doesn't copy the instance. The monitor and the code using the lock both have a reference to the same instance.

Identity Equality vs. Value Equality

When we say we're comparing variables to see whether they're equal, what we really mean is that we're comparing the variables' *values*. If two variables have the same value, they're considered equal. The type of each value plays an important role: the values being compared must be the same type, although one or both values may have resulted from an implicit conversion.

If we compare the values of two variables of the same reference type, their respective values are references, which compare equal by default if they both refer to the same object in memory. This is known as an *identity comparison*. We can override the default identity comparison behavior in our own reference types (a topic we'll examine in detail in Chapter 5), but two references to separate instances that have identical field values compare *unequal* according to the default identity comparison because they refer to different objects.

By contrast, two value type instances compare equal—again by default, because we can modify this behavior—if all the fields of one compare equal with their counterparts on the other. The difference in equality comparison behavior between value type instances and reference type instances is directly related to their respective copy semantics. Since a copy of a value type instance is a new independent instance with identical *state*, an identity comparison makes no sense. The two concepts of copying and equality are therefore intimately related.

The ability to compare two values to see whether they are equal is often underappreciated. Even if we rarely need to compare variables in our own code, commonly used classes such as `List<T>`, `Dictionary<T>`, and the LINQ methods that work on collections may be making those comparisons out of sight. `Equals` is a virtual method defined by the `object` base class, which is a clue to how fundamental it really is, because it means we can call the `Equals` method on *any* value to compare it with any other.

However, the `object.Equals` implementation always performs an identity comparison, which, again, is pointless for value types. For this reason, all structs implicitly inherit the `ValueType` class. `ValueType` overrides the `Equals` method to perform a value-based comparison.

The difference between what equality means for reference types and value types affects the way our code behaves at run time. Consider Listing 2-11, where the `Thing` type has not yet been allocated as a reference type or value type and does not explicitly override the `Equals` method. Here, we create two instances of `Thing` with the same value for their `Host` property. What happens when we call `Equals` depends entirely on whether `Thing` is a class, record, struct, or record struct.

```
public ??? Thing
{
    public string Host { get; set; }
}

var thing = new Thing { Host = "Palmer" };
var clone = new Thing { Host = "Palmer" };

Assert.That(clone.Equals(thing), Is.True);
```

Listing 2-11: Comparing equality of two independent variables

This assertion will fail if `Thing` is a class, because the `object.Equals` method will return true only if both `clone` and `thing` are references to the same instance, and they're not. The assertion will pass if `Thing` is a struct, because the `ValueType` implementation of `Equals` returns true if both `clone` and `thing` have the same value; that is, all their fields compare equal.

The `clone` and `thing` variables also compare equal if `Thing` is either a record or a record struct because they also use a value-based comparison for equality.

Records, Structs, and Value Semantics

Records are reference types but have value-like behavior when it comes to comparing two record variables for equality. When a record type is compiled, the compiler generates a class definition with an overridden implementation of the `Equals` method unless we define one ourselves. The `Equals` method generated for records compares two instances to determine if they have the same state, rather than just comparing two references to determine if they refer to the same instance.

In a struct, on the other hand, if we don't override `Equals`, the equality comparison relies on the implementation of `Equals` provided by the `ValueType` base class. Records, as reference types, don't inherit from `ValueType`. Record structs do inherit from `ValueType`, but, as with records, `Equals` is overridden by a compiler-generated implementation, because `ValueType.Equals` might not be the optimal implementation.

The `ValueType` implementation is necessarily general; it must work for *any* struct type, regardless of the types of the struct's fields. If a field of the type has a custom implementation of `Equals`, instances of the containing type must use that field's implementation for comparisons; a simple structural or bitwise comparison of the instances may not always be correct. The implementation of `Equals` provided by `ValueType` relies on reflection at run time to determine how to compare the fields and will use an overridden implementation of `Equals` to compare a field if the type of that field has one.

If we want to avoid the overhead of reflection in a struct, we must override `Equals` with our own implementation to compare each field and property with its corresponding field or property in the instance being compared. If each field and property value compares equal, using its `Equals` method where required, then the two instances are equal. This is essentially the implementation provided by the compiler for records and record structs.

To reiterate, structs, records, and record structs all employ a value-based comparison of their state to implement the `Equals` method, but for records and record structs, the implementation is generated automatically by the compiler, freeing us from the responsibility of providing our own custom implementation.

The variables we use for records—but not record structs—are references, and when we assign one record reference to another variable, we still get two references to the same record instance, just as we do if the type is a class. Records therefore have reference semantics for copying and value semantics for equality comparison.

The different comparison and copy semantics for value types and reference types have important consequences for the way instances of those types behave at run time. However, important differences also exist in the way those instances are created in the first place. In the next section, we'll look at how construction and initialization differ depending on whether the type of the instance is a value type or reference type.

Construction and Initialization

Creating a new object is superficially a simple operation, but behind the scenes the compiler goes to a great deal of trouble to make the process as efficient as possible. In principle, creating an object involves allocating the memory for an instance of a type and then calling a constructor whose job is to initialize the instance's fields. The syntax is identical for both value types and reference types, but `new` treats them differently and hides some complexity around how and where different types are allocated in memory.

In other words, the new expression is an abstraction that shields us from the implementation details of how memory is allocated and used.

Specifically, the memory for reference type instances is allocated dynamically. When a new instance of a class or record type is created, the memory is allocated on the heap at run time. Instances of struct and record struct types are allocated differently, depending on how the resulting instance is used. Consider this code, which initializes a variable with a new instance of a type named Thing:

```
var thing = new Thing();
```

This basic syntax for creating an object and assigning it to a variable is the same whether Thing is a class, struct, record, or record struct. As you'll see over the coming sections, this code depends on Thing having an accessible constructor that can be invoked with no arguments, which isn't necessarily the case when Thing is a reference type. For the time being, though, let's assume that Thing instances can be created this way. If Thing is a class or a record, new causes memory to be allocated on the heap at run time and returns a reference to the new object, which is assigned to the thing variable.

If Thing is a struct or a record struct, the new instance is assigned to the thing variable. However, this code may or may not allocate memory for a new instance of Thing and may or may not call a constructor. The reason is that construction and initialization are separate processes. Part of the difference is related to whether a Thing is a value type or reference type.

Default Initialization

Default initialization means that each of a type's fields, including the backing fields for properties, is given a default value, which is defined in the language to mean one of the following:

- References are set to null.
- Built-in numeric value type variables are set to 0.
- All other value types are default-initialized.

Default-initialized reference type fields are a common cause of errors. For example, the simple MusicTrack struct in Listing 2-12 relies on us manually initializing an instance by setting its properties. If we neglect to set suitable values for the properties of a MusicTrack instance, we may be rewarded with an exception when we use the instance.

```
public struct MusicTrack
{
    public string Artist { get; set; }
    public string Name { get; set; }

    public override string ToString()
        => $"{Artist.ToUpper()}: {Name.ToUpper()}";
}
```

```
var defaultTrack = new MusicTrack();

var print = defaultTrack.ToString();
```

Listing 2-12: Initializing reference type fields

The call to ToString causes a null reference exception because the defaultTrack value has been default-initialized. The ToString method calls ToUpper on its Artist and Name properties, whose default-initialized value is null. We need to be alert to any uses of default-initialized references in order to avoid such problems resulting from accessing a null reference. One way to minimize the impact of default-initialized values is by providing our own instance constructors.

Instance Constructors

An instance constructor, like a method, can have zero or more parameters. Also like methods, constructors can be overloaded, so we can define several constructors for a type, each with a different number of parameters, or parameters of different types. Constructor definitions for classes, structs, records, and record structs have many similarities, but several important differences exist.

In Listing 2-13, we add a constructor for the MusicTrack struct and use the parameter values to initialize the instance's property values. We use the null-coalescing operator ?? to assign an empty string for each property if its corresponding parameter is null.

```
public readonly struct MusicTrack
{
    public MusicTrack(string artist, string name)
    => (Artist, Name) = (artist ?? string.Empty, name ?? string.Empty);

    public string Artist { get; }
    public string Name { get; }

    public override string ToString()
        => $"{Artist.ToUpper()}: {Name.ToUpper()}";
}
```

Listing 2-13: Adding an instance constructor with parameters

By adding a constructor, we no longer have to rely on MusicTrack users setting the properties explicitly, since the initial values for those properties are set in the constructor. We have made those properties get-only—that is, they can be given a value only in the constructor—and made MusicTrack a readonly struct. However, we must still be cautious of using the property values inside the ToString method because instances of any value type can always be default-initialized, regardless of the presence of a user-defined constructor definition. Adding our own constructor for MusicTrack to give meaningful values to the properties isn't sufficient protection against exceptions that occur from calling methods using a null reference, because MusicTrack is a struct type.

If the nullable reference type feature is enabled (see "Nullable Reference Types" on page 64 for more), the constructor's parameters will be non-nullable variables, meaning that passing null for either argument would cause a compiler warning. Using non-nullable parameters doesn't mean that null can't be passed as an argument, but we may decide that the warning is sufficient protection, potentially allowing us to omit the null-coalescing assignments in the constructor. The nullable reference type feature doesn't, however, mean we can avoid verifying that the property values are not null prior to using them in the ToString method. Fortunately, the null-conditional operator makes the check straightforward and safe:

```
public override string ToString()
    => $"{Artist?.ToUpper()}: {Name?.ToUpper()}";
```

Here the presence of the null-conditional operator, a ? appended to each property name, means that in each case the ToUpper method will be called only if the property is a non-null value. If either property is null, the result of the expression between the braces within the string is null, which the string interpolation treats as an empty string.

If MusicTrack were a class or record, the presence of our own constructor would mean we could no longer create an instance without passing arguments like this:

```
var track = new MusicTrack();
```

If we attempt to create a default-constructed instance, we get the following compiler error:

```
[CS7036] There is no argument given that corresponds to the required formal parameter 'artist'
of 'MusicTrack.MusicTrack(string, string)'
```

If we don't provide any constructors for a class or record, the compiler inserts a default constructor for us. If we define a constructor when we define our own reference type, however, the compiler will not generate the default constructor. The compiler doesn't create a default constructor for value types, but an instance of a struct or record struct can be default-initialized whether or not we define our own constructor.

Default and Generated Constructors

The behavior of reference types and value types differs partly because reference types are allocated on the heap, but value types might not be. The compiler generates a default constructor for reference types because instances of such types are allocated dynamically, and their instances are initialized at run time. When a reference type instance is allocated on the heap, the memory for it is set to zero, effectively default-initializing the instance.

Value types are treated differently because their memory isn't necessarily allocated at run time: for local value type variables, the compiler may *reserve* memory for the instance data, and the program accesses that memory directly. The underlying Common Intermediate Language (CIL) has an efficient instruction for default-initializing value type instances that effectively zeroes out the memory used by the instance, wherever its memory actually resides.

We can think of the default initialization of a struct or record struct as being performed by a compiler-provided default constructor, because the result is identical in any case. Default-initializing value types offers a minor performance advantage because it doesn't require a method call to a constructor, although it's almost never the most significant optimization.

In a positional record or a positional record struct, the compiler generates a public constructor based on the parameters we use in the type definition, like this:

```
public sealed record Color(int Red, int Green, int Blue);
```

The parameters to `Color` in this example tell the compiler to create public properties using those names and their types. The compiler also creates a constructor with the same signature as the record's parameter list, where the properties are assigned their values. The constructor generated by the compiler is the equivalent of this:

```
public Color(int Red, int Green, int Blue)
    => (this.Red, this.Green, this.Blue) = (Red, Green, Blue);
```

Although the constructor has been generated by the compiler, it's still considered a user-defined constructor and therefore still suppresses the default constructor for the `Color` record.

Regardless of its type, an instance is always default-initialized when it's first created, whether its memory is being allocated on the heap or elsewhere.

When we define our own constructor for a class, we can rely on all the fields having been default-initialized prior to the constructor's body; the fields of a class are considered *initially assigned* within the constructor. In a struct's constructor, the fields are *initially unassigned*, so we must definitely assign a value for every field of a struct or record struct, even if it's simply to replace the value with its default-initialized equivalent.

Overloaded Constructors

We can provide a constructor with parameters for any type, and we can overload the constructor by defining several constructors that have different numbers or types of parameters. This is useful when we want to support different ways to construct our type. For instance, Listing 2-14 shows a struct that has two constructors with differing signatures.

```
public readonly struct Color
{
    public Color(int red, int green, int blue)
        => (Red, Green, Blue) = (red, green, blue);

    public Color(uint rgb)
        => (Red, Green, Blue) = Unpack(rgb);

    public int Red { get; }
    public int Green { get; }
    public int Blue { get; }
}
```

Listing 2-14: Overloading constructors

The first constructor initializes the three properties from three separate parameters (red, green, blue). The second constructor receives a numeric representation of an RGB value and initializes the Red, Green, and Blue properties by calling the Unpack method (not shown here) to unpack the number into its component parts. We select the different overloads when using the constructor by passing different arguments, as shown in Listing 2-15.

```
var orange = new Color(0xFFA500);
var yellow = new Color(0xFF, 0xFF, 0);
```

Listing 2-15: Selecting the correct overload

Here, the orange variable is created using the constructor with a single uint parameter (the second constructor in Listing 2-14), and the yellow variable uses the constructor with three int parameters (the first constructor in Listing 2-14).

Parameterless Constructors

As noted earlier, defining our own constructor for a class type will inhibit the compiler-generated default constructor, meaning that we can create new instances of the type only by passing arguments to our own constructor's parameters. If we need to create instances of such a reference type without arguments, we can define our own *parameterless constructor*, which we might use to initialize reference type fields and properties to non-null values. This is common when a class contains a collection that needs to be initialized but can be empty, as demonstrated in Listing 2-16.

```
public sealed class Playlist
{
    public Playlist(IEnumerable<MusicTrack> items)
      ❶ => queue = new(items);

    public Playlist()
      ❷ => queue = new();
```

```
    public void Append(MusicTrack item)
        => queue.Add(item);
--snip--

    private Queue<MusicTrack> queue;
}
```

Listing 2-16: Defining a parameterless constructor

The two constructors defined here allow us to create a Playlist either by passing a sequence of items to populate the queue ❶ or by passing no arguments ❷. If we pass no arguments, the queue field is initialized as an empty queue, ensuring that it isn't null.

Both constructors initialize the queue field by using type inference, a feature called *target-typed new*, introduced in C# v9.0. The compiler deduces the type required by new from the type of the target variable being initialized—in this example, a Queue<MusicTrack>. The queue field is guaranteed to be non-null for any Playlist instance, so we don't need to check for null in the Playlist.Append method.

In a positional record, the compiler creates a constructor based on the positional arguments for the record, so by default, instances of a positional record can't be created without arguments. We can define our own parameterless constructor for a positional record if we require that behavior. A struct or positional record struct, on the other hand, can *always* be created without arguments, whether or not we define our own constructors.

Structs and Default Values

As of C# v10.0, we can define our own parameterless constructors for value types to help ensure that any reference fields are non-null. However, we still need to check for null in a value type's implementation because an instance of a struct or record struct can always be default-initialized, effectively bypassing any constructors we define. This is illustrated in Listing 2-17, where we add a parameterless constructor for the MusicTrack struct that explicitly initializes the two string properties.

```
public readonly struct MusicTrack
{
    public MusicTrack()
        => (Artist, Name) = (string.Empty, string.Empty);

    public MusicTrack(string artist, string name)
        => (Artist, Name) = (artist, name);

    public string Artist { get; }
    public string Name { get; }

    public override string ToString()
        => $"{Artist?.ToUpper()}: {Name?.ToUpper()}";
}
```

Listing 2-17: Adding a parameterless constructor for a struct

The parameterless constructor sets both reference type properties to a non-null value, so calling ToUpper on either property is safe when we're using a MusicTrack instance that was created using new MusicTrack. However, this doesn't mean we can omit the null-conditional checks in ToString. It's still possible for Artist or Name to be null if the instance is a default-initialized MusicTrack—for example, when it's an element in an array:

```
var favorites = new MusicTrack[3];

var print = favorites[0].ToString();
```

Without the checks for null in ToString, this code would cause ToString to throw a NullReferenceException because the creation of the favorites array doesn't call our parameterless constructor on its elements. Each element is default-initialized, leaving the Name and Artist properties with their default value of null, so attempting to call the ToUpper method on a null reference causes the exception.

Array elements are default-initialized without invoking any parameterless constructor we provide. The parameterless constructor is reserved for when we create a new instance by using the new keyword.

Value Type Initialization

One quite subtle consequence of the way value type instances are allocated in memory is that if a value type's fields are all public, we can definitely assign a value for each field outside the constructor (as long as they're not read-only), which results in the whole instance being fully assigned.

For example, Listing 2-18 assigns a value to each field of an uninitialized struct variable.

```
public struct Color
{
    public int red;
    public int green;
    public int blue;
}

Color background;    // initially unassigned variable

background.red = 0xFF;
background.green = 0xA5;
background.blue = 0;

Assert.That(background.red, Is.EqualTo(0xFF));
```

Listing 2-18: Definitely assigning a struct

This code compiles, and the test passes. We can read the value of the red field, even though we've never allocated the background variable with new or invoked a constructor for it. The same would be true if Color were a record struct instead.

This example demonstrates that value type variables directly contain an instance of their type. Assigning to each field means we don't need to explicitly construct an instance. However, relying on this behavior is likely to cause other problems, not the least of which is that using public fields leaves the Color type open to misuse, intended or not. In practice, a constructor is a much better way to initialize a value type's fields, which should all be private and read-only.

Note that if we alter the public fields to be publicly mutable properties, this code will fail to compile. We can't access a property of a value type in any way until the instance itself has been fully, and definitely, assigned. Every property has a backing field generated by the compiler, and that backing field is always private.

Constructor Accessibility

Constructors with parameters can be made public or private in any type. Private constructors are useful when we want to prevent users from creating instances with certain arguments. We used this technique in "Static Creation Methods" in Chapter 1 to force users to call the static class factory methods we defined in order to create certain values, rather than using the new keyword directly. In a class or record, we can make the parameterless constructor private to prevent users from creating default-constructed instances, shown for the Color record in Listing 2-19.

```
public sealed record Color
{
    private Color() { }

    public static Color Black { get; } = new Color();


--snip--
}
```

Listing 2-19: Making constructors private for reference types

Since the constructor for Color is marked private, we can use it to initialize the static Black property value and any other static or instance members of Color, but it's inaccessible to code outside of the Color type. If users of Color forget and attempt to create an instance with new, the compiler forbids it:

```
var black = new Color();

[CS0122] 'Color.Color()' is inaccessible due to its protection level
```

Classes and records can also use the protected keyword on a constructor, making it available to inheriting types. Since structs and record structs can't be inherited, the compiler will prevent the use of protected in a value type.

In a struct or record struct, if we define our own parameterless constructor, it *must* be public. Struct and record struct instances can *always* be default-initialized, whether or not we provide a parameterless constructor.

Field Initializers

In a class or record definition, and in structs or record structs after C# v10.0, we can assign initial values to fields inline by using *field initializers*. We can do the same with automatic properties by using *property initializers*, which initialize the hidden backing field associated with the property. Listing 2-20 uses a field initializer for the `queue` field of the `Playlist` class from Listing 2-16 to assign an initial value and adds a `Name` property for `Playlist` that we also assign an initial value by using a property initializer.

```
public sealed class Playlist
{
--snip--

    public string Name { get; set; } = "_playlist";

    private Queue<MusicTrack> queue = new();
}
```

Listing 2-20: Assigning initial values for fields and properties

Field and property initializers are part of object construction but are not applied when a value type instance is being default-initialized. Conceptually, initializers are applied just before the body of a constructor. As noted previously, the compiler creates a default constructor for class and record types if no user-defined or positional constructors are present; however, the compiler won't synthesize a parameterless constructor for any value type. Therefore, if we want to use field or property initializers for struct or record struct types, we must also define at least one constructor of our own. This can be a parameterless constructor or a constructor taking one or more parameters.

Field initializers can't reference any instance members. However, since static fields are guaranteed to be definitely assigned before any instance fields, a field initializer can reference a static value. Static fields can also have initializers and can reference other static fields. However, we need to take care when referencing one static field from another static field because they're initialized in the order in which they appear in the class.

Object Initializers

With *object initializers*, we set values for publicly mutable properties of a variable at the point of creating a new instance, like this:

```
var fineBrush = new Brush { Width = 2 };
```

Classes, records, structs, and record structs accept this syntax, and they all behave the same way. The initialization process is the same for each: a constructor is invoked in the usual way to create an instance, and then the value is assigned to the property of the instance. In this example, a `Brush` is created using a parameterless constructor (or one with all-optional parameters), but we can call any constructor before the initialization expression inside the braces. In the special case of a constructor that requires no arguments, we can leave out the parentheses for the constructor.

Classes and records require an accessible parameterless constructor to use this syntax. If the parameterless constructor of a class or record is hidden or nonpublic, we *must* invoke a valid constructor before the object initialization within the braces. We don't have to worry about this for struct or record struct types because they can always be default-initialized if the type has no parameterless constructor.

init-Only Properties

As of C# v9.0, any property can be *init-only*, meaning it can be written to only during the creation of a new instance. Prior to C# v9.0, object initialization required properties to have a public set accessor, meaning object initialization couldn't be used with immutable properties. Object initialization requires the value of the property to be set after the constructor has completed, which wasn't permitted for properties without a public set accessor. An init accessor allows a property to be set during object initialization and then makes the property immutable after the initialization is complete.

The Color struct in Listing 2-21 demonstrates how init-only properties are used during object initialization.

```
public readonly struct Color
{
    public int Red { get; init; }
    public int Green { get; init; }
    public int Blue { get; init; }
}
var orange = new Color { Red = 0xFF, Green = 0xA5 };

Assert.That(orange.Red, Is.EqualTo(0xFF));
Assert.That(orange.Green, Is.EqualTo(0xA5));
Assert.That(orange.Blue, Is.EqualTo(0));
```

Listing 2-21: Setting properties as init-only

When we create the orange variable, a new Color is first default-constructed, giving each property its default value of 0. The object initializer between the braces gives new values to the Red and Green properties, leaving the Blue property with its default value. Note that Color is a readonly struct, which requires that the struct has no mutable properties.

We can assign a value to an init-only property in an instance constructor or by using object initialization, but we can't assign a new value after the instance has been created. An init-only property is immutable. The init accessor syntax can be used for properties and indexers for any type, although it was introduced in C# v9.0 to support a special initialization syntax supported by records and known as *non-destructive mutation*.

Non-destructive Mutation

Records and record structs support the non-destructive mutation syntax, and as of C# v10.0, so do structs and anonymous types. Syntactically, non-destructive mutation is similar to object initialization, except that it initializes a new instance by copying an existing one and providing new values for selected properties in that copy. Listing 2-22 demonstrates this syntax, using the with keyword to copy the orange record variable to a new variable named yellow, and then assigning a new value to one of the properties of the copy.

```
public sealed record Color(int Red, int Green, int Blue);
var orange = new Color(0xFF, 0xA5, 0);

var yellow = orange with { Green = 0xFF };

Assert.That(yellow.Red, Is.EqualTo(0xFF));
Assert.That(yellow.Green, Is.EqualTo(0xFF));

Assert.That(orange.Green, Is.EqualTo(0xA5)); // unchanged in orange
Assert.That(orange.Blue, Is.EqualTo(0));
```

Listing 2-22: Initializing a copy of a record with non-destructive mutation

The with expression we use when we create the yellow variable creates a new instance of the Color record with property values identical to the original orange instance. Those properties specified between the braces following with are then assigned the values by using the same syntax as object initialization. This approach is called *non-destructive* mutation because no changes are made to the original record.

Constructors and initializers are both ways we can create new instances with known values. However, sometimes we can't provide an initial value for a variable, but leaving it uninitialized is too restrictive: we can't even test it to see whether it has a value, owing to the rules governing definite assignment. In the next section, we'll examine the options open to us when we need a variable with no value, and how value types and reference types differ here too.

null Values and Default Values

A plain value type variable can never be null. An instance of a value type directly contains all of its fields, and there's not necessarily a representation of "no value." A default-initialized instance of a value type is not the same thing—it's a complete instance of the type, just with the default-initialized values for each of its fields.

We can employ a nullable value type, which can be assigned and compared with the value null, as you'll see shortly, but plain value type instances are incompatible with null. The null constant expression is a reference and therefore can be assigned only to reference variables. One of the implications of not being able to assign `null` to a value type variable is that we can't pass `null` as an argument to a value type method parameter.

Similarly, attempting to *compare* a value with `null` makes no sense. If we do, as shown in Listing 2-23, the compiler rejects the code.

```
public readonly struct Speed
{
--snip--
}

var c = new Speed();

Assert.That(c == null, Is.False);
```

Listing 2-23: Comparing a value type variable with `null`

The error from the compiler is shown here:

```
[CS0019] Operator '==' cannot be applied to operands of type 'Speed' and '<null>'
```

We can, however, compare any reference type with `null`, and, as of C# v8.0, we can use a constant pattern to make this comparison more direct by using the is keyword:

```
Assert.That(someObject is null, Is.True);
```

Comparing any value type with `null` makes no sense, whatever method we choose, because `null` is a reference and as such is represented differently than a value type. That said, the rule against comparing value types with `null` has one exception: generic types.

Generics and null

In a generic class or method, an unconstrained type parameter variable can be compared with `null`. An unconstrained generic type can be either a value type or a reference type. To illustrate, the simple example in Listing 2-24 compares an instance of a generic parameter type with `null`.

```
public static int Compare<T>(T left, T right)
{
    if(left is null) return right is null ? 0 : -1;
--snip--
}
```

Listing 2-24: Comparing a generic type parameter instance with `null`

The Compare generic method has a type parameter named T that might represent either a value type or a reference type, because it has no type constraints. In this instance, T is not known to be a value type, so the compiler allows the syntax. If T's type is determined at run time to be a value type, the whole expression simply evaluates as false.

The compiler still prevents us from assigning null to a variable of type T, because if T were a value type, the assignment would fail at run time. Similarly, we can't return null through an unconstrained type parameter, demonstrated in Listing 2-25.

```
public static T Consume<T>(IProducerConsumerCollection<T> collection)
    => collection.TryTake(out var item) ? item : null;
```

Listing 2-25: Trying to return null as a generic parameter type

This gives the following error:

```
[CS0403] Cannot convert null to type parameter 'T' because it could be a non-nullable value
type. Consider using 'default(T)' instead.
```

In this example, the difficulty arises because T is unconstrained. It might represent a struct or record struct type, for which null is not a valid value. The error message gives us a clue that instead of returning null, we can return a *default* value for T. Default values have other, more significant use cases too, but also some limitations.

Generics and Default Values

The concept of a default value is closely related to a null value, especially in the context of generic types and methods. At times, we—and the compiler—must ensure that an instance of a generic parameter type T is definitely assigned, even when T's type is not known at compile time. We can't just use new to make a new instance of type T because the compiler isn't able to determine which constructors are available for T.

If T is a value type, we can *always* make a default instance by using default initialization or by calling a parameterless constructor, but if T is a reference type, it might not have an accessible default or parameterless constructor. We can use the new constraint on T, meaning that our generic type or method will work only with types that have an accessible parameterless constructor, but this might be too restrictive.

In a generic type, we can use the generic parameter to denote a field or property of the generic parameter type. Generic value types must ensure that *all* their fields are definitely assigned before control leaves the constructor. To make that possible, we use the default keyword to initialize a default instance of T, as in the generic struct shown in Listing 2-26.

```
public readonly struct Node<T>
{
    public Node(int index)
    {
        idx = index;
        contained = default;
    }
```

```
    private readonly int idx;
    private readonly T contained;
}
```

Listing 2-26: Initializing a default instance of a type parameter

In the `Node` constructor, the `contained` field is assigned the default value of its type by using the target-typed default literal (available since C# v7.1), which is equivalent to the expression `default(T)`. Where `T` is a class or record, its default value is `null`, and where `T` is a struct or record struct, the default value is a default-initialized instance. Note that initializing a value by using `default` does not invoke a parameterless constructor, if we have defined one. This code is valid because we can always create a default *value* for a variable of type `T`: if `T` is a value type, the value is a default instance of `T`, and if `T` is a reference type, a default `T` is `null`. The `default` keyword has many uses outside of generic types and methods, but within generic code it's indispensable.

Default values are useful, but they're not sufficient to identify a particular value type instance as invalid. In other words, we can't use a default when what we really mean is *no value present*. The default value of a struct or record struct is a default-initialized instance and might therefore be a *valid* value. Consider Listing 2-27.

```
int x = default;
int y = 0;

Assert.That(x.Equals(y), Is.True);
```

Listing 2-27: Default values can be valid.

The default value for an `int` type is `0`, which we may use to indicate an invalid number in some circumstances but not all. Whether that matters, especially for our own value types, depends on the context in which instances of the type are used, but limiting valid integers to only nonzero values would be very restrictive. Fortunately, we have an alternative.

Nullable Value Types

Nullable value types allow us to have a representation of a value type that means *no value present*. A nullable value type is a wrapper around a value type, and a nullable value type variable may or may not have a value. A nullable value type variable can also be assigned the value `null`, demonstrated by using a simple test in Listing 2-28.

```
int? x = null;
int y = 0;

Assert.That(x.Equals(y), Is.False);
```

Listing 2-28: Using nullable values

The ? following the int type of the x variable is shorthand for saying that x is a Nullable<int>. We can now represent an invalid value for x that's distinct from any valid values for int. We can use a nullable variable for any value type, not just built-ins. The default value for a nullable is null, as shown here:

```
int? x = default;
int? y = null;

Assert.That(x.Equals(y), Is.True);
```

This test passes because x and y are both null. The declaration of x in the first line doesn't initialize a default int but rather a default Nullable<int>. Equality comparison between nullable values compares the underlying value if there is one. Two nullable values are equal if they both have no value, or values that themselves compare equal. Nullable<T> is a struct and overrides the Equals method to provide this behavior.

As a consequence of not being able to assign null to a plain value type variable, we can't use a plain value type on the right-hand side of an as expression, like this:

```
object speed = new Speed();
var actual = speed as Speed;
```

If Speed is a struct or record struct, this code won't compile, because if the cast fails, the as operator will return null. As we know, null can't be assigned to a value. The solution is to use a nullable value type as the source of the conversion, as shown here:

```
var actual = speed as Speed?;
```

The type of the actual variable is a nullable Speed in this example and will have the value null if the conversion fails—that is, if the speed variable is not in fact a Speed type.

Nullable Reference Types

C# v8.0 introduced *nullable reference types*, a feature that allows the compiler to warn us when a reference is or might be null and we expect it to have a real value. While reference variables have always been able to have a null value, the nullable reference type feature allows us to express whether we *intend* for them to. In other words, when we use a nullable reference type variable, we're being explicit about our intention that null is an *expected* potential value for a variable.

Reference variables are non-nullable by default. In the declaration in Listing 2-29, the brush variable is a *non-nullable* reference.

```
object brush = null;
```

Listing 2-29: Declaring a non-nullable reference variable

The compiler performs static analysis that enables it to issue a warning if a non-nullable reference can't be guaranteed to be non-null. To state that with fewer negatives, the compiler issues a warning if a value that may be null is assigned to a non-nullable reference. In particular, assigning null to a non-nullable reference, as we just did, provokes this warning:

```
[CS8600] Converting null literal or possible null value to non-nullable type
```

If we attempt to pass a possibly null value as an argument to a non-nullable method parameter, we'll get a warning from the compiler. Consider the method in Listing 2-30, which capitalizes the first character of each word in a string.

```
public static string ToTitleCase(string original)
{
    var txtInfo = Thread.CurrentThread.CurrentCulture.TextInfo;
    return txtInfo.ToTitleCase(original.Trim());
}
```

Listing 2-30: Defining the ToTitleCase method with a non-nullable reference parameter

Within the ToTitleCase method, we should be able to depend on the original parameter having a real, non-null value, because it's a non-nullable string. That means we can avoid explicitly writing code to check that it isn't null. When we call ToTitleCase, if the compiler can't guarantee that the argument we pass isn't null, it will give us a warning.

We might have a legitimate need for a null reference, however, in which case we mark the type of a variable as nullable to suppress the compiler warnings about possible null assignment. The syntax is the same as for nullable value types: we append a ? to the type. Listing 2-31 shows a collection of nullable string elements designated by the string? type name.

```
var names = new List<string?>();
// Load names from somewhere, may contain null elements
--snip--
var properNames = names.Select(name => ToTitleCase(name));
```

Listing 2-31: Passing a possibly null argument for a non-nullable parameter

If we apply the ToTitleCase method from Listing 2-30 to this collection, we get a similar compiler warning as with Listing 2-29, where we explicitly assigned null to a non-nullable reference type variable:

```
[CS8604] Possible null reference argument for parameter 'original' in 'string
ToTitleCase(string original)'.
```

We're given this warning because the compiler can't guarantee that the collection contains no null elements. The compiler assumes any of the elements may be null because the element type of the collection is a nullable reference.

If we explicitly check each element before making the call to ToTitleCase, the compiler can determine that we're not using a null reference as an argument to the method. To achieve that, we could unpack the Select expression into a loop, such as the foreach loop in Listing 2-32.

```
foreach (var name in names)
{
    if(name is not null)
        properNames.Add(ToTitleCase(name));
}
```

Listing 2-32: Explicitly using a non-null reference

This code doesn't prompt a warning about the argument in the call to ToTitleCase because the compiler can perform enough analysis on the code preceding the method call to guarantee that the name argument isn't null.

However, sometimes the compiler needs our help to determine whether it's safe to assign a variable to a non-nullable reference or to call a method with a non-nullable parameter. Listing 2-33 shows a slightly modified version of Listing 2-31 calling ToTitleCase, where any null elements are filtered out before the method is called.

```
var properNames = names
    .Where(name => name is not null)
    .Select(name => ToTitleCase(name));
```

Listing 2-33: Removing null elements before the method call

This code gives us the same warning as in Listing 2-31, however, because the compiler can't be certain ToTitleCase won't be invoked with a null argument. Although it looks as if the check for null is being made inline, in fact we're calling a lambda function to make that comparison, and the compiler doesn't attempt to analyze every possible code path to make this safe. Fortunately, we have a workaround.

The Null-Forgiving Operator

We can use the *null-forgiving operator* to inform the compiler that we definitely know what we're doing and that no null references are used as arguments to a non-nullable parameter. The null-forgiving operator is an ! appended to the variable, which is why it's also referred to as the *dammit operator,* as in, "It's definitely not null, dammit!" When we've filtered out all the null elements from our collection, we apply the dammit operator to the argument for ToTitleCase, as shown in Listing 2-34.

```
var properNames = names
    .Where(name => name is not null)
    .Select(name => ToTitleCase(name!));
```

Listing 2-34: Using the null-forgiving operator

Using the null-forgiving operator with the argument to `ToTitleCase` convinces the compiler that it is safe to call the method having a non-null reference type parameter. If we were to inadvertently pass a `null` reference, we'd (justifiably) get the dreaded `Object reference not set to an instance of an object` exception. We must take care when using the null-forgiving operator that we really do know that the variable can't be `null`.

Nullable reference types, while having the same syntax as nullable value types, are just a device that indicates to the compiler that we're making certain assumptions about the variable. Unlike nullable value types, which are underpinned by a distinct type with behavior injected by the compiler, nullable reference types are a purely compile-time mechanism, used for static analysis, and do not change the behavior of our code in any way. At run time, nullable and non-nullable references are just references. Nevertheless, distinguishing between them in code is useful for encoding our assumptions about nullability.

Unexpected `null` reference exceptions are the curse of many programs and a class of error that programmers everywhere go to great lengths to try to avoid. The nullable reference type feature of modern C# is one that shifts some of that responsibility away from the programmer and onto the compiler.

Summary

My goal was to ensure that all use of references should be absolutely safe, with checking performed automatically by the compiler. But I couldn't resist the temptation to put in a null reference, simply because it was so easy to implement. This has led to innumerable errors, vulnerabilities, and system crashes, which have probably caused a billion dollars of pain and damage in the last forty years.
—Tony (C.A.R.) Hoare

The type system in C# is broadly similar to many other programming languages, including its support for user-defined types. C# differs in its distinction between reference types and value types. Although there are various recommendations on when to choose to define a value type instead of a reference type, including documentation from Microsoft, those guidelines often take only part of the story into consideration.

The technical purpose of distinguishing value types from reference types is to allow the compiler and Common Language Runtime to make assumptions about values that may allow certain opportunities for optimization. Some of the differences we've discussed result from the way reference and value type instances are stored and managed in memory. That value type variables are not independently subject to garbage collection can itself be a big win. However, we can't just turn our classes into structs or record structs and expect that our programs will suddenly use less memory or run more quickly. Value semantics involves much more than just declaring something as a value type.

Likewise, the copy-by-value behavior of value types is more than just a side effect of the way values use memory. Copying by value gives rise to many of the constraints that are imposed on value types and for which reference types have no need. Using value types where they're appropriate can make our code clearer and simpler in subtle ways, like not having to check for null values on every use of a value. The characteristics of copying values also affect the behavior of the Equals method; although comparing variables to see if they are equal may sound inconsequential, it's an essential aspect of working with variables.

The distinction between value types and reference types, then, is not just a list of *restrictions*. Genuine semantic differences affect our programs' behavior and can bring tangible benefits. One advantage of value types is that they can never be null. Constantly having to check references to ensure that they're valid can be tiresome and error-prone. Using the non-nullable reference type feature is one way we reduce the occurrence of unexpected errors arising from dereferencing a null reference.

One of the great strengths of C# being a compiled and type-safe language is that the compiler can identify many kinds of errors *before* our program is ever run.

3

REFERENCE AND
VALUE PARAMETERS

In this chapter, we'll look at how method parameters and arguments relate to reference and value types. We'll revisit the idea that all variables have a value, regardless of their type, and see how to pass values of different types *by value* or *by reference* as arguments for methods.

We'll explore the following:

- How *reference* and *by reference* differ in meaning
- Why aliasing and mutability are so closely related
- How avoiding side effects can make our code clearer
- When to pass values by reference as an optimization

Passing method parameters by value or by reference isn't the same as those parameters being value or reference types. In other words, the parameter's type (value or reference) differs from how the method uses that parameter (by value or by reference). *Passing* in this context refers to the mechanism for supplying values to a method's parameters and receiving the result the method returns.

Before we get into those distinctions in detail, let's look at how method parameters and arguments work.

Method Parameters and Arguments

As explained in Chapter 2, method parameters are a particular kind of variable. A parameter variable is declared with a name and explicit type in the method's definition and goes out of scope when the method ends. If the method is defined in a generic type or the method itself is generic, the parameter type can be generic. When we call the method, we pass arguments to each parameter.

C# has four kinds of method parameters:

Value parameters

The most common kind of parameter, value parameters, behave as if they're local variables in the method. A value parameter is initialized with the value of the argument passed to it.

Reference parameters

These parameters take the `ref` modifier, signifying that they're passed by reference. The arguments passed also use the `ref` modifier to reinforce that the argument and the parameter both refer to the same memory location.

Output parameters

These are parameters that use the `out` modifier, meaning they're given a new value by the method. Output parameters are also passed by reference. As with the `ref` modifier for reference parameters, we use the `out` modifier for both the argument being passed and the parameter.

Input parameters

This special kind of reference parameter uses the `in` modifier to indicate that its value doesn't change within the method. Unlike `ref` or `out` parameters, the argument passed to an input parameter doesn't require the `in` modifier, because `in` is designed to be transparent to calling code.

Reference, output, and input parameters are special variables in that they indicate a level of indirection to an actual variable. They are known collectively as *by-reference parameters*.

When we call a method, the arguments we pass populate the parameters we've declared for that method. When the parameter is a value parameter, our argument for it is passed by value. When the parameter is any of the by-reference parameters, our argument is passed by reference.

Reference Types vs. By-Reference Parameters

By-reference parameters are sometimes confused with reference type variables, in part because the phrase *pass by reference* is often used along with its companion, *pass by value*, to describe how reference types differ from value types. Consider Microsoft's guide to framework design (*http://msdn.microsoft .com/en-us/library/ms229017.aspx*), which includes the following statement:

> Reference types are passed by reference, whereas value types are passed by value.

This is a not-quite-accurate description of the mechanics of passing by reference. To say that reference types are passed by reference is conflating the concepts of type and passing. Arguments for by-reference parameters are passed by reference, no matter the argument's type. Put another way, arguments of either reference or value type may be passed either by reference or by value, according to the presence or absence of a ref, out, or in modifier for the method's parameters. A by-reference parameter is not itself a reference, but the variable it refers to might be. Terminology is fun, isn't it?

In Chapter 2, we explored how reference types and value types have different copy semantics, and passing arguments and copying variable values are related ideas. In particular, when we pass an argument by value, we make a copy of its value. The Microsoft documentation article quoted earlier goes on to say this:

> Changes to an instance of a reference type affect all references pointing to the instance. [. . .] When an instance of a value type is changed, it of course does not affect any of its copies.

The operative word here is *instance*. We can have multiple references to a single instance of a reference type. Copying a reference doesn't make a copy of the *instance*, just a copy of the reference's value. By contrast, a copy of a value type variable is a new instance, independent of the original value. The value *is* the instance.

Value Types and Parameters

A *value type variable* directly contains the data represented by the member fields of the type. This is true whether the variable is a local instance, a field stored in another object, or a parameter for a method. Consider the simple value type in Listing 3-1 representing a two-dimensional coordinate.

```
public readonly struct Coordinate
{
    public int X { get; init; }
    public int Y { get; init; }
}

var position = new Coordinate { X = 10, Y = 20 };
```

Listing 3-1: A simple Coordinate value type

The Coordinate type has two int fields, each of which takes up a single location in memory. A variable of this type, such as the position variable in Listing 3-1, will directly contain the entire instance. The memory used by the position variable would look more or less like Figure 3-1.

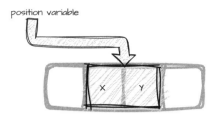

position variable

Figure 3-1: Memory representation of a simple value

The position variable doesn't refer to the data in memory but rather stores the contents of each field of a Coordinate directly in place. If a type has multiple fields, those fields are stored in consecutive locations. If we copy position into another variable, each field's value in the new variable is an independent copy of the corresponding field's value in the original position variable.

If we pass a Coordinate value as an argument to a method's value parameter, the whole value is copied into the parameter. In Listing 3-2, we have a method, Difference, with two Coordinate value parameters, start and end, and we pass the position variable as an argument to both parameters.

```
public Coordinate Difference(Coordinate start, Coordinate end)
{
    --snip--
}

var position = new Coordinate { X = 10, Y = 20 };

var distance = Difference(position, position);
```

Listing 3-2: A method with two value parameters

Because the Difference method's parameters are both taken by value, each parameter receives its own copy that's independent of the original value. The result looks something like Figure 3-2 in memory.

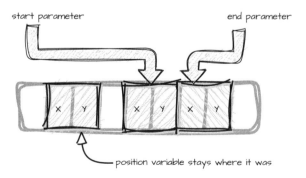

start parameter   end parameter

position variable stays where it was

Figure 3-2: Memory representation of a copied value

The start and end parameters are initialized with the value of the position argument passed to them, and each has its own copy within the method itself.

When we assign one value to another or pass a value type instance as an argument by value, we copy the value. Two value type variables are always independent instances. This is the essence of *copy-by-value* semantics.

Reference type variables behave differently because their value is a reference. A reference's value is used to identify an instance of the type on the heap or is null.

The Value of a Reference

When we create an instance of a reference type, memory is allocated on the heap, and a reference identifying the location of that memory is stored in the variable. Syntactically, it appears that the type of a reference variable is the type of the instance to which it refers, as illustrated here with a string variable:

```
string name = "Alfred";
```

We'd normally refer to the name variable as a string. However, that's not completely accurate. It's more precise to say that name is a variable whose *type* is string and whose *value* is a *reference* to an instance of the string type. The type of a reference variable need not exactly match the type of the instance. For example, we can use a base class reference variable, such as object, to refer to a more specific reference type instance, such as string.

A reference's value is an opaque handle used by the Common Language Runtime (CLR) to identify an object. We're not really interested in what the value of a reference is; references are just the mechanism by which we access and manipulate instances of a reference type, as illustrated in Figure 3-3.

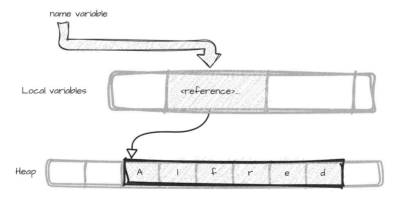

Figure 3-3: Memory representation of a string reference

In Figure 3-3, name is a variable whose value is a reference. A reference does not itself have a distinct type (certainly not one we can name), but it does have a value. The value of a non-null reference is a handle to an area of memory allocated on the heap that contains the instance of a reference type.

This precision matters because when we're talking about passing or copying variables, we really mean passing or copying *values*. For value types, this distinction doesn't exist: the value of a struct variable *is* the instance. However, reference variables are distinct from the instances they refer to—when we copy a reference variable's value, we're making a copy of the reference, not the instance.

Some languages use pointers to objects in memory, but a reference isn't quite the same as a pointer. References can't be used for just anything in memory. They're specifically used to access reference type objects on the heap and to track those objects when they move around as a result of garbage collection and memory compaction. The details of those processes are hidden from us and handled automatically as part of the memory management for reference types.

We can think of the value of a reference as being a kind of address. In this respect, a reference value behaves very much like a value type instance. Like a value type variable, a reference type variable directly contains its value (an address) and lives within the scope of its parent, which might be the stack frame for the local variables of a method.

With that in mind, consider this: *all* variables, whether they represent reference or value types, have values that may be copied. More than that, by default, all variable values are copied—and passed—*by value.*

Reference Variables and Aliasing

Aliasing refers to accessing a single memory location via multiple variables. As you've seen, when we copy one reference to another, such as when we pass a reference as an argument to a method, we create two aliasing references—the argument variable and the parameter variable—to the same object in memory.

In contrast, when we pass a value type instance as an argument, the argument variable and parameter variable are identical but independent copies of each other. The difference between reference types and values in this respect is most significant when the instances are mutable (that is, their state can be altered).

Aliasing can be intentional and useful, such as when we want changes to an object to be observable by all references to it, wherever they might be. For example, see the Command and DataStore classes in Listing 3-3; we create an instance of the Command type by using the CreateCommand method of DataStore, and the Command object stores a reference to the DataStore instance used to create the Command instance.

```
public class Command
{
    public Command(DataStore store)
        => Connection = store;

    public DataStore Connection { get; }
}
```

```
public class DataStore
{
    public enum ConnectionState { Closed, Open }

    public Command CreateCommand()
        => new Command(this);

    public void Open() => State = ConnectionState.Open;
    public void Close() => State = ConnectionState.Closed;

    public ConnectionState State { get; private set; }
}
```

Listing 3-3: Storing a reference to a DataStore as a property of Command

The CreateCommand method returns a reference to the newly created Command object, with its reference to the DataStore instance. We can *mutate*—change the state of—the DataStore object by using its Open or Close methods, and whether we use a local DataStore variable or the Connection property of a Command object returned from CreateCommand, we'll update the same DataStore instance because both references are aliases for the same object, as demonstrated in Listing 3-4.

```
var store = new DataStore(...);

Command command = store.CreateCommand();

// Open the connection.
command.Connection.Open();

Assert.That(store.State, Is.EqualTo(ConnectionState.Open));
```

Listing 3-4: Mutating the DataStore instance via an alias

We call the Open method by using the Connection property of the command variable and test that the state of the local variable named store has been changed.

Value type variables are never aliases for a single instance, so changes to an instance are visible only in the variable used to make the change. Value type instances are copied by value, so each copy is an independent instance. This process is analogous to me sending you a document as an email attachment: we both have our own copy of the document, so if I change my copy, your copy is unaffected, and vice versa.

However, if I instead send a link to a shared document that we can both edit, any change either of us makes will be visible to us both via that link. The link is similar to a reference; it's a kind of address for the document, but it's not the document itself. The link represents a level of indirection to the real document. In exactly the same way, a reference variable doesn't contain an object but instead a reference, and the object's instance is accessed indirectly via that reference.

Mutable By-Reference Parameters

By default, method parameters are value parameters, meaning that arguments passed to them are passed by value, regardless of the argument's type. In this section, we'll look at the *mutable by-reference parameters*, ref and out, which cause arguments to be passed instead by reference.

Value type instances and references can both be passed by reference by using the ref or out modifiers, so it's important to understand that by-reference parameters are different from reference type *value* parameters. When we pass a reference as an argument to a reference type value parameter, the same object instance is referenced by both the argument and parameter variables, and any change to the instance is visible via either variable. A by-reference parameter, in contrast, is an alias for the value of the argument variable, whether that value is a reference or value type instance.

The presence of a ref or out modifier on a parameter means that when we call the method, the address of the argument's value is passed rather than a copy of the value. This extra level of indirection means that regardless of the argument's type, both the caller and the method directly access the same value. If the argument's value is a reference, we can change it to refer to a new instance or assign null to it, and that change is visible via both the argument and the parameter variables.

To illustrate the difference between reference variables and by-reference parameters, consider Listing 3-5, where we pass a reference by value to the AutoAppend method that attempts to change its name parameter.

```
public void AutoAppend(string name, string extension)
{
    if(!name.EndsWith(extension))
        name += extension;
}

var saveName = "Alfred";
AutoAppend(saveName, ".docx");

Assert.That(saveName, Is.EqualTo("Alfred.docx"));
```

Listing 3-5: Creating a new instance versus changing an instance

This test fails, even though string is a reference type. Although the += operator appears as though it's mutating the string, it actually creates a new string with the updated contents and returns a new reference to it. The new reference and instance are visible within the AutoAppend method but not outside it. The original string is unchanged.

The AutoAppend method isn't changing the shared string instance, but rather the *value* of its name parameter. Calling += here changes the reference to refer to a new, different instance. The saveName variable used as an argument for AutoAppend still refers to the original, unchanged instance.

This demonstrates clearly that when we pass a reference as an argument, it is, by default, passed by value. For the AutoAppend method in Listing 3-5 to work as expected, we need to pass the saveName reference by reference so that when the method alters the value of the reference *variable*, the change is visible to the calling code.

Passing References by Reference

The most direct way to make our test in Listing 3-5 pass is to use the `ref` modifier to make `name` a by-reference parameter. Listing 3-6 shows the same `AutoAppend` method as Listing 3-5, except in this version we pass the `name` parameter by reference by using the `ref` modifier on it.

```
public void AutoAppend(ref string name, string extension)
{
    if(!name.EndsWith(extension))
        name += extension;
}

var saveName = "Alfred";
AutoAppend(ref saveName, ".docx");

Assert.That(saveName, Is.EqualTo("Alfred.docx"));
```

Listing 3-6: Using the ref *modifier to pass* name *by reference*

We use the `ref` modifier on both the method's parameter and the argument we pass to it because we're passing a reference to a variable. The test now passes because the changes that the `AutoAppend` method makes to the value of the reference variable are visible via the `saveName` variable in the calling code.

The `name` parameter is, in effect, an alias for the `saveName` variable, as illustrated in Figure 3-4.

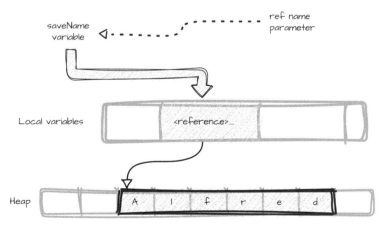

Figure 3-4: A by-reference parameter aliases a variable.

The consequence of using a by-reference parameter is that the argument and the parameter variables don't just refer to the same instance—they're effectively the same reference. We can still use the `name` parameter to access the string instance (for example, to access properties or call methods), and the compiler hides the extra level of indirection afforded by the ref modifier on the parameter.

Passing Values by Reference

We can pass value type variables by reference too. Keep in mind that passing arguments by reference doesn't imply that the parameter is a reference variable.

When we pass a value type instance as an argument to a method, the method normally gets a copy of the instance because of the copy-by-value semantics of value types. As you've seen previously, any changes made to the fields of the instance inside the method aren't visible to the calling code.

If we require those changes to be visible outside the method, we need to pass the value by reference. In Listing 3-7, we introduce an Increment method that takes a mutable Speed value type parameter by reference and changes its value. Value types like Speed should almost always be immutable, and you'll see in "Mutation vs. Creation" on page 89 how to express this differently. This example merely demonstrates that the mechanism for passing value types by reference is identical to passing references by reference.

```
public struct Speed
{
    public double InMetersPerSecond { get; set; }
}

public void Increment(ref Speed initial, double amount)
    => initial.InMetersPerSecond += amount;
```

Listing 3-7: Value type by-reference parameters

When we call the Increment method, we use the ref modifier to pass the argument for the initial parameter by reference, just as we did for the name parameter in Listing 3-6. As a result, the change to initial's InMetersPerSecond property within Increment is visible to the calling code, as shown in Listing 3-8.

```
var speed = new Speed { InMetersPerSecond = 50.0 };
Increment(ref speed, 20);

Assert.That(speed.InMetersPerSecond, Is.EqualTo(70.0));
```

Listing 3-8: Using the ref modifier to pass speed by reference

Because the speed variable is passed to Increment by reference, speed is aliased in the Increment method. Both the calling code and Increment are effectively using the same variable, so any changes to the value of the initial parameter are visible within both the Increment method and the code that calls it. The test shows that we're expecting the value to be changed.

NOTE *To reiterate, by-reference parameters aren't the same as reference type variables. A reference type variable refers to an instance of a reference type, whereas a by-reference parameter refers to a variable, which can be either a reference type or a value type.*

References can refer only to an object on the heap. If we assign a reference type variable to an instance of a value type, the value is boxed onto the heap, and the variable refers to the boxed copy. A by-reference parameter adds an extra level of indirection to a variable's value. When we pass a value type instance by reference, the value is neither boxed nor copied.

Working with Output Parameters

Output parameters, designated by the out modifier, are mutable by-reference parameters and are usually used when we require a method to create a new instance of an object for that parameter variable. They're similar to reference parameters in that they, too, alias the variable used as the argument. The argument we pass to the method is usually uninitialized, and the method will initialize it by assigning a value to populate the output parameter variable.

More formally, the difference between a reference parameter and an output parameter is that a reference argument must be definitely assigned before it's passed, whereas an output argument may or may not be initialized when it's passed, but the parameter must be assigned a value within the method either way.

Output parameters are typically used when acquiring a new instance of an object could fail without the failure being a fatal or even serious problem. Examples include parsing a string for a specifically formatted value, connecting to an unreliable service, and reading a value from a shared resource such as a queue, which could be empty. In cases like these, we often want a way to attempt the process and be able to either ignore a failure or retry the operation. If the operation succeeds, we receive a valid object as a result.

The common approach to this use case is to define a method that takes at least one output parameter and returns a bool indicating success or failure. If the method succeeds, the out parameter is initialized with a new object, and the method returns true, indicating that the argument passed has been successfully initialized. If the operation is unsuccessful, the method returns false, indicating to the caller that the output argument's value should be ignored. This is a common technique in C# known as Try*XXX*.

Using the TryXXX Idiom

The Standard Library has several examples of using Try*XXX* to parse a string for a specific kind of value, such as a DateTime object. The DateTime.TryParse method takes a string parameter and an output parameter for a DateTime value. If the parse fails, the method returns false. If the parse succeeds, the

`DateTime` value will contain the date parsed from the string. Listing 3-9 demonstrates how we might use this idiom.

```
string logTime = --snip--
if(DateTime.TryParse(logTime, out DateTime timeStamp))
{
    var elapsed = DateTime.Now - timeStamp;
    --snip--
```

Listing 3-9: The TryXXX idiom

The `logTime` variable passed as an argument to `TryParse` may come from an unreliable source, such as user input or a file. Incorrectly formatted dates are an error but shouldn't be considered an exceptional case. A successful call to `TryParse` means the `timeStamp` variable is a valid `DateTime` instance. If `TryParse` returns `false`, the `timeStamp` variable is default-initialized instead.

NOTE *The documentation for `DateTime` specifies that the failure case initializes the variable to the value of the `MinValue` property, but that's equivalent to a default `DateTime`.*

`TryXXX` methods often have a companion version that *will* throw an exception when the operation fails. The exception version of the `DateTime.TryParse` method, for example, is `DateTime.Parse`, which returns a `DateTime` value upon success and throws a `FormatException` error upon failure. Handling exceptions can be intrusive, and failing to parse a string for a valid `DateTime` is the kind of error we'd probably want to handle as soon as it occurs.

If we had used the plain `Parse` method, we might have wrapped the call in a `try...catch` block, but this could become cumbersome if we had several strings to parse: to catch a failure on any one value, we'd have to wrap *each call* in its own `try` block. Using `TryParse` instead is more direct and less verbose.

Making a Definite Assignment

The underlying mechanism for `ref` and `out` parameters is identical in the CIL, which has native support for by-reference parameters and arguments. They differ in the semantics imposed by the compiler: a `ref` parameter is considered initially assigned within the method, meaning a `ref` argument must be definitely assigned before being passed; an `out` parameter, on the other hand, is considered initially unassigned within the method, regardless of whether it had been assigned a value before the call. We must therefore definitely assign all `out` parameters before the method returns. Not doing so results in a compile-time failure, as shown by this method, which attempts to return before the `connection` parameter has been assigned:

```
public bool TryRemote(string address, out DataStore connection)
{
    if(string.IsNullOrEmpty(address))
        return false;
    --snip--
```

We receive this error:

```
[CS0177] The out parameter 'connection' must be assigned to before control
leaves the current method
```

The most straightforward way to avoid the error in this example would be to preemptively assign null to the connection parameter before returning false. By convention, an argument passed to the out parameter of a TryXXX method should be considered to have a valid value in the calling code only if the method returns true.

The target out variables in the calling code are considered definitely assigned only after a *normal* return from a method. It's possible for control to leave the method *abnormally* by throwing an exception before all of its out parameters have been assigned. If the method exits with an exception, the variables used as out arguments that weren't definitely assigned prior to the method call remain not definitely assigned. Any arguments that were already definitely assigned before the call remain definitely assigned, although they may still have been given a new value within the method before the exception was thrown.

However, we'd usually use the TryXXX idiom to *avoid* exceptions, as most users will expect such methods to not throw any exceptions.

Selecting Operations

Using the TryXXX idiom with an out parameter, like that shown in Listing 3-9, is appealing because the method can be used inline in a simple if statement to test the return value and capture the required output argument's value all in one place. In Listing 3-10, we use the TryRemote method to determine how to obtain a list of results, using the ternary conditional operator ?: rather than if...else blocks. The connection output variable is declared inline in the argument list for the method.

```
List<Record> results = TryRemote(remoteName, out DataStore connection)
    ? connection.LoadData()
    : LoadFromCache();
```

Listing 3-10: Using a simple out parameter

If TryRemote returns true, the branch following ? is taken, and we can use the connection output variable in the call to TryRemote. If the method returns false, indicating the connection to the remote resource failed, our code takes the branch following the : and loads the results from a cache instead.

Note that we can also use var to declare the type of the inline connection argument, in which case the compiler will determine its type according to the type of the parameter in the method's definition. The TryRemote method allows us to handle the failure to connect without the extra cost and complexity of handling an exception, and to attempt a different approach to obtain the list of results.

We can think of a TryXXX method as returning multiple values: a bool to indicate the success or failure of attempting to obtain a resource, and the resource itself when its acquisition succeeds.

Limitations of By-Reference Parameters

While methods with by-reference parameters are well suited for certain situations, such as the TryXXX technique, by-reference parameters are not appropriate for every case, and the rules around definite assignment can sometimes require a different approach. Other restrictions can also affect where we can use these parameters. We'll look at these restrictions in this section.

Property Values

The result of getting a property or indexer value can't be used directly as a ref or out argument. In Listing 3-11, we attempt to pass the Speed property of a Velocity instance as an argument to a ref parameter.

```
public readonly struct Velocity
{
    public Speed Speed { get; }
    public Angle Direction { get; }
}

public void Increment(ref Speed initial, double amount)
    => initial.InMetersPerSecond += amount;

var start = new Velocity ( --snip-- );
Increment(ref start.Speed, 25);
```

Listing 3-11: Passing properties to ref parameters

The compiler rejects this code with the following error:

```
[CS0206] A property or indexer may not be passed as an out or ref parameter
```

The compiler doesn't allow this code because a property result is a value and not a variable. In Chapter 2, you saw how variables can be assigned to, but values can't. Accessing a property is exactly the same as reading the return value from a method call—something we look at in detail in Chapter 4—and methods return values, not variables. We usually use a ref parameter when we expect the called method to modify its argument, but because a property isn't a variable, it *can't* be modified.

It makes no difference whether Speed is a reference type or a value type. Passing a ref or out argument is essentially passing the address of the argument, and we can't pass the address of a nonvariable.

Overloading on By-Reference Parameters

By-reference parameter modifiers are part of the signature of a method. A reference or output parameter is effectively a different type than its value parameter equivalent. If we have a method that takes a ref parameter, we can overload it with a method that takes that parameter by value.

Method overloads can have different return types, so we can write a method that takes its parameters by value and returns a new object, and overload it with a version taking a ref parameter that modifies the object in place, as shown in Listing 3-12.

```
public Speed Increment(Speed initial, double amount)
    => new Speed { InMetersPerSecond = initial.InMetersPerSecond + amount };

public void Increment(ref Speed initial, double amount)
    => initial.InMetersPerSecond += amount;
```

Listing 3-12: Overloading on by-reference modifiers

When we call the Increment method, the compiler selects the correct overload based on whether we modify the Speed argument with the ref keyword to pass it by reference or omit the modifier to call the version with a value parameter.

We can't, however, overload a method when the only difference is the kind of by-reference modifier for its parameters, as we try to do in Listing 3-13.

```
public void Increment(ref Speed initial, double amount)
    => initial.InMetersPerSecond += amount;

public void Increment(out Speed initial, double amount)
    => initial = new Speed { InMetersPerSecond = amount };
```

Listing 3-13: Overloading on different modifiers

This might seem an arbitrary restriction. After all, calling code must differentiate between passing a ref argument and passing an out argument. However, the compiler rejects this overload because the Common Language Infrastructure (CLI) has no way to distinguish between ref and out in the method signature. Both are just by-reference parameters, so the two overloads have the same signature, as far as the CLI is concerned, resulting in ambiguity.

The same restriction applies with in parameters, which we cover in "Read-Only References and Returning by Reference" on page 92. As with ref and out parameters, an in parameter is simply another kind of by-reference parameter, as far as the CLI is concerned.

Overloading a method based purely on whether one or more parameters is taken by reference or by value is probably best avoided in any case. Anyone calling such a method needs a thorough knowledge of this somewhat arcane corner of overloading rules, so such code could easily be confusing.

Using Fields

Making a field a by-reference variable is impossible. Again, this might seem arbitrary, but otherwise a by-reference field could become a *dangling* reference—that is, it could refer to an object that no longer exists.

NOTE   *As of C# v11.0, by-reference fields are permitted within `ref struct` types, which are specialized value types intended for high-performance applications. Numerous restrictions on `ref struct` types make them less suitable for most general-purpose code, so we don't cover them in this book.*

Consider a class like `Reminder` in Listing 3-14, which attempts to store a ref parameter in a ref field.

```
public class Reminder
{
    public Reminder(ref DateTime start)
        => time = start;

    private readonly ref DateTime time;
}
```

Listing 3-14: A hypothetical `Reminder` class that stores a field by reference

Although this approach might seem attractive in principle—say, if we want the `Reminder` class to deliberately alias the argument to its constructor, or we want to avoid copying the `DateTime` instance—this code doesn't compile. The compiler rejects it as simply invalid syntax because the `Reminder` instance could be used after the referenced `DateTime` variable has gone out of scope, meaning the field would become a reference to memory that no longer exists or, perhaps worse, memory that has been allocated to something else. The `time` field would be a dangling reference, something the rules of C# go to great lengths to prevent.

Although reference types have different lifetimes and enjoy automatic memory management, allowing `ref` fields only for reference types would indeed be arbitrary and a source of potential confusion and error. This capability would also serve little purpose because reference variables already exhibit aliasing behavior, and by-reference variables are the same size as references for the purposes of copying, so the compiler forbids it.

Closures

The prohibition of `ref` and `out` fields is also the reason we can't use a by-reference parameter inside a closure. A *closure* is a method that encapsulates behavior along with its *context*—that is, the state of any variables declared outside the method's own scope but used within its implementation. Those external variables are said to have been *closed over* by the method, hence the term *closure*. Listing 3-15 shows a method trying to use a ref parameter inside a lambda expression.

```
public static Reminder
NextAppointment(ref DateTime time, IEnumerable<Reminder> items)
{
    var results = items.Where(item => item.Date == time.Date);
    return results.FirstOrDefault();
}
```

Listing 3-15: Anonymous closure capturing a ref parameter

The compiler rejects the NextAppointment method, giving us the following error:

```
[CS1628] Cannot use ref, out, or in parameter 'time' inside an anonymous method, lambda
expression, query expression, or local function
```

The closure in the NextAppointment method is the lambda expression used by the Where method. The lambda is an anonymous method that uses the captured time parameter, which belongs to the scope of NextAppointment. Closure functions are implemented by the compiler as a small, unnamable class with fields for each of the closed-over variables. In this example, the variable being captured is a ref parameter, which, as you saw in Listing 3-14, isn't a valid field.

As the error message indicates, the same problem applies equally to nested local functions and anonymous methods, which can also capture the outer method's variables, including its parameters. Anonymous methods, lambda expressions, and local functions are all implemented the same way: using a hidden class synthesized by the compiler. Any captured variables become fields of that class.

Iterator Blocks

An *iterator block* is a compiler-generated class that implements the standard IEnumerable<T> interface to iterate over the elements of a sequence, such as an array or a List<T>, using deferred execution. Also known as *lazy enumeration*, *deferred execution* means that the next element is obtained from the sequence only when the user requests it; the sequence is produced on demand and theoretically may even be infinite.

An iterator block is created whenever we use the yield statement, as shown in Listing 3-16. However, the compiler rejects the AppointmentsForDay method because it has a ref parameter.

```
public static IEnumerable<Reminder>
AppointmentsForDay(ref DateTime time, IEnumerable<Reminder> items)
{
    foreach (var item in items)
```

```
    {
        if(item.Time.Date == time.Date)
            yield return item;
    }
}
```

Listing 3-16: A ref parameter in an iterator

Here the `AppointmentsForDay` method is attempting to filter the `items` sequence passed as a parameter for elements that match the `time` parameter. However, like closures, methods that use iterator blocks can't have by-reference parameters, so the method in Listing 3-16 fails to compile, with this error:

```
[CS1623] Iterators cannot have ref, in or out parameters
```

Each time the method yields a value, control returns to the calling code. When the next item is requested, the method must continue at the statement following the `yield` and must do so with the same state. The compiler transforms the `yield` statement to return an instance of the iterator block class that captures the state between requests for each element, similar to the way closures work.

The compiler-generated class needs to capture *all* the method parameters and any local variables as fields to preserve the method's state between each request for a value, which is why iterator methods can't have by-reference parameters.

Asynchronous Methods

Lastly, and for exactly the same reason as closures and iterator blocks, we can't declare by-reference parameters for async methods like the `TryGetResponse` method in Listing 3-17.

```
public static async Task<bool> TryGetResponse(out string response)
{
    response = await Task.Run(() => GetUserInput());
    return !string.IsNullOrEmpty(response);
}
```

Listing 3-17: An out parameter in an asynchronous method

This method fails to compile with the following error:

```
[CS1988] Async methods cannot have ref, in or out parameters
```

In this instance, the compiler synthesizes a hidden class to manage the asynchronous invocation of the `Task.Run` method. Asynchronous methods return control to their caller when the `await` statement is reached, and so, like iterator blocks, they must preserve the state of *all* their variables. The compiler-generated class captures all local variables and parameters as fields, so by-reference parameters aren't allowed for any method that has the async modifier.

Extension Methods

We can use by-reference parameters in any method that doesn't use a closure, an iterator block, or asynchronous operations using the await keyword. However, caveats exist for *extension methods*, static methods that extend the interface of another type. The first parameter of an extension method is of the type being extended and uses the special this modifier. Extension methods have some restrictions on using by-reference parameters for the this parameter. First, the this parameter of an extension method can't be an out parameter, as demonstrated by Listing 3-18.

```
public static void
FormatConnection(out this string connString, string host, string source)
{
    connString = $"Server={host};Database={source};Trusted_Connection=True;";
}
```

Listing 3-18: Extension method using an out parameter

This code produces the following error message:

```
[CS8328] The parameter modifier 'this' cannot be used with 'out'
```

If this syntax were permitted, code using the FormatConnection method could *appear* to call a method using an uninitialized variable, like this:

```
string connection;  // uninitialized variable
connection.FormatConnection(host, source);
```

Most users would probably find this code confusing because using an uninitialized variable to invoke a method isn't allowed in any other circumstances. In any case, we have much better alternatives to achieve the same result, and the syntax for this parameters is also an error. We can use an out modifier with any of the other parameters, just as we can with any regular method, but we can't make this an output parameter.

Using ref for the this parameter is permitted if the parameter is a value type, but not if it's a reference type. This restriction might also seem unreasonable at first glance, but it's intended to explicitly prohibit code like the following:

```
public static void Nullify(ref this string val)
    => val = null;
```

The compiler rejects the Nullify method with the following error:

```
[CS8337] The first parameter of a 'ref' extension method 'Nullify' must be a value type or a
generic type constrained to struct.
```

If this code were permitted, the variable used to call the method could refer to a different variable, or—as in this example—be set to null after the method returned. Most users would likely be surprised by such behavior, so, once again, the compiler forbids it.

We can use ref for the this parameter when the parameter is a value type, which avoids copying the this argument's value. While there's no benefit to avoiding the copy of a reference, copying a large value might be relatively expensive. A value type variable can't be assigned the value null, but the method can assign a new value to the ref this parameter, thus changing the argument's value. Again, doing so would likely surprise most users of the method, so even though the syntax is legal, we should avoid using ref this parameters. If we really want to avoid copying the argument for a this parameter, then instead of using ref, we can use the in modifier to make this a read-only reference parameter, as discussed in more detail in "Read-Only References and Returning by Reference" on page 92.

In spite of their limitations, by-reference parameters are a core part of C#, and understanding their semantics is important. None of these restrictions is particularly onerous, not least because the use cases for these parameters are limited. The use of ref this value type parameters in extension methods would be considered unusual by most programmers and is a niche-enough feature that it's probably best avoided in any case.

Fields *must* be real variables, and C# provides no way to store a by-reference variable as a field of a general-purpose type. Every other example in this section can be expressed differently to achieve the same result.

Side Effects and Direct Effects

Methods with by-reference parameters intentionally alias variables in the calling code, and therefore changes made to those parameters within the method are visible outside the method's scope. Altering the state of an aliased object is an example of a *side effect*, which is more generally defined as any change of state that's visible to code outside the scope where the change occurs.

Side effects aren't intrinsically bad, but programs that depend on them heavily can be more difficult to follow than those that rely only on direct effects. The *direct effect* of a method is whatever it returns, normally referred to as the method's output, with the inputs being the method's formal parameters. By-reference parameters, especially out parameters, blur the distinction between the inputs and outputs of a method, since side effects may alter state that is unrelated to the method's direct effect.

Consider how TryXXX methods are commonly used to initialize variables, as shown in Listing 3-19.

```
if(TryRemote(remoteName, out var connection))
{
    // Perform activities using connection
}
```

Listing 3-19 Using TryRemote with an output parameter to initialize the connection variable

The direct effect of the `TryRemote` method is the `bool` return value indicating the success or failure of initializing its output parameter. We use the return value to determine whether the `connection` variable has been initialized; in other words, the direct effect tells us whether the side effect was successful. In this case, a connection exists between the side and direct effects of `TryRemote`, but, as with other `TryXXX` methods, the direct effect seems secondary to the side effect!

Methods with by-reference parameters, and more generally those that rely substantially on operating by side effect, often result in very procedural code comprising a set of logical steps or instructions to accomplish a task. Procedural solutions are described as *imperative code* because they're an explicit sequence of instructions to be processed to achieve a result. The contrasting approach is *declarative code*, which emphasizes outcomes over specific implementation. A more declarative approach pulls the focus away from *how* things get done and allows us to concentrate instead on the outcomes.

One aspect of a declarative style is that we attach more importance to the direct effect of a method and make a clear separation between a method's inputs and its output.

We could make our `TryRemote` method in Listing 3-19 more declarative by removing the `out` parameter and returning the required `DataStore` reference directly; since `DataStore` is a reference type, we can return `null` if the `TryRemote` method fails. However, the side effects associated with by-reference parameters aren't really an issue when those parameters are reference types. Reference types are often mutable—by design, and for good reason—and the fact that multiple variables can refer to a single instance is often desirable behavior, as you saw in "Reference Variables and Aliasing" on page 74. The benefits of declarative code are much more important when we're using value types, which should be immutable.

Mutation vs. Creation

A method that uses `ref` and `out` parameters is giving a strong signal that those parameters will change within the method. Since such parameters are aliases for the variables passed as arguments to them, we need to pay attention to which variables may be changed. Unexpected modifications to variables can cause errors that are hard to identify, especially in code that uses multiple threads. If we follow the common advice to make our own value types immutable, we reduce the likelihood of such problems occurring, which means we should also avoid mutable by-reference parameters of value type. Then, there's only one way that a value type variable can change: by assignment.

If we have an instance of a value and require an instance with different properties, we simply create a new one with the state we want, leaving the original unchanged. Compare the `Incremented` method in Listing 3-20 with the similar `Increment` method in Listing 3-7.

```
public Speed Incremented(Speed initial, double amount)
    => Speed.FromMetersPerSecond(initial.InMetersPerSecond + amount);
```

Listing 3-20: Creating a new value rather than mutating an existing variable

We create and return a new instance of a Speed that's initialized using the InMetersPerSecond property of a parameter variable, instead of altering the properties of a value that has been passed by reference. Note that the method name is Incremented rather than Increment. The name Increment is a direct verb and might imply that the Speed parameter was somehow being altered. In contrast, the name Incremented is an adjective describing the result. Using adjectives for nonmutating methods is another indication that no state is being altered. Other examples of this naming convention include Sorted, UpperCased, and Rounded.

To call the Incremented method, we pass an existing Speed value along with a numeric amount by which to increment its value, as shown here:

```
var speed = Speed.FromMetersPerSecond(50.0);
var newSpeed = Incremented(speed, 20);

Assert.That(speed.InMetersPerSecond, Is.EqualTo(50));
Assert.That(newSpeed.InMetersPerSecond, Is.EqualTo(70));
```

The speed variable in the calling code isn't changed; the Incremented method returns a *new* Speed instance with the required value. We assign the new value to a different variable here, but we could have overwritten the original speed variable with the new instance instead.

Not all objects are values, and sometimes it's convenient for certain objects to be mutable; the DataStore object you saw earlier has mutable state that can be changed via its Open and Close methods.

Aliasing is useful when we require changes to an object to be visible via all *references* to that object, but the benefits of such side effects aren't so clear for value types. Side effects aren't limited to output parameters. They occur anytime we can modify the state of an object that's visible outside the scope in which we make the change, including via a plain reference variable.

Changing the state of any object requires special care and attention, especially in the presence of multiple threads, so if we limit the need to modify our objects, we reduce the potential for problems. If we make all value types immutable, we reduce the prevalence of side effects, which can be difficult to identify and sometimes make our logic less clear.

An alternative approach to creating a new value based on the properties of an existing instance is to use the non-destructive mutation syntax, introduced in Chapter 2. Listing 3-21 uses the with keyword to copy an existing Velocity variable and provide a new value for the Direction property of the copy.

```
public readonly struct Velocity
{
    public Speed Speed { get; init; }
    public Angle Direction { get; init; }
}
```

```
var velocity = new Velocity
    {
        Speed = Speed.FromMetersPerSecond(10),
        Direction = Angle.FromRadians(.88)
    };

var copy = velocity with { Direction = Angle.FromRadians(.99) };
```

Listing 3-21: Copying an instance as a template

The init accessors on each property of the Velocity type enable us
to copy an instance and change selected properties for the new instance
by using the with keyword. Non-destructive mutation was introduced for
record types in C# v9.0, and since C# v10.0, we can also use it with structs
and record structs, and even anonymous types.

The init accessor also allows us to give a property a value by using
object initialization (as shown for the velocity variable in Listing 3-21) or
via a constructor, but once its value is set via init, the property is immutable. If we'd used private set accessors for the properties instead of init, the
object initialization and non-destructive mutation syntax wouldn't be possible. Non-destructive mutation and object initialization both require either
a public init or public set accessor.

Copying selected properties of immutable values is another aspect of a
declarative approach to problem-solving, and in some circumstances makes
it simpler and more direct to create new values by using existing variables as
a kind of template.

Declarative Code and Performance

Using a declarative style can lead to code that is clearer and more direct
but often results in more copies of variables being created, adding storage expense. This is particularly relevant for value types for which the cost
of copying large instances may impact a program's performance. Up to
this point, we have considered only quite small instances, which would be
unlikely to negatively impact performance significantly. While reference
variables are always all the same size, values can be any size. To an extent,
size matters when we're copying values around. A value type that simply
wraps a single int field will be cheaper to copy than one that has lots of
fields, which is why we're often advised to keep value types small.

The definition of *small* varies but is commonly between 16 and 24 bytes.
Note that on a 64-bit architecture, references are 8 bytes each, so it's not
hard to imagine a useful value type that exceeds the recommended size
limit. We'll explore some of the performance characteristics of large value
types in Chapter 8.

Nevertheless, the size of a value type shouldn't be the primary motivation for choosing a class or record over a struct or record struct. If we want
instances of a type to have value semantics, we should make it a value type,
regardless of how large it might be. When we pass value type variables as
arguments for ref or out parameters, no copy of the instance is made because

those arguments are passed by reference. Might the preference for returning values over using ref or out parameters affect the efficiency of our code?

For values with several fields, avoiding the copying might well represent a net performance gain, but we should also consider the impact of our choices on *human* readers. It might seem attractive to use by-reference parameters to avoid copying large values, except that using a ref or out parameter strongly implies that the argument passed is likely to change. If we want our code to be as self-documenting as possible, using ref parameters as an *optimization* might be surprising.

Rather than using the mutable out or ref parameters, we can use in parameters, which are *immutable* by-reference parameters. Arguments for in parameters are passed by reference in exactly the same way as ref and out arguments, but an in parameter variable is read-only within the method. In the next section, we'll explore how to avoid copying value type method arguments by using read-only reference parameters, as well as how to return values by reference.

Read-Only References and Returning by Reference

Read-only references and returning by reference are related concepts, and both can help us reduce the number of copies of value type instances in our code. First we'll look at read-only reference parameters, which we denote using the in keyword on a method parameter. The in modifier, like the ref and out modifiers, makes a by-reference parameter, but, unlike ref or out parameters, it prevents the value of the underlying variable from being changed. In other words, an in parameter variable is immutable. Using in parameters when we're passing large value type instances as arguments might be beneficial because we avoid copying the instance.

Technically, we can also pass a reference to an in parameter, but there's no reason to do so. Passing a reference by reference is useful only if we need to change the reference to refer to a new instance. For that to work, we need a ref or out parameter. No performance benefit is associated with passing a reference by reference, as there may be with value types.

Listing 3-22 shows a simple expression-bodied method, DistanceInKm, that calculates a distance from its speed and time parameter values, both of which are value types.

```
public double DistanceInKm(in Speed speed, in TimeSpan time)
    => speed.InKmh * time.TotalHours;
```

Listing 3-22: Read-only reference parameters

Both the speed and time variables use the in modifier, making them read-only reference parameters in the DistanceInKm method. Since the parameter variables are read-only, the compiler will reject any attempt to set mutable properties, change public fields, or assign a new value to either of them.

When we call a method that has a ref or out parameter, we must also modify the argument we're passing with the ref or out keyword. By contrast, arguments passed to in parameters do *not* require the in modifier, as shown here:

```
var time = TimeSpan.FromHours(2.5);
var speed = Speed.FromKmh(20);

var distance = DistanceInKm(speed, time);

Assert.That(distance, Is.EqualTo(50.0));
```

As with reference and output parameters, we can overload DistanceInKm with a version that has value parameters. The overload *without* modifiers takes precedence in overload resolution if we don't specify the in modifier for the argument. We can explicitly use in for an argument passed to an input parameter to select the version taking its parameters by reference. As mentioned earlier in the chapter, overloading methods based solely on whether a parameter is passed by reference or by value is likely to be a source of confusion.

Read-only reference parameters are designed to be transparent in the calling code; that is, passing an argument to an in parameter appears the same as passing an argument by value. One consequence is that a method may be modified to receive its parameters by read-only reference instead of by value, but without requiring changes to the calling code. Arguments that were previously passed by value would then be passed by reference. This matters only if the *argument* variables may change—perhaps within a different thread. Bear in mind that only the parameter variables within the method are read-only; the argument variables usually aren't. Since the argument passed to an in parameter is passed by reference, any change to the argument's value will be reflected in the value of the parameter variable inside the method. Listing 3-23 demonstrates that it's possible to modify the value of an argument passed to an in parameter even without multiple threads.

```
void ModifyByCallback(in int value, Action callback)
{
  ❶ var temp = value;

  ❷ callback();
     Assert.That(value, Is.Not.EqualTo(temp));
}

int input = 100;

❸ ModifyByCallback(value: input, callback: () => input = 200);
```

Listing 3-23: Modifying a read-only parameter's value via a callback delegate

The ModifyByCallback method takes an int value by read-only reference and an Action delegate. A *delegate* is a variable that refers to a method; here, we use the standard `Action` type for the delegate that represents a method with no parameters and returns void. Within the `ModifyByCallback` method, we copy the *value* of the value parameter into a temporary variable ❶. Then we call the `callback` delegate before testing that the value parameter's value is now different from the value copied to `temp` before we called the delegate ❷. When we call `ModifyByCallback`, we pass the input value along with a lambda for the `callback` parameter. The lambda closes over the input variable, whose value is changed by the lambda ❸.

The test within the `ModifyByCallback` method passes because the value parameter is an alias to the calling code's `input` variable. When the `input` variable's value changes inside the lambda, the value parameter's value is also changed. We should therefore be cautious of methods that have both in parameters and delegate parameters. More generally, we should be suspicious of code that changes the values of any variable passed as an argument to a method, especially if the method and calling code can run on different threads of execution. The potential errors caused by changing an apparently read-only variable could be difficult to track down.

Returning Values by Reference

Although instances of value type aren't generally copied by reference, we can return a value type instance by reference, and receive the returned reference by using a by-reference variable. This can be useful if we're particularly sensitive to the cost of copying large instances, although the technique is sufficiently complex that we probably shouldn't use it routinely. Listing 3-24 shows a struct whose instances will be larger than a reference variable.

```
public readonly struct Address
{
    public Address(string street, string city, string state, string zip)
        => (Street, City, State, Zip) = (street, city, state, zip);

    public string Street { get; }
    public string City   { get; }
    public string State  { get; }
    public string Zip    { get; }
}
```

Listing 3-24: An Address struct with multiple fields

This `Address` struct has four string backing fields, so an instance of the struct is somewhat larger and more expensive to copy than a single reference. If huge numbers of instances were being copied around, we might want to address the cost of some of those copies. However, returning by reference isn't guaranteed to be cheaper than returning even large values by value, and may even represent a performance cost. Even so, if careful performance analysis identified instance copying as an issue, returning values by reference might prove beneficial.

When we access a property, we inadvertently make a copy of the property's value. We can avoid making this copy by returning the value by reference, known as a *reference return value*, or simply a *ref return*. We mark a value as being a ref return by adding the ref keyword, as we do when modifying by-reference method parameters. The Mail class in Listing 3-25 has a Destination property that returns the destination field value by reference.

```
public sealed class Mail
{
    public Mail(string name, Address address)
        => (Addressee, destination) = (name, address);

    public string Addressee { get; }

    public ref Address Destination => ref destination;

    private Address destination;
}
```

Listing 3-25: The Destination property returning the destination field value by reference

Note that we need to add the ref keyword to the property and to the variable being returned by reference.

When we access a property that returns its value by reference, we can also receive that value by reference without copying it at all. A *by-reference variable*, or *ref local*, is a local variable that refers to the same variable as the ref return. This is best illustrated with a simple example. In Listing 3-26, we receive the ref return value from Mail.Destination by using a local reference variable.

```
var address = new Address ("62 West Wallaby Street",
                           "Wigan", "Lancashire", "WG7 7FU");

var letter = new Mail("G Lad Esq.", address);

ref var local = ref letter.Destination;
```

Listing 3-26: Consuming a value returned by reference

This local variable is an alias to the destination field within the letter instance, not a copy of its value. Again, note that we have to use the ref modifier on both the target variable and the property access; if we forget either, the compiler will give us an error. If we omit both, we simply copy the property's value by value into a normal variable.

Preventing Modifications to Data

Just as with by-reference parameters, ref return values and ref locals introduce an alias to a value. If we modify a value through such an alias, we need to make sure we know where those changes will be visible.

We can use the ref local reference to mutate the field in letter too, although in this example we can only assign it a completely new value, since Address is a read-only struct. Listing 3-27 demonstrates that modifying the ref local also changes the field of the letter variable.

```
var letter = new Mail("G Lad Esq.",
    new ("62 West Wallaby Street", "Wigan", "Lancashire", "WG7 7FU"));

ref var address = ref letter.Destination;

Assert.That(address.Street, Is.EqualTo("62 West Wallaby Street"));

address = new Address("1619 Pine Street", "Boulder", "CO", "80302");

Assert.That(letter.Destination.Street,
    Is.EqualTo("1619 Pine Street"));
```

Listing 3-27: Mutating a field by using a ref local variable

Being able to modify a *private* field of an instance in this way might not be desirable. First, it violates the encapsulation of the field in the Mail class, and second, as with any alias, directly altering an object would likely cause problems in multithreaded code. A *race condition* occurs whenever an object's state can be altered by multiple threads simultaneously, or when one thread can read an object before another thread has finished changing it. The size of the Address type means that assigning a new value won't be an atomic operation, meaning that a second thread could read a partly initialized instance.

One common approach to addressing race conditions is to protect access to a variable from multiple threads by using a lock. Locking access to the data within the property itself isn't sufficient in this situation because the underlying data can be modified outside the property definition; we'd need to lock every use of the property, which would likely hamper our code's performance. Fortunately, we have a less intrusive solution: we can simply make the property immutable. Sharing immutable state has none of the drawbacks associated with changing data from multiple threads.

To protect the destination field in Mail from modifications, we can change the Destination property to return a read-only reference to the destination field. If we return such a ref readonly variable, the calling code needs to also use the readonly keyword for the target variable, as Listing 3-28 shows.

```
public sealed class Mail
{
    --snip--

    public ref readonly Address Destination => ref destination;

    private readonly Address destination;
}

var address = new Address ("62 West Wallaby Street", "Wigan", "Lancashire", "WG7 7FU");
var letter = new Mail("G Lad Esq.", address);

ref readonly var local = ref letter.Destination;
```

Listing 3-28: Preventing mutation of a ref return

The compiler won't allow any modifications via the read-only `local` reference variable. We've also made the `destination` field read-only in the `Mail` class. This means that we *must* use a read-only reference if we return a reference to the `destination` field. If we attempt to return a read-only field by reference without the `readonly ref` modifier, the compiler gives us this error:

```
[CS8160] A readonly field cannot be returned by writable reference
```

We can assign one ref variable to another by using the same syntax as assigning a ref local to the result of a property. Note that a `ref readonly` variable can be assigned from a non-read-only reference. An automatic and implicit conversion occurs from a plain—or *writable*—ref return or a ref local *to* a `ref readonly` variable, but not in the other direction. A read-only reference can't be assigned to a writable ref local. Doing so would break the immutability guarantees of a read-only reference.

Keeping By-Reference Variables Within Scope

Methods can return values by reference too, and the syntax is the same as for properties. However, the lifetime of the variable returned by reference must be guaranteed to last at least as long as the reference's lifetime. More formally, the scope of the variable being referenced must *include* the method or property that returns a reference to that variable.

One implication of this rule is that we can't return a reference to a local variable, because the variable will go out of scope as soon as the method or property implementation returns. This is most clearly apparent for value types. The lifetime of a value ends when the scope ends, so its lifetime is *shorter* than that of the reference. The method in Listing 3-29 fails to compile because it's attempting to return a reference to a local variable.

```
public ref Address Get()
{
    var val = new Address();
    return ref val;
}
```

Listing 3-29: Trying to return a reference to a local variable

If we *could* return a reference to the `val` variable, the code calling this method would get a reference to a value that no longer exists. The compiler prevents such a situation by refusing to compile the code, giving this error:

```
[CS8168] Cannot return local 'val' by reference because it is not a ref local
```

This rule applies regardless of whether the value of the local variable is a reference or an instance of a struct. The *variable* still goes out of scope, even when the *instance* exists on the heap. By-reference variables and by-reference returns are references to variables, not instances, in exactly the same way as by-reference parameters.

Instance Fields of Value Types

The compiler will prevent us from returning a variable by reference if it can't guarantee that the variable will be valid for at least as long as any reference to it. A less obvious consequence of this rule is that a method or property of a value type can't return a reference to one of that type's instance fields. The code in Listing 3-30, for instance, won't compile.

```
public readonly struct Color
{
    --snip--
    public ref readonly uint Rgb => ref rgbValue;

    private readonly uint rgbValue;
}
```

Listing 3-30: Returning a struct field by reference

The compiler gives us this error message:

```
[CS8170] Struct members cannot return 'this' or other instance members by reference
```

This operation is prohibited because the compiler can't easily determine that the Color instance will outlive any reference to a field within it. Listing 3-31 shows a pathological example to demonstrate why that might be a problem.

```
public ref readonly uint DefaultRgb()
{
    var source = new Color();

    ref readonly var rgb = ref source.Rgb;
    return ref rgb;
}
```

Listing 3-31: Invalid code returning a reference to a struct's field

If the Color struct in Listing 3-30 could legally return one of its fields by reference, the DefaultRgb method in Listing 3-31 would be returning a reference to a field of an object that has gone out of scope. This is a similar problem to returning a reference to a local variable, but this time the problem is directly related to Color being a struct. When a Color variable goes out of scope, each of its fields goes out of scope too. The compiler forbids returning any instance field of a value type by reference to avoid even the possibility of this happening.

Member methods and properties of a value type are also prevented from returning this by reference. It's disallowed for exactly the same reason as for instance fields: if it were permitted, we would be returning a reference to a local value—an instance of the type—that goes out of scope.

References to References

When a reference variable goes out of scope, the instance it represented still exists on the heap until it is garbage collected. We can, therefore, safely return a reference to an instance field from a property or method of a class or a record. In fact, holding such a by-reference variable *prevents* the instance from being garbage collected. In Listing 3-32, we take a reference to an instance field of a local reference type object and return it.

```
public ref readonly Address GetAddress()
{
    var local = new Mail("G Lad Esq.",
        new ("62 West Wallaby Street", "Wigan", "Lancashire", "WG7 7FU"));

    ref readonly var address = ref local.Destination;
    return ref address;
}
```

Listing 3-32: Returning a reference to a field of a local object

The compiler accepts this code, and it's safe to use this method, although we should certainly be cautious because this technique relies on a somewhat esoteric feature of the garbage collector. When GetAddress returns, the local variable goes out of scope, leaving no live reference variables directly to the Mail instance created inside the GetAddress method. Normally, that instance would then become eligible for garbage collection, making the by-reference return value a dangling reference. However, the returned by-reference variable is enough to prevent the garbage collector from destroying the Mail instance, so holding a by-reference variable to one of its fields remains valid.

Behind the scenes, a by-reference variable or parameter to a field within a class or record instance represents a managed pointer. *Managed pointers* are an implementation detail of the CLR, but the takeaway here is that they're tracked by the garbage collector and considered *object roots*—simply put, references or managed pointers to objects known to be live when the garbage collector runs. Those objects, in turn, may contain references to other objects on the heap, so the chain of references forms a graph of objects currently in use at the time the garbage collector runs.

The garbage collector uses object roots to determine whether object instances can be collected: any instance it can't reach from an object root by following the object graph is eligible for collection, and any object that *is* reachable survives. Storing a ref local variable is enough to keep the owning object from being garbage collected.

We can always safely return a by-reference parameter variable by reference because the variable aliased by the parameter must be in scope for the calling code. Strictly, the scope of the variable includes the method accepting the parameter by reference, as shown in Listing 3-33.

```
public ref Color RemoveRed(ref Color color)
{
    color = new Color(0, color.Green, color.Blue);
    return ref color;
}

var hasRed = new Color(0x77, 0xFF, 0x11);

ref var noRed = ref RemoveRed(ref hasRed);

Assert.That(noRed.Red, Is.EqualTo(0));
Assert.That(hasRed.Red, Is.EqualTo(0));
```

Listing 3-33: Returning a ref parameter by reference

The RemoveRed method's color parameter can be returned by reference because the reference can't outlive the variable underlying it, since the scope of the hasRed variable in the calling code *includes* RemoveRed. Listing 3-34 shows that the same is true of out parameters, even though they look like they're returning a reference to a local variable.

```
public ref Color CreateColor(out Color result)
{
    result = new Color();
    return ref result;
}

ref var created = ref CreateColor(out Color color);

Assert.That(created.Red, Is.EqualTo(0));
Assert.That(color.Red, Is.EqualTo(0));
```

Listing 3-34: Returning an out parameter by reference

The result parameter in the CreateColor method is a reference to a variable in the calling code, whose scope also includes the CreateColor method itself.

NOTE *Returning out parameters by reference is prohibited as of C# v11.0, although returning ref parameters by reference is still permitted.*

We can also return in parameters by reference, but they must be returned as ref readonly, because an in parameter is immutable. If we forget to make the returned reference readonly, the compiler gives us a predictable error:

```
[CS8333] Cannot return variable 'in Color' by writable reference because it is a readonly
variable
```

Given that the variable used to populate the in parameter must already be part of the calling code and we can't modify it in any way, returning an in parameter by reference typically isn't useful. We can pass the variable to an in parameter to avoid copying it, but the method could just as easily return void because the calling code must already know about the variable, which could not be modified by the method.

Mutable Immutable Properties

Properties that return by reference can't have a set accessor and thus are apparently immutable. However, ref returns have a peculiarity: if we return by *writable* reference, as shown in the Color property in Listing 3-35, we can use the reference to mutate the underlying value, just as we would use a setter for the property.

```
public class Brush
{
    public Brush(Color c) => color = c;

    public ref Color Color => ref color;

    private Color color;
}

var brush = new Brush(new Color(0x77, 0x33, 0xFF));

brush.Color = new Color();

Assert.That(brush.Color.Red, Is.EqualTo(0));
```

Listing 3-35: Setting a new value for a writable reference property

It may look like we're setting the Color property of the brush variable to a new instance of Color, but in fact we're assigning a new value to the *field* in the Brush class directly, by reference. The semantic difference is somewhat subtle. Part of the purpose of a property is to *encapsulate* access to a value, but here we deliberately sidestep that encapsulation by returning a reference to the field.

If the Color property returned a ref readonly, this code wouldn't compile because we'd be attempting to modify a read-only variable. A set accessor for the Color property would enable us to change its value, but permitting a set accessor for something that is read-only seems perverse.

Considering Performance vs. Simplicity

Ref returns, used in conjunction with ref locals, may be beneficial when we'd otherwise be copying large value type instances around, particularly if *many* copies would be generated. Ref locals and ref returns are a relatively complex optimization feature and need to be introduced with care. When the values are small, creating references to them carries no benefit and might even result in added cost due to the extra indirection required to access the value. We can use ref returns and ref locals for reference variables too, but, again, doing so provides no advantage; C# allows it just for the symmetry.

We need to be aware of the costs of *all* by-reference variables, whether they're parameters, return values, or locals. Any by-reference variable introduces extra indirection in order to obtain the *actual* underlying value.

Final Word on Mutable By-Reference Parameters

As mentioned previously, using the mutable by-reference parameter types ref and out often indicates very procedural code. In general, if we prefer a more declarative style, we make our code more self-describing and often more compact. However, output parameters have one use in modern C# that supports that same declarative approach. The term of art is *object deconstruction*, although the relevance of out parameters here may not be immediately obvious.

We begin with the value tuple, introduced in C# v7.0 to simplify the creation of lightweight aggregate types such as the point variable in Listing 3-36.

```
var point = (X: 30, Y: 50);

Assert.That(point.X, Is.EqualTo(30));
Assert.That(point.Y, Is.EqualTo(50));
```

Listing 3-36: A value tuple for a point

This point variable is a *named tuple*, where we give a name to each component. The tests show how we use those names like properties to obtain their respective values. Value tuples support deconstruction: we can decompose the point variable into individual variables with names unrelated to the names we gave the components. Listing 3-37 uses the deconstruction syntax to assign two separate variables from the fields of the point tuple from Listing 3-36.

```
var (horizontal, vertical) = point;

Assert.That(horizontal, Is.EqualTo(30));
Assert.That(vertical, Is.EqualTo(50));
```

Listing 3-37: Tuple deconstruction

In this code, the types of the horizontal and vertical variables are inferred from the components of the point value tuple, and we use them individually without needing to refer to point at all. We can support this same syntax in our own types by writing a public Deconstruct method, which uses out parameters to take all of its parameters by reference. Listing 3-38 shows a Coordinate struct type with such a method.

```
public readonly struct Coordinate
{
    public Coordinate(int x, int y) => (X, Y) = (x, y);
```

```
    int X { get; init; }
    int Y { get; init; }

    public void Deconstruct(out int x, out int y)
    {
        x = X;
        y = Y;
    }
}
```

Listing 3-38: User-defined type deconstruction

We can use identical syntax to that shown in Listing 3-37 to deconstruct a `Coordinate` value into individual variables:

```
var point = new Coordinate(30, 50);

var (horizontal, vertical) = point;
```

The compiler translates this code to call the `Deconstruct` method of the `Coordinate` struct, so the calling code has no mention of out arguments, or even a call to a method. The compiler's support for object deconstruction allows the code using `Coordinate` to access its properties as individual variables in a compact and clear way.

The same syntax for the `Deconstruct` method is also supported for classes. The compiler generates a `Deconstruct` method for both records and record structs, saving us from having to define our own implementation of it.

Simple value types like `Coordinate` and the `point` value tuple are common in functional programs because they encapsulate simple abstractions with a minimum of syntactical overhead. They also present little or no performance overhead, allowing us to write expressive and efficient programs more simply.

Summary

> *How do we convince people that in programming simplicity and clarity [. . .] are not a*
> *dispensable luxury, but a crucial matter that decides between success and failure?*
> —Edsger W. Dijkstra, *Selected Writings on Computing:*
> *A Personal Perspective*

The concept of pass-by-reference, and how it differs from pass-by-value, is much less straightforward than a first glance might suggest. The common explanation—that value types are passed by value and reference types by reference—is misleading. We don't pass types around; we pass values. What's more, by default all values are passed by value.

Understanding what the value of a variable actually *is* helps us more precisely define what passing by reference really entails. Passing by value is merely the default; we have to actively choose to pass a value by reference. Reference and value types differ semantically because the value of a reference variable isn't the same as the instance of the type it represents. For value type variables, however, the value and the instance are the same thing.

Moreover, we can pass a variable by reference in several ways, each with different behavior and restrictions. We've looked at using by-reference method parameters to change variables in different ways, as well as at alternatives that can make our programs more direct and comprehensible by avoiding side effects and making values immutable. Immutability is an important aspect of avoiding problems associated with unwanted aliasing, even when by-reference variables are being used. If we use read-only properties and read-only structs judiciously, we can take advantage of some of the performance benefits of passing by reference, without suffering from the complications of managing access to shared mutable data.

When an immutable value is shared by several references, aliasing can never present a problem. This is the basic principle behind in parameters and read-only local references, but it's also a consideration when we want value semantics for a type but also want the benefits of reference semantics for performance.

However, passing by reference isn't without cost. Every access to a by-reference parameter involves an extra level of indirection. This cost is likely to be negligible but could adversely affect performance if the method is used in "hot paths" through the code. As with any performance optimization, we must measure the outcome to determine whether the optimization is worthwhile.

4

IMPLICIT AND EXPLICIT COPYING

In almost any useful program, the values of variables are constantly being copied, even when we don't realize it. In this chapter, we'll examine the causes and the possible consequences of copying. This topic might seem trivial, but copying can have hidden costs that can prove problematic when it's not clear that a section of code *is* making copies.

We'll explore the following:

- Why knowing whether a value is a copy is vital to understanding a program
- How to avoid copying values in certain circumstances
- Where the compiler may be making hidden copies of values
- What we can do to prevent the need for the compiler to make hidden copies

You know from previous chapters that copying references is always a cheap operation, because it doesn't also copy the instance. When we copy a value type instance, however, the value of each field is also copied, costing time and memory space, especially if the instance consists of several fields. Knowing when copying might occur, then, may help us identify opportunities to avoid some copies, thereby improving our program's memory usage and speed.

The relative cost difference between copying a reference and copying an instance is part of the rationale behind the common advice to make value types small. However, the cost of copying is only one part of the story. Copying value type instances around is usually cheap, although some pathological cases may be cause for concern, but working with a copy might also have *semantic* implications. In particular, if we haven't noticed that we've made a copy, we might be surprised that changes we've made to a value aren't visible in the way we expect. Correspondingly, unexpected changes to an instance that have occurred using a copied reference can be the cause of subtle problems.

Copying by Simple Assignment

The differences in copy behavior of value types and reference types can have subtle consequences that can be hidden in apparently simple expressions that make a copy. The simplest example of copying occurs as the result of assignment:

```
var copy = existing;
```

Assigning the value of one variable to another like this is called *simple assignment*, and the left side—the target of the assignment—must be either a variable, or a property or indexer with an accessible set accessor. The right side is an *expression*, which describes anything that can be evaluated to produce a value. The expression might be a simple value like a literal or an enum member, another variable, or a more complex expression, such as a call to a method.

Both variables and values are associated with a type. Since in the preceding example we use type deduction for copy with the var declaration, the compiler deduces the type of the copy variable from the type of the *value* of existing. The type of the target variable doesn't necessarily need to be identical to the type of the value being assigned. If we specify a different type for the target variable, the type of the value on the right must be *implicitly convertible* to the type of the variable on the left.

We can try to explicitly coerce the value to the target type by using an explicit cast, which you saw in Chapter 2. For example, a double can be explicitly cast to an int, although the conversion may lose information because the value is truncated. If the compiler detects that an explicit conversion can never succeed, such as from a string to an int, the code won't compile. Otherwise, the conversion happens at run time and may fail with an `InvalidCastException` if the conversion fails.

Value Copy Behavior

We know a copy of a non-null reference refers to the same instance in memory as the original reference. That means any change we make to an instance of a reference type is visible via *all* the references to that instance. By comparison, when we copy an instance of a value type, the copy is a new, independent instance of the type, with copies of the original value's fields.

However, it's not always the case that changes to one instance of a value type can't be observed by other instances. If any of the fields copied from the original value type instance are references, the copied instances will have copies of those references. Therefore, a copy of a value type instance can still alias an object on the heap via its fields. To illustrate, consider the ill-advised example in Listing 4-1, where the `Item` property of the `Purchase` struct is a reference to a mutable `Product` class.

```
public sealed class Product
{
    public int     Id { get; set; }
    public decimal Price { get; set; }
}

public readonly struct Purchase
{
    public Product  Item { get; init; }
    public DateTime Ordered { get; init; }
    public int      Quantity { get; init; }
}
```

Listing 4-1: Mutable reference fields

Here, `Product` is a simple data-carrier class, similar to types often used to read data from a database or message queue. A common characteristic of simple data carriers like `Product` is to have mutable properties to read and write their values. The `Purchase` type, meanwhile, is a struct and a well-behaved value type; it's marked `readonly`, and all of its properties are init-only, meaning they can be given a value only when a new `Purchase` instance is initialized.

Even though `Purchase` is a readonly struct, it is *not* immutable because its `Item` property is a mutable type. Moreover, that property is a reference because `Product` is a reference type. Two `Purchase` instances, therefore, can refer to the same *mutable* `Product` instance on the heap. To illustrate this, let's look at how instances of these types are set out in memory.

We create instances of the `Purchase` type and its properties from Listing 4-1 like this:

```
var existing = new Purchase
    {
        Item = new Product { Id = 10990, Price = 12.99m },
        Ordered = DateTime.Parse("2024-02-02"),
        Quantity = 12
    };
```

The memory used by the existing variable might look something like Figure 4-1.

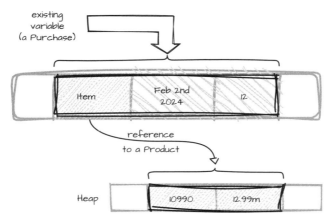

Figure 4-1: The memory layout of a reference in a struct

Since `Purchase` is a value type, a variable of type `Purchase` contains a complete instance in place wherever the variable is declared. In Figure 4-1, the existing identifier is a name representing a memory location containing the values of the three fields of a `Purchase` type. One of those fields is a backing field for the `Item` property, whose type is the `Product` class. As a reference type, the `Product` instance is allocated on the heap, and the `Item` property stores a reference to it. The content of the other property values, being value type instances, is stored directly within the existing variable. Now consider what happens when we *copy* the existing variable in Listing 4-2.

```
var existing = new Purchase
    {
        Item = new Product { Id = 10990, Price = 12.99m },
        Ordered = DateTime.Parse("2024-02-02"),
        Quantity = 12
    };
--snip--
var copy = existing;
```

Listing 4-2: Copying the value of the existing variable

Because the type of the Item property is a class, only the *reference* is copied to the new copy variable's instance, leaving both the existing and copy variables referring to the same Product instance on the heap, as depicted in Figure 4-2.

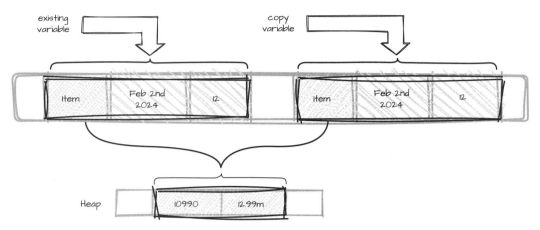

Figure 4-2: The memory layout after copying a struct instance

Having copied existing to copy, we now have two Purchase instances in memory, but the instance data for Item hasn't been copied. Each Purchase instance has a reference to the same Product on the heap.

Read-Only Properties vs. Immutable Types

Making the Purchase struct in Listing 4-1 read-only doesn't protect it from unintended side effects associated with aliasing references, nor does the fact that its Item property has no set accessor. We could still inadvertently modify the object referred to by the Item property because even though Purchase.Item has no set accessor, the Product type it refers to has mutable properties. If we alter a property of the Product instance via the copy variable, that change is visible in the existing variable, as demonstrated in Listing 4-3.

```
var existing = new Purchase
    {
        Item = new Product { Id = 10990, Price = 12.99m },
        Ordered = DateTime.Parse("2024-02-02"),
        Quantity = 12
    };

var copy = existing;

copy.Item.Price = 14.99;
Assert.That(existing.Item.Price, Is.EqualTo(14.99));
```

Listing 4-3: Altering the state of a Product via a shared reference

Because the properties of the Product type are writable, we can change the instance by using any reference to it. If we make the Product type immutable, we can't change the data in a Product instance via *any* reference to it, so it doesn't matter that it's shared among multiple reference variables. It isn't especially unusual for value types to contain references as fields or properties, but we must be cautious about the *kinds* of references we store in a value type. If we want to avoid the issues associated with unexpected changes to Purchase instances, we must make sure that the object referred to by Purchase. Item can't be changed via *any* reference; it's not enough to simply ensure that the referenced object can't be changed via Purchase itself. The simplest way to achieve that would be to make Product immutable. More generally, value types with reference type fields should refer only to immutable types.

Knowing whether we have a copy of a reference or a copy of a complete instance is valuable information. Assigning one variable to another is the most visible example of how values are copied in a program. In the next few sections, we'll look at some less obvious examples of values being copied and see how our programs may be making more copies than we think.

Creating New Objects

Most of the time, we don't need to worry about how object instances use memory; that's the CLR's responsibility. We create object instances with the new expression, which abstracts the details of how and where memory for the object is allocated. New objects are always created by calling a constructor, although, as you saw in Chapter 2, when we use the object initialization syntax, the constructor call may be implicitly inserted by the compiler. Either approach may require an extra copy of a new value type instance, so to more closely monitor the memory our programs use, we need to pay extra attention to *how* we construct new objects.

For example, Listing 4-4 shows an instance of a Purchase value type being created via object initialization. Although not visible in the code, an extra copy of the Purchase instance is used to perform the initialization.

```
public readonly struct Purchase
{
    public Product   Item { get; init; }
    public DateTime  Ordered { get; init; }
    public int       Quantity { get; init; }
}

var order = new Purchase
    {
        Item = new Product { Id = 10990, Price = 12.99m },
        Ordered = DateTime.Parse("2024-02-02"),
        Quantity = 12
    };
```

Listing 4-4: Creating a new instance of the Purchase value type via object initialization

NOTE *The extra copy of Purchase is required only if we actually access its properties, but setting property values that are never read probably isn't common.*

When we use object initialization to create a new object, the constructor is still invoked, even when it isn't specified. Since `Purchase` is a struct and has no user-defined constructors, the new instance is first default-initialized and then its properties are assigned according to the values specified between the braces.

The default-initialized instance created by the constructor call is *not* observable by our code. The properties of the new instance are initialized via a hidden variable, which is then copied to the target variable—the `order` variable in Listing 4-4—after the object initialization has completed. When the code to initialize a `Purchase` is compiled, the compiler emits the equivalent of Listing 4-5.

```
var __temp = new Purchase();
__temp.Item = new Product { Id = 10990, Price = 12.99m };
__temp.Ordered = DateTime.Parse("2024-02-02");
__temp.Quantity = 12;
var order = __temp;
```

Listing 4-5: Code that's equivalent to object initialization syntax

NOTE *We couldn't have written the same code ourselves, because the `Purchase` type's `Item`, `Ordered`, and `Quantity` properties are init-only. The compiler would also translate the initialization of the `Item` property into a call to the constructor and separately set its properties, but for brevity's sake, the object-initialization syntax has been left intact here.*

After the constructor has completed, the instance has only been default-initialized, and, in particular, the `Item` property will be `null` since it's a reference type. The purpose of this two-stage initialization is to prevent that incomplete instance from being observed. The value of the hidden `__temp` variable is copied to the target `order` variable when the initialization is complete, after all the properties have been assigned.

Overwriting a Value

A hidden variable also allows us to reassign a variable by using properties of its previous value. Listing 4-6 reinitializes the `order` variable with a new instance and uses the existing value of `order.Item` for the `Item` property of the new instance.

```
order = new Purchase
    {
        Item = order.Item,
        Ordered = DateTime.Parse("2024-02-03"),
        Quantity = 5
    };
```

Listing 4-6: Reinitializing the order variable by using its own properties

Without the hidden `__temp` variable introduced by the compiler, the result of the `new` expression would be assigned to `order` before the value of the Item property had been obtained. The initialization of the order variable would be similar to the following:

```
order = new Purchase();
order.Item = order.Item;
order.Ordered = DateTime.Parse("2024-02-03");
order.Quantity = 5;
```

Notice that the order variable being assigned to is default-initialized before its properties are set. The Item property is effectively being used to reinitialize itself. Without the hidden __temp variable, Item will be initialized to null during the order variable's initialization and then reassigned that same null value. As a result, the order variable's Item property will end up with the value null, which is certainly not what we intend. The approach shown in Listing 4-5 correctly handles this behavior by not overwriting the order instance until the temporary copy has been fully initialized.

When Purchase is a value type, as in these examples, the extra __temp copy might be significant, because it's a copy of the whole instance value. When the type is a class or a record, the copy is just a new reference to the same instance, so the cost of the extra copy is negligible.

Prior to C# v9.0, object initialization could be used only for properties with a public set accessor. This restriction was removed with the introduction of init-only properties, but in general a constructor is a more direct method for initializing an instance, at least in part because it avoids the need for a hidden variable—well, *most* of the time. As you'll see next, this is not universally true for value types.

Constructing Value Types

When we create a local variable instance of a struct or record struct type via a user-defined constructor, the compiler can introduce a variation on the two-stage initialization we saw with object initialization. The compiler still inserts a hidden variable, but instead of setting properties, it adds code to directly call the required constructor on the hidden instance before copying its value to the target variable.

Listing 4-7 shows a Color struct whose properties have neither set nor init accessors, so we must use a constructor to initialize the properties.

```
public readonly struct Color
{
    public Color(int red, int green, int blue)
        => (Red, Green, Blue) = (red, green, blue);

    public int Red { get; }
    public int Green { get; }
    public int Blue { get; }
}

var background = new Color(red: 0xFF, green: 0xA5, blue: 0x0);
```

Listing 4-7: Calling a constructor to initialize the Color struct's properties

A constructor has the special name `.ctor` in the compiled code, so creating an instance of `Color` with arguments is broadly equivalent to this:

```
Color __temp;
__temp..ctor(red: 0xFF, green: 0xA5, blue: 0x0);
Color background = __temp;
```

The constructor is invoked on the `__temp` value *in place* on the second line. The declaration of the `__temp` variable causes the compiler to reserve enough space for a default instance of `Color`, and, at run time, the constructor is invoked on that instance as if it were a normal method.

Since `Color` is a value type, the hidden variable represents a full instance, and that instance is copied in full to the target variable. This behavior applies only to user-defined constructors of struct and record struct types; the default constructor for a value type simply default-initializes each field and thus doesn't require a hidden copy.

As we saw with object initialization, the hidden `__temp` variable prevents a partially constructed instance from ever being observable. In practice, the compiler can typically optimize away the hidden instance altogether, but in some circumstances, such as when constructing an instance might fail with an exception, a hidden copy can't be avoided. Consider the `Brush` class in Listing 4-8, whose background field is initialized using a field initializer. In the `Assign` method, we assign a new value for background.

```
public class Brush
{
    public void Assign(int r, int g, int b)
    {
        background = new Color(red: r, green: g, blue: b);
    }

    private Color background = new Color(red: 0xFF, green: 0xA5, blue: 0);
}
```

Listing 4-8: Calling a struct constructor that might throw an exception

The hidden temporary copy of `Color` is essential when we reassign the background field within the `Assign` method of `Brush`, as it ensures that background always has a valid and predictable value. If the `Color` constructor were called directly on the background instance and failed with an exception, it might leave background in an indeterminate state. In the `Assign` method, the compiler must ensure that the existing value for the background field can be used, even if the constructor for `Color` throws an exception.

By separating the construction of the `Color` instance from assigning to the background field, the compiler ensures that the only *observable* states for the variable are either the fully constructed value, if no exception occurred, or its previous value, if the constructor throws an exception. Note that copying a value type instance will never throw an exception; copying the value from one memory location to another is always safe and doesn't require new memory to be allocated at run time.

Copying value type instances isn't guaranteed to be atomic. For example, if the type has multiple fields or floating-point values, a different thread could observe the target value partway through the copy operation, a risk known as *memory tearing*. This is an issue only when multiple threads share memory that can be written. However, it's important to remember that mutability isn't just about setting properties; immutable values can be copied as well. The simplest protection against memory tearing is to make sure that memory accessible to multiple threads is truly read-only.

Copying Records Like Value Types

Chapter 2 showed how to use non-destructive mutation to copy an existing record instance and alter selected properties of that copy by using the with keyword. Listing 4-9 shows how a Color record can be cloned this way.

```
public sealed record Color(int Red, int Green, int Blue);

var pink = new Color(Red: 0xFF, Green: 0xA5, Blue: 0xFF);

var orange = pink with { Blue = 0 };
```

Listing 4-9: Cloning a record instance by using with

Cloning an instance by using non-destructive mutation means that the original instance is preserved while the copied instance is changed. In Listing 4-9, the cloned variable orange takes all the properties from pink *except* the Blue property, which is explicitly given the value 0.

The same syntax can be used to copy structs and record structs and provides a convenient way to set init-only properties on the target variable. Record types have an additional benefit because they're reference types and thus don't have the copy-by-value semantics of a true value type. If we just assign a record variable to another variable, we still get two references to the same instance, as shown here:

```
var black = pink;
Assert.That(ReferenceEquals(black, pink), Is.True);
```

If the pink variable were a value type, black would be a copy of the instance. The with keyword always copies an instance, regardless of whether it's a value type or reference type.

Just as with object initialization, the compiler creates a hidden temporary instance and sets its properties before copying it to the target variable. Non-destructive mutation differs from object initialization in that, for records, the new instance is created using a virtual compiler-generated Clone method. This method is essential because, by default, positional records like the Color record in this example do not have an accessible parameterless constructor.

Record structs and structs can always be constructed without arguments and are always copied by value, meaning they don't have or need a

Clone method. The with syntax isn't supported by class types because, among other challenges, most classes aren't intended to model value semantics.

The initialization process for reference type instances differs from the process for value types, mainly because of the way the different types are allocated and stored in memory. That has consequences for the variables we use to access those instances too, especially when we need to use a reference variable to refer to a value type instance, causing the value to be boxed.

Identifying Unnecessary Boxing

Value type instances don't exist on the heap except as part of another object, so we can't use a reference to refer to them directly. Boxing, as you know from Chapter 2, solves this by copying the value to a known place on the heap and allowing us to reference that copy.

However, because boxing always copies to the heap, the box is subject to garbage collection and other heap management tasks. If we box values indiscriminately, then our program's performance and memory use will suffer. Taking the time to identify and remove unnecessary boxing will improve our code's efficiency.

Boxing occurs anytime we use a reference type variable to refer to a value type instance. It usually happens implicitly (although we can explicitly box a value, it's rarely necessary). Recall from Chapter 2 that all types ultimately derive from object, so we can always implicitly cast a value of any type to object. When that value isn't already a reference, the result is a reference to a boxed instance.

Let's look at an example. The Clone method in Listing 4-10 creates a new local instance of the Coordinate value type and returns an object reference to it. The returned value is a reference to a Coordinate that has been boxed.

```
public readonly struct Coordinate
{
    public int X { get; init; }
    public int Y { get; init; }

    public object Clone()
    {
        var item = new Coordinate { X = this.X, Y = this.Y };
        return item;
    }
    --snip--
}
```

Listing 4-10: Returning a reference to a boxed value type variable

When we call the Clone method, we are returned an object reference to a boxed Coordinate instance. The boxing occurs just before the method exits; space is allocated on the heap for a copy of item's value, and a reference to that box is returned from the method.

Unboxing, the reverse of boxing, copies the value inside a box on the heap into an instance of its original value type. Unboxing must always be done explicitly and is syntactically the same as an explicit cast from the boxed value to the target type, as shown in Listing 4-11.

```
var original = new Coordinate( --snip-- );
object box = original.Clone();

Coordinate clone = (Coordinate)box;
```

Listing 4-11: Unboxing to the original type

When a value type implements one or more interfaces, instances can also be referred to by a variable of any of those interface types, and this also requires the instance to be boxed.

To an Interface

A value can be boxed only when it can be implicitly converted to the target reference type. Since all value types are sealed—meaning inheritance is prohibited—that valid conversion can be to an `object` variable reference, a `System.ValueType` (which itself is *not* a value type), or an interface implemented by the value type. If the value is an `enum` member, it can also be converted to the `System.Enum` class or any of the interfaces implemented by `System.Enum`.

We need a direct `object` reference to a value in only a very few cases, and there's no excuse for boxing to a `System.ValueType`, except perhaps for purely didactic examples. A value type variable can implicitly convert to any interface implemented by the type, such as the `IComparable` interface implemented by the `Color` struct in Listing 4-12.

```
public readonly struct Color : IComparable<Color>
{
    public Color(uint val) => rgb = val;

    int IComparable<Color>.CompareTo(Color other)
        => rgb.CompareTo(other.rgb);

    private readonly uint rgb;
}
```

Listing 4-12: The IComparable interface implemented by the Color struct

The `IComparable<T>` interface specifies a single method named `CompareTo`, in which we define the comparison operation allowing collections of `T` to be sorted. The implementation for `Color` here simply defers to its `uint` field, which implements the `IComparable<uint>` interface.

Note that the implementation of `IComparable<Color>.CompareTo` is an *explicit* implementation, meaning we can invoke `CompareTo` only by using a reference to the interface type. Any attempt to call `CompareTo` directly on a `Color` variable results in a compile error. If we cast a `Color` variable to the `IComparable<Color>` interface, the value will be boxed into an `IComparable<Color>` reference, as in Listing 4-13.

```
var red = new Color(0xFF0000);
var green = new Color(0x00FF00);

IComparable<Color> compare = red;
var less = compare.CompareTo(green);
```

Listing 4-13: Explicitly boxing to an interface type

When we initialize this `compare` variable, the value of red is boxed, because variables of any interface type are references. We could avoid the box by making `CompareTo` nonexplicit, allowing us to call it directly using the red variable without casting to the interface. That's not to say that we should prefer nonexplicit implementations; explicit interface methods are a good way to segregate the public interface of a type.

We can call an explicit interface implementation by using a generic type parameter that has been constrained to the interface type. In this case, no cast is needed, and no boxing takes place. To demonstrate, the generic `LessThan` method in Listing 4-14 doesn't box its parameters, even when we pass Color values as arguments for it, because the generic parameter T is constrained to the `IComparable<T>` interface.

```
public static bool LessThan<T>(T left, T right)
    where T : IComparable<T>
{
    return left.CompareTo(right) < 0;
}

var red = new Color(0xFF0000);
var green = new Color(0x00FF00);

Assert.That(LessThan(green, red), Is.True);
```

Listing 4-14: Constraining the generic type parameter T to the IComparable<T> interface type

When a generic type parameter is constrained in this way, a variable of the generic type is considered to be of the type used for the constraint. In this example, `left` is used as if it were an `IComparable<T>` variable. We can invoke the method directly on whatever value T represents, even when the implementing method is an explicit implementation.

In Method Calls

Boxing a value type instance by assigning it to a reference variable is often conspicuous in our code, but boxing also occurs when we pass a value type instance as an argument for a reference type method parameter. As with assigning to a reference variable, the value is boxed implicitly if an implicit conversion to the type of the parameter exists. Since boxing is usually implicit, it can be hard to spot. For example, Listing 4-15 boxes the now variable because `DateTime` is a value type, and `Console.WriteLine` takes an `object?` parameter following the format string parameter.

```
DateTime now = DateTime.Now;
--snip--
Console.WriteLine("Time now: {0}", now);
```

Listing 4-15: Boxing the now argument for `Console.WriteLine`

If we remain aware when we're passing value types as arguments for reference type parameters, we can minimize the need to box the arguments or alter the code to avoid the box. However, it's important to weigh the costs of boxing against the context of the rest of the code.

For example, rather than just passing the now variable as the argument to `Console.WriteLine` in Listing 4-15, we could pass now.`ToString`, which doesn't need a box because the `DateTime` struct overrides the `ToString` method, and the `WriteLine` method would call it anyway. Arguably, though, explicitly calling `ToString` reduces the directness of the code, and the cost of boxing the now variable is minimal compared to that of writing to the console.

When we call a base class virtual method on a value type instance that doesn't specifically override that method, the instance is boxed in order to call the base class implementation. If the method is overridden by the type, as `ToString` is in `DateTime`, then no boxing occurs. We avoid the need to box our own value types in such situations by overriding all the virtual methods inherited from `object`: `ToString`, `Equals`, and `GetHashCode`.

Calling the `GetType` method on a value, however, will *always* cause the value to be boxed. The `GetType` method is used to obtain the run-time type of a variable and is implemented on `object`. However, `GetType` isn't virtual, so it can't be overridden.

The lesson here is that we should avoid calling `GetType` for value types. If we need type information on a value, we can use `typeof` instead. Since value types are sealed and can't inherit any other type, the compile-time type returned by `typeof` will always match the run-time type given by `GetType`.

Method Parameters and Arguments

Most copies of values aren't so easily avoided, and passing arguments to methods is perhaps where the majority of copies are made. Trying to avoid such copying is not always beneficial, but understanding the mechanics of method calls is essential. This section examines where hidden copies can be found in properties, indexers, operators, and conversions, often as the result of behind-the-scenes method calls.

Methods can take their parameters either by value or by reference. As you saw in Chapter 3, reference parameters are distinctive in that we need to use one of the `ref`, `out`, or `in` keywords to declare them as well as, for `ref` and `out` parameters, on the arguments passed to them. Parameters that are not reference parameters are known as *value parameters*. Passing an argument to a value parameter is so common that it's easy to forget it results in a copy. Capturing the result of a method call also generally makes a copy of the returned value.

Additionally, the semantic and behavioral differences between value types and reference types have important consequences when we're using the value returned from a method. It's not even always obvious that we are calling a method or using a value returned from one. However, before we investigate those circumstances, let's revisit the essential mechanics of value parameters and return values.

Passing and Returning by Value

Listing 4-16 shows a simple value type, Speed, that has a static Incremented method that takes a value parameter, original, and returns a new value. Both the parameter and the return statement in the Incremented method represent copies of Speed instances.

```
public readonly struct Speed
{
    private Speed(double ms) => InMetersPerSecond = ms;

    public double InMetersPerSecond { get; }
    public static Speed FromMetersPerSecond(double val) => new Speed(val);

    public static Speed Incremented(Speed original)
    {
        var result =
            Speed.FromMetersPerSecond(original.InMetersPerSecond + 10);
        return result;
    }
}

var start = Speed.FromMetersPerSecond(40);
var end = Speed.Incremented(start);

Assert.That(end.InMetersPerSecond, Is.EqualTo(50));
```

Listing 4-16: Passing and returning Speed instances by value

The Incremented method receives its original parameter by value, meaning original is a local variable within the method. The return is also by value, so a whole new instance of Speed is returned as a new value when we call the method. As an optimization, the compiler may be able to avoid that copy by using the result local variable to assign the target variable directly, as long as the observable effect is identical to making a copy. We can either assign the value to a new variable, as we do here, or use the new value to overwrite the value of the start variable passed as the argument in the first place.

Instead of a plain static method, we could use an extension method, which we call as if it were an instance method. The first parameter of an extension method is special because it represents the this identifier that would be implicitly available within an ordinary instance member. An extension method is a good candidate for providing different, perhaps less common, units of measurement. Listing 4-17 uses an extension method called InMph to obtain the value of a Speed in miles per hour.

```
public static class SpeedExtensions
{
    public static double InMph(this Speed speed)
        => speed.InMetersPerSecond * 2.236936;
}

var mph = initial.InMph();
```

Listing 4-17: Defining the InMph extension method for Speed

Despite the special this syntax in the InMph extension method's declaration, the first parameter is still just a value parameter, taking its argument by value. The initial variable's value will therefore be copied into the speed parameter in order to call the method. The Speed type is a struct, so every copy we make represents a whole instance of Speed.

NOTE   *We have many online converters to choose from for this type of conversion. The one used for Listing 4-17 is from the Inch Calculator website,* https://www.inch calculator.com/convert/meter-per-second-to-mile-per-hour/.

Accessing Properties

Whenever we access a property, we're really making a call to a method, either to obtain its value or to set a new one. Both get and set accessors are implemented as hidden methods on a type. By default, set has a value parameter, and get returns by value. In either case, therefore, when we access the property, we make a copy of the value. This process is easy to overlook because the syntax for using a property looks like it's directly getting or setting a field.

Consider the Speed property of the Velocity value type shown in Listing 4-18.

```
public readonly struct Velocity
{
    public Velocity(Speed speed, Angle angle)
        => (Speed, Direction) = (speed, angle);

    public Speed Speed { get; }
    public Angle Direction { get; }
}
```

Listing 4-18: Defining properties of the Velocity struct

Looking at the compiled CIL for the Speed property of the Velocity struct, we see that the property accessor is emitted as a call to the hidden get_Speed method:

```
.property instance valuetype Speed Speed()
{
    .get instance valuetype Speed Velocity::get_Speed()
} // end of property Velocity::Speed
```

Apart from the CIL-specific markers .property, instance, and valuetype, the call to get_Speed is a regular method call. The compiler has synthesized the get_Speed method too, and its signature looks like this in the CIL:

```
.method public hidebysig specialname instance valuetype Speed
    get_Speed() cil managed
{
    --snip--
```

If Speed had a corresponding set accessor, it would be emitted as a method named set_Speed that takes a Speed parameter and returns void. The CIL markers hidebysig and specialname aren't used during execution, but they're used by tools that work with CIL.

The compiler implements the get_Speed accessor as a method that takes no parameters and returns a value of Speed *by value*. It's almost exactly as if we'd written our own method returning a Speed like this:

```
public Speed get_Speed()
{
    // return a Speed value
}
```

The Speed property's get accessor returns a *copy* of a Speed instance by value, in exactly the same way as any method returning a Speed by value.

It's easy to mistake using a property or indexer for directly accessing a field, since the method calls injected by the compiler are conveniently hidden. However, it's important to be aware that accessing a property or indexer calls a method and typically copies values.

NOTE *Indexers are special instance methods that allow an object to be accessed as if it were an array or similar sequence-like object. They're implemented via methods in the same way as properties.*

Using Expressions with Operators

Expressions with operators, such as + or ==, often also represent method calls, requiring copies for parameters and return values and perhaps making other copies internally. For example, in Listing 4-19 we add two Speed values.

```
var start = Speed.FromMetersPerSecond(55);
var increase = Speed.FromMetersPerSecond(15);

var final = start + increase;
```

Listing 4-19: Adding two Speed values

The method call behind this addition may not be immediately apparent, but a closer look shows that simply adding instances together might represent several copies. Listing 4-20 shows the canonical form of operator+ for adding two Speed values.

```
public static Speed operator+(Speed left, Speed right)
    => new Speed(left.InMetersPerSecond + right.InMetersPerSecond);
```

Listing 4-20: Defining the addition operator for Speed

The left and right parameters for operator+ represent one copy each. Conceptually, a copy is also made for the return value, although the compiler is free to optimize that copy away and construct the new Speed instance directly in the target variable being assigned.

We might also overload the == equality operator, comparisons like operator<, the binary combination operators | and &, and even the truth operators true and false, allowing us to include a variable in a Boolean test expression like if(speed) {...}. Hopefully, we would *not* be tempted to overload the truth operators for a type like Speed.

All such operator overloads are implemented as static methods for a type, and all take at least one parameter, which is the type to which they belong. That parameter is usually taken by value and thus represents a copy.

User-defined conversion operators are methods too, and when their parameter or return type is a value type, it is copied by value in the same way. Spotting where an implicit conversion is being invoked can be particularly difficult because the process leaves few syntactic clues in the code. To illustrate, consider the Velocity type in Listing 4-21, which defines an implicit conversion from a Velocity to a Speed.

```
public readonly struct Velocity
{
    public Velocity(Speed speed, Angle angle)
        => (Speed, Direction) = (speed, angle);

    public Speed Speed { get; }
    public Angle Direction { get; }

    public static implicit operator Speed(Velocity velocity)
        => velocity.Speed;
}
```

Listing 4-21: A user-defined implicit conversion

This conversion operator uses one copy of Velocity for the parameter, and two copies of Speed—one to access the property of the velocity parameter, and another to return the value. As with other methods, the compiler may be able to avoid an explicit copy of the return value. In Listing 4-22, the DistanceInKm method takes a Speed parameter and is called with an instance of Velocity, rather than the velocity.Speed property.

```
public double DistanceInKm(Speed speed, TimeSpan elapsed)
    => speed.InMetersPerSecond / 1000 * elapsed.TotalSeconds;

var velocity = new Velocity(initial, direction);

var distance = DistanceInKm(velocity, TimeSpan.FromHours(2));
```

Listing 4-22: Using an implicit conversion to pass an argument

Although this looks to be a regular call to the DistanceInKm method, the velocity argument first needs to be converted to a Speed. Our type conversion operator makes this possible, and since we made the conversion implicit, the compiler simply inserts the call to that operator when we call DistanceInKm, copying the Velocity argument and Speed return value in the process.

Type conversions need to be used wisely. They can hide all sorts of complexity, quite apart from the copies they usually represent. Implicit conversions happen invisibly by design, leaving only subtle clues in code that employs them, such as in method calls like DistanceInKm in Listing 4-22. Explicit user-defined conversions are syntactically more obvious in the code that uses them, but it's still easy to overlook that they, too, represent a call to a method.

When a method returns a variable by reference—which we first examined in Chapter 3—we can use that by-reference variable to directly alter the underlying variable, provided neither is read-only. However, remember that ref returns are an optimization feature and shouldn't be introduced indiscriminately.

All other non-void methods produce values, not variables, meaning we can't assign to the result directly. If we forget this and misuse a return value, it can result in surprising behavior.

Modifying Return Type Instances

You saw in Chapter 2 that a variable can be assigned to, but a value can't. Values are the result of expressions, including method calls, and are immutable. We can't directly modify the value returned from any method.

One common source of confusion is that value type instances and reference type instances have different behavior in this regard: if the method returns a reference to a mutable type, we can use the returned reference to directly modify the instance in memory, but we can't modify a mutable value type instance unless we first copy the returned value to a variable. Understanding how value types differ from reference types in this respect will help us avoid some common hazards and better appreciate the best practice of making all value types immutable.

When a return value is a value type instance, we can't use it to set property values or change any of the value's public fields. We must assign that value to a variable before we can change it. To demonstrate, Listing 4-23 shows a struct with an intentionally mutable InMetersPerSecond property and a static class factory method named FromKmh.

```
public struct Speed
{
    public double InMetersPerSecond { get; set; }

    public static Speed FromKmh(double val)
        => new Speed(val * 1000 / 3600);

    private Speed(double ms) => InMetersPerSecond = ms;
}

Speed.FromKmh(70).InMetersPerSecond = 15.2;
```

Listing 4-23: Attempting to modify the return value of FromKmh

On the last line, we attempt to set a value for the InMetersPerSecond property of the value returned from the static method, which gives us a compilation error:

```
[CS1612] Cannot modify the return value of 'Speed.FromKmh(double)' because it is not a variable
```

This example fails to compile because the FromKmh method returns a Speed *value*. The compiler rejects any modifications to the value, even though the InMetersPerSecond property has a public set accessor.

NOTE *C++ programmers would refer to the returned value as an rvalue.*

If modifications to a return value were permitted, they would be made on a temporary instance introduced by the compiler to capture the value returned by the method. The lifetime of the Speed instance created in the FromKmh method in Listing 4-23 ends when the method returns, so the return value needs to be stored somewhere—namely, in a hidden copy of the instance.

In any case, we would normally assign the Speed value returned by FromKmh to another variable. We are permitted to modify the InMetersPerSecond property of the target *variable* because Speed has a public set accessor, as shown here:

```
var start = Speed.FromKmh(70);
start.InMetersPerSecond = 15.2;
```

The prohibition against modifying a returned value is not specific to properties; it also applies if we try to modify a public field on the return value. The compiler prevents such modifications because the return value from a method isn't a variable. However, as you've already seen, several parts of code don't look like methods but are represented in the compiled code as methods. This restriction on modifying return values applies equally to them because they also produce temporary copies.

Reference Type Properties

If the value returned from a method—or property, indexer, or operator—is a reference, we can modify the instance referred to because the temporary copy of the value is another reference to that same instance. We can therefore use the returned reference to set publicly mutable properties, although we can't change the value of the reference itself by assigning it to refer to a different object.

Consider Listing 4-24, which uses the value returned from the `Data` method to set a property of a reference type instance.

```
public class ReadBuffer
{
    public StringBuilder Data()
        => buffer;

    private readonly StringBuilder buffer = new();
}

var buffer = new ReadBuffer();

buffer.Data().Capacity = 128;
```

Listing 4-24: Setting a reference type property

The `StringBuilder` type is a class with a publicly writable `Capacity` property. The value returned from `ReadBuffer.Data` is a reference to the `StringBuilder` instance stored as a field of `ReadBuffer`. Therefore, we can use the reference returned from the `Data` method to set the `Capacity` of the instance stored as a field of `buffer`.

We can't assign that reference to a new instance of `StringBuilder`, however, as that would be changing the value being returned, not the instance:

```
buffer.Data() = new StringBuilder();
```

This fails to compile because we're attempting to assign to a value, not a variable:

```
[CS0131] The left-hand side of an assignment must be a variable, property or indexer
```

The difference in behavior between methods returning references and those returning value type instances is one of the reasons it's recommended to make all value types immutable. By doing so, we remove any confusion over where a value type instance can be modified, because it can't be modified by anything. When we attempt to modify a returned value, our code fails to compile. When the value is a value type instance, the failure to compile is a good thing: if the modification were permitted, we wouldn't be changing the instance we might think we were changing. Unless a value type is truly immutable, preferably by being a read-only struct or read-only record struct, an instance can still be modified by its instance methods, even when it's a hidden copy.

Instance Methods and Mutability

Although we can't set the value of a property on a returned value type instance, we can call methods on that instance. If the type has non-read-only fields, or properties with a set accessor, the method we call can mutate the instance. In this next example, we have a mutable `Speed` struct with a `Reset` method that changes the value of the `InMetersPerSecond` property:

```
public struct Speed
{
    public double InMetersPerSecond { get; set; }

    public void Reset() => InMetersPerSecond = 0;

    --snip--
}
```

The `Reset` method can be called on any `Speed` value, including one returned from a method or property. In Listing 4-25, we use the value of the `Speed` property of a `Velocity` object to call `Reset`.

```
var velocity = new Velocity(Speed.FromKmh(55), Angle.FromDegrees(45));

velocity.Speed.Reset();

Assert.That(velocity.Speed.InMetersPerSecond, Is.EqualTo(0));
```

Listing 4-25: Calling the `Reset` method on the value returned by `Velocity`'s `Speed` property

When we call `Reset` on `velocity.Speed`, we might be tempted to think we've changed the value stored in the `velocity` variable, but `velocity` doesn't change here, and the test fails, because the `Reset` method mutates only the instance used to call it. The instance returned from the `Speed` property is a temporary value. Recall from Listing 4-23 that we can't use the value to directly set the `InMetersPerSecond` property, but we can change that property via an instance method of `Speed`.

We can mutate a value obtained from an indexer in a similar way, and we can just as easily overlook that only the hidden copy gets altered. Consider Listing 4-26, which calls a method on the value returned from the `Journey` type's indexer.

```
public class Journey
{
    --snip--

    public Velocity this[int idx]
    {
        get => legs[idx];
```

```
                set => legs[idx] = value;
        }

        private List<Velocity> legs = new List<Velocity>();
}
```

journey[0].Speed.Reset();

Listing 4-26: Calling a method on the value returned by Journey's indexer

An indexer is implemented as a method, in the same way as a property, and has precisely the same behavior. Again, it's easy to forget that properties are not variables, especially when they're value type instances. The compiler can't prevent us from calling a method on a returned value, because it's a perfectly reasonable thing to want to do. The only way to prevent this erroneous behavior is to make Speed an immutable type, thereby disallowing any mutating methods entirely. This is another good reason to make all value types immutable.

Properties as Arguments for Read-Only Parameters

Another consequence of method returns being values rather than variables is that they can't be directly passed as arguments for ref or out parameters. As you saw in Chapter 3, by-reference parameters receive the address of their arguments, but only variables have addresses. If we first assign a method return or property result to a variable, we can pass the variable by reference.

Chapter 3 also explained that an in parameter is an immutable by-reference variable. Although in parameters take the address of their argument in exactly the same way that ref and out parameters do, they're designed to behave as if they're value parameters. The compiler therefore allows us to pass a nonvariable as an argument for an in parameter but copies the value to a hidden variable, and it's that variable's address that's passed.

Listing 4-27 defines a BallisticRange method with two in parameters, and calls it using the Speed and Direction properties of a Velocity type.

```
public static double BallisticRange(in Speed initialSpeed, in Angle initialDirection)
{
    const double Gravity = 9.81;

    return initialSpeed.InMetersPerSecond * initialSpeed.InMetersPerSecond *
        Math.Sin(initialDirection.InRadians * 2) / Gravity;
}

public readonly struct Velocity
{
    public Velocity(Speed speed, Angle angle)
        => (Speed, Direction) = (speed, angle);
```

```
    public Speed Speed { get; }
    public Angle Direction { get; }
}

var velocity = new Velocity(Speed.FromMetersPerSecond(55),
                            Angle.FromRadians(0.78));

var distance = BallisticRange(velocity.Speed, velocity.Direction);
```

Listing 4-27: Passing properties as in arguments

Recall that, unlike with ref and out arguments, we don't need to modify the arguments passed for in parameters with the in keyword.

Here, the compiler takes copies of the values it has obtained from velocity.Speed and velocity.Direction and passes references to those copies to the BallisticRange method's in parameters. It's as if we'd written this:

```
var __temp_Speed = velocity.Speed;
var __temp_Angle = velocity.Direction;
var distance = BallisticRange(in __temp_Speed, in __temp_Angle);
```

The __temp_Speed and __temp_Angle copies are made because accessing a property's get accessor produces a value, not a variable. Passing an argument by reference effectively requires the compiler to take its address in memory, but only variables have addresses. The get accessor returns a temporary value that needs to be either assigned to a variable so its address can be taken or passed to a value parameter, which makes a copy of the value. Although in parameters can help reduce the number of copies our applications make, we see their benefits only when we're passing variables as arguments.

A hidden copy is also made for other expressions that are not variables, such as constants and value type method return values. These copies are made only for the read-only in parameters. If we try to pass a property value or other nonvariable to a ref or out parameter, the compiler simply rejects our code. Such *mutable* reference variables are intended to be modified by the called method, and those modifications would be illegal on a constant or the temporary value returned by a get accessor.

Defensive Copies

Whenever the compiler requires a read-only variable but can't guarantee that its value will never change, the compiler will make a *defensive copy*. As a result, any change, however inadvertent, is made to the hidden copy and not the visible variable, so the change can't be observed.

You saw one example of the compiler making a defensive copy of a value type instance in Listing 4-8, where constructing a value type with arguments makes a hidden temporary instance, and then the compiler copies it to the target variable when the constructor has completed. This process protects an existing value from any exceptions that may occur inside the constructor body. If an exception occurs, the original value remains intact.

The compiler may also make a defensive copy of a value type instance to protect a read-only variable from modifications.

Defensive copies aren't required for references because the compiler can always detect a change to the value of a reference. If a reference variable is read-only, any attempt to assign a new reference to it fails to compile. Whether or not the instance being referred to is immutable makes no difference here; if we require the instance to be read-only, it's up to us to ensure that it doesn't change. The value of a value type variable is the instance, and a mutable value can be changed by its instance methods, so the compiler may introduce a defensive copy when we call those methods if the variable is supposed to be read-only.

Mutable Value Types and in Parameters

In Chapter 3, you saw how to use the in modifier for a method parameter to avoid copying the argument if the method's implementation won't modify the corresponding parameter variable's value. However, unless the compiler can guarantee that even inadvertent changes to the parameter values aren't possible, it will make defensive copies of those values.

Listing 4-27 showed the BallisticRange method, which has two read-only reference parameters, initialSpeed and initialDirection. The method implementation uses properties of those parameter variables (InMetersPerSecond and InRadians, respectively) to calculate its return value. If the types of those properties aren't explicitly immutable, the compiler will make defensive copies of their values to guarantee the read-only characteristics of the in parameters. The Speed and Angle struct types used by BallisticRange are shown in Listing 4-28. Neither type's properties are mutable, but note that the types themselves aren't marked readonly.

```
public struct Speed
{
    --snip--
    public double InMetersPerSecond => amount;

    private readonly double amount;
}
public struct Angle
{
    public double InRadians { get; }
    --snip--
}

public static double BallisticRange(in Speed initialSpeed, in Angle initialDirection)
{
    const double Gravity = 9.81;

    return initialSpeed.InMetersPerSecond * initialSpeed.InMetersPerSecond *
            Math.Sin(initialDirection.InRadians * 2) / Gravity;
}
```

Listing 4-28: Using in parameter properties for the BallisticRange method

Within `BallisticRange`, the compiler makes a copy of the initial parameter for each use of the `initialspeed.InMetersPerSecond` property (so two copies in all), even though there's no attempt to modify the `initialSpeed` parameter variable in `BallisticRange`. The `initialDirection` parameter, on the other hand, isn't copied when its `InRadians` property is accessed, although, like `Speed`, the `Angle` struct isn't a read-only type.

To determine why the `Speed` parameter is copied, but the `Angle` parameter is not, we need to understand what the compiler provides and what assumptions it makes.

Automatic vs. Nonautomatic Properties

Although the properties of both the `Speed` and `Angle` types in Listing 4-28 are get-only, they differ in the way they're implemented. The `InRadians` property of `Angle` is an *automatic property*, meaning the compiler introduces a hidden backing field for it and generates the implementation of the get accessor to obtain the field's value. If we had also specified a set accessor for `InRadians`, the compiler would generate the corresponding implementation to set the backing field's value.

By contrast, the `InMetersPerSecond` property of `Speed` is an *expression-bodied property*, meaning it returns the value of an explicitly declared private field. An expression-bodied property is equivalent to a *nonautomatic* property with no set accessor, like this:

```
public double InMetersPerSecond
{
    get { return amount; }
}
```

We'd normally understand this to be a read-only property, since we can't usually change the value of a property with no set accessor. However, C# has no rule that says get accessors *can't* modify the fields of a type; it's merely a convention. Within `BallisticRange`, the `InMetersPerSecond` property is accessed via an immutable reference; if the get accessor did indeed modify the value of the parameter, that change would be visible outside the `BallisticRange` method because the argument was passed by reference.

If the parameter variable is supposed to be immutable, as with in parameters, the compiler must satisfy itself that using the variable in any way won't change its value. Without this guarantee, the compiler makes defensive copies of the value everywhere the parameter is used to access a property or call a method. If the method or property *did* mutate the value, only the hidden copy would be affected. The change would never be observable outside the `BallisticRange` method via the argument passed to the method's parameter.

The `InRadians` property of `Angle` in Listing 4-28 is also get-only, but because it's an automatic property, the compiler adds a special attribute to the get accessor method to indicate that it's a read-only implementation. Listing 4-29 shows the generated CIL for the get_InRadians method.

```
.method public hidebysig specialname instance float64
get_InRadians() cil managed
{
    .custom instance void [System.Runtime]
            System.Runtime.CompilerServices.IsReadOnlyAttribute::.ctor()
    = (01 00 00 00 )
--snip--
```

Listing 4-29: A read-only automatic property

The compiler adds the IsReadOnlyAttribute indicator for automatic properties in the compiled code and can check for the presence of the attribute cheaply, even when the type of the parameter is declared in a different compiled assembly. In a positional record struct, the compiler generates the properties for the parameters given to the type. The get accessors of those generated properties also have IsReadOnlyAttribute applied.

When we use an in parameter variable to call methods or access property values, the compiler checks those methods and properties. If this attribute is present, the compiler knows it can avoid making defensive copies.

Read-Only Reference Variables

Defensive copies are also required when we use read-only local reference variables, unless the compiler is satisfied that accessing the variable can't change its value. We explored in Chapter 3 how local reference variables are used in cooperation with reference return values.

A method or property of a class or a record—but not a struct or record struct—can return an instance field by reference. If we return a value by reference, no copy of the value is made. Making it read-only ensures that the value can't be modified using that reference. For example, the Projectile class in Listing 4-30 has properties that return instance fields by reference.

```
public sealed class Projectile
{
    public Projectile(Speed speed, Angle angle)
        => (initial, direction) = (speed, angle);

    public ref readonly Speed Speed => ref initialSpeed;
    public ref readonly Angle Angle => ref initialDirection;

    private readonly Speed initialSpeed;
    private readonly Angle initialDirection;
}
```

Listing 4-30: Defining ref return values for the Projectile class

The references returned by these Angle and Speed properties can never outlive the Projectile instance because Projectile is a class, so its instances are allocated on the heap and their lifetimes are governed by the garbage collector. Value types are not permitted to return their fields by reference because the instance's lifetime might end before any reference to its internals.

With ref readonly properties, we would usually also capture the returned reference in a local read-only reference variable, also called a *ref readonly local*. In the following code, we use ref readonly locals to receive the references returned from the properties of Projectile from Listing 4-30:

```
var dart = new Projectile(initial, direction);

ref readonly var speed = ref dart.Speed;
ref readonly var angle = ref dart.Angle;

var kmh = speed.InMetersPerSecond;
var degrees = angle.InRadians;
```

Because the properties of Projectile return read-only references, we must assign them to read-only reference variables, or explicitly copy their value by omitting the ref keyword altogether on the target variables.

A read-only reference variable must be guaranteed to be immutable in the same way as an in parameter. The compiler therefore makes a defensive copy of the speed variable when we later use its InMetersPerSecond property, in case that property mutates the value.

The InRadians property of Angle, being an automatic property, has the IsReadOnlyAttribute indicator, so the compiler doesn't require a copy of the angle variable. If we manually copy the value of a ref return, there's no danger of Projectile's read-only field being changed via that variable, so the compiler doesn't introduce an additional copy in that case.

Read-Only Fields

Each access to a property of a read-only field will produce a defensive copy, unless the compiler is satisfied that the property doesn't change its instance. The same is true when we call an instance method of a read-only field.

In Listing 4-31, we make the BallisticRange method from Listing 4-28 an instance member of the Projectile class and alter its implementation to use instance fields of the class instead of taking in parameters.

```
public sealed class Projectile
{
    public double BallisticRange()
    {
        const double Gravity = 9.81;

        return initialSpeed.InMetersPerSecond * initialSpeed.InMetersPerSecond *
            Math.Sin(initialDirection.InRadians * 2) / Gravity;
    }

    private readonly Speed initialSpeed;
    private readonly Angle initialDirection;
}
```

Listing 4-31: Accessing properties of read-only fields of the Projectile class

The `Speed` and `Angle` types are the same as those in Listing 4-28, but they're read-only fields rather than parameters. Since read-only fields must be immutable, the compiler makes a defensive copy of the `initialSpeed` field's value for each access to the field's `InMetersPerSecond` property. Using the `Angle.InRadians` property doesn't cause a defensive copy, because it's an automatic property.

Interestingly, if we made the fields of `Projectile` *non*-read-only, the compiler would omit the defensive copies. The reason should be clear by now: the defensive copies are required to prevent *unwanted* modifications to read-only variables from being visible. If the variables are not read-only, allowing them to be altered causes no problems and requires no defensive intervention by the compiler.

However, making conceptually immutable fields and properties mutable isn't really a solution. What we'd really like are stronger guarantees of immutability, rather than sacrificing immutability in favor of fewer defensive copies. We can take measures that allow us to use `in` parameters, `ref` local variables, and read-only fields without incurring the cost of extra defensive copies made by the compiler.

THE CAUSES OF DEFENSIVE COPIES

Many caveats exist around read-only references and read-only fields, so if we're to avoid the potential copies introduced by the compiler, we have a lot to consider. The compiler may introduce defensive copying in several situations, but the rules can be summarized quite simply:

For some expression *x.Y*, where *Y* might be a property or a method, the compiler makes a defensive copy of the value of *x* if all of the following are true:

- *x* is a read-only field, an `in` parameter, or a `ref readonly` local.
- The type of *x* is a non-read-only value type.
- *Y* is not marked `readonly`.

If *Y* is a field, no defensive copy is needed in any circumstance because just reading a field can't possibly mutate it. Any attempt to write to *Y* will be caught by the compiler because *x* is read-only. However, avoiding defensive copies isn't a good reason to expose public fields on structs or record structs, because in doing so we lose all the benefits of encapsulated data. Using the `readonly` modifier on the type, or at least the properties and methods, encodes the intent of immutability much more effectively.

Defending Against Mutation

We can alter our code in a few ways to avoid the need for defensive copying. In each approach, we provide a guarantee that a method or property never alters the value of an instance, meaning the compiler doesn't need to make a copy to protect a read-only variable.

To recap, the following kinds of variables are read-only:

- in parameters
- ref readonly local variables
- Read-only fields

When we use read-only value type variables to access a property or call a method, the compiler may require a defensive copy of the value. If the variable's type is a reference type, there's no need for a defensive copy, although we must remember that even when a reference variable is read-only, the instance can still be changed. Defensive copies of value type instances are required when the compiler can't guarantee that the value is immutable.

One simple way to avoid many defensive copies is to use automatic rather than manually implemented properties. As we've discussed, the compiler adds the IsReadOnlyAttribute marker to the get accessor of an automatic property to confirm that it doesn't alter the value in any way. When the property is accessed, the presence of the attribute proves to the compiler that a defensive copy isn't required.

However, using automatic properties is not always possible or desirable, such as when we want a common backing field that's used by several properties, or a property that performs a calculation. Making properties automatic also doesn't prevent the compiler from making defensive copies when calling methods via a read-only variable. Fortunately, we can employ several alternatives to automatic properties to help avoid defensive copying. Which approach we choose will depend on the specific needs of an application, but in each case we're explicitly guaranteeing that calling a method or accessing a property can't alter the state of the instance.

Read-Only Accessors and Methods

One option for avoiding defensive copies when accessing a nonautomatic property is to add the readonly modifier to the property, as shown for the InMetersPerSecond property in Listing 4-32. For properties that also need a set accessor, like the InKmh property shown here, we can use readonly just for the get accessor.

```
public struct Speed
{
    --snip--

    public readonly double InMetersPerSecond => amount;

    public double InKmh
    {
        readonly get => amount / 1000 * 3600;
```

```
        private set { amount = value / 3.6; }
    }

    private double amount;
}
```

Listing 4-32: Declaring a read-only get accessor

Note that if we attempt to set a value for the mutable InKmh property by using a read-only variable, such as an in parameter, the compiler will give an error message saying that the variable is read-only. Similarly, a read-only property can't modify instance fields of the type; attempting to do so results in a compiler error.

Individual instance methods of structs and record structs can also be marked readonly, as shown here with the Sin method for our Angle type:

```
public struct Angle
{
    public readonly double InRadians { get; }

    public readonly double Sin()
        => Math.Sin(InRadians);
}
```

Adding the readonly modifier for property accessors and methods causes the compiler to annotate the compiled methods with the IsReadOnlyAttribute, which the compiler can easily check for when the property or method is used with a read-only variable.

Read-Only Types

When a struct or record struct doesn't need to modify its fields or properties, we can make the whole type read-only. Listing 4-33 makes the Speed struct entirely immutable by adding the readonly keyword to the type declaration.

```
public readonly struct Speed
{
    public Speed(double amount) => this.amount = amount;

    public double InMetersPerSecond => amount;
    public double InKmh => amount / 1000 * 3600;

    private readonly double amount;
}
```

Listing 4-33: Declaring a read-only struct

This is the ultimate move in immutability: all fields of a read-only struct must be read-only, and its properties can't have set accessors. We don't need to add the readonly modifier to the individual properties or any methods of

Speed. The compiler adds the `IsReadOnlyAttribute` attribute to every method and property of a read-only type.

We can avoid almost all defensive copies by making our value types read-only because this provides the strongest possible guarantee to the compiler that its instance methods and properties don't mutate the value.

Making a value type read-only isn't sufficient to avoid *all* invisible copies the compiler makes. Using a property as an argument to an in parameter will always copy the property value if it's a value type. Regardless of the type's immutability, a property isn't a variable, so the compiler must copy its value so that a reference to it can be passed to an in parameter.

When the compiler determines that a defensive copy is required to protect a value from potential change, the copy is invisible. The purpose of reference parameters, and local reference variables in particular, is to *avoid* unnecessary copying to make our code more efficient. Defensive copies negate any advantage of passing value type instances by reference. Using the `readonly` keyword on all structs and record structs is the most effective way to reduce the need for those invisible copies.

Summary

The real problem is that programmers have spent far too much time worrying about efficiency in the wrong places and at the wrong times.
—Donald E. Knuth, "Computer Programming as an Art,"
Communications of the ACM 1974

Values are copied a lot in most programs—perhaps more than many programmers think. It's easy, for example, to overlook the fact that when we access a property, we're making a copy of the value, and the pass-by-value nature of value type instances can make this a hidden cost. Practically every access of a value type instance involves a copy. Some copies are obvious, immediately apparent when we read the code. Other copies are more subtle, and still others are completely invisible and might even be surprising. Whether it's references or instances that we're copying, those copies happen frequently, often implicitly, and sometimes unexpectedly.

It's widely recommended to make value types small to minimize the cost of copying them. In practice, however, too much emphasis is placed on their size. Making copies of values, even when they're instances with several fields, is generally inexpensive but may still be costlier than copying a reference.

We can model values as classes or use records that have value-like behavior to try to alleviate the cost of copies. Knowing when copies occur—and how often—can help us choose between implementing a value as a value type or a reference type. This knowledge can also play an important role in identifying algorithm bottlenecks in existing programs. Minimizing copying is certainly a micro-optimization, however, and whether the cost of copying is significant is something we can judge only by measuring it. We need to weigh the cost of copying value type instances against other penalties, such as the garbage-collection overhead we'd add by introducing a reference type instead.

Even hidden copies might represent little or no performance impact. In many cases, even if the compiler introduces defensive copies, the just-in-time (JIT) compiler may be able to optimize those copies away. Nevertheless, we can employ some useful techniques to help both the compiler and the JIT compiler maximize performance. We shouldn't be too careless with copies because memory is a finite resource.

Making our value types immutable can make our programs more efficient, but doing so has other important benefits. Mutable values can lead to surprising behavior, which in turn leads to errors. If we make our value types immutable by default, we won't suffer many of the problems associated with unexpected aliasing. We also get the best advantage from the assumptions the compiler makes for truly read-only values. This is not premature optimization—it's deliberately choosing not to make our programs less efficient.

Copying values is usually not expensive, unless the instances are exceedingly large. We face many other considerations beyond how performance is affected by copying value type instances. If the behavior we want from a type is best modeled by a value type, we should choose to implement it as a struct or a record struct.

5

TYPES OF EQUALITY

Programs frequently compare variables to see if their values are equal, although this operation is often overlooked because it's done implicitly. Every type inherits the Equals method from the object base class, so given any two values x and y, the expression x.Equals(y) is always valid.

C# also provides ==, or the *equals-equals* operator, for explicitly checking equality of two values. Using == for comparisons differs from using the Equals method in multiple ways. In this chapter, we'll look at why C# supports two techniques for equality comparison and how each is affected by the differences between types.

We'll explore the following:

- How the differences between comparisons using the Equals method versus == affect our programs
- What support the compiler provides for comparisons, and what we must provide ourselves
- Why equality comparisons and hash codes are so closely related

- When we need to customize equality comparisons for our own types
- How a variable's type affects equality behavior

We'll take a forensic approach to see how the compiler treats equality for different types and explore why there's more to the topic of equality than just Equals and ==. Having more than one way to compare values underscores just how important this most basic comparison is. First, let's look at how equality works for the built-in types.

Built-in Equality

In this section, we'll look at the basics of equality comparisons between C#'s built-in types—including integers and floating-point numbers, reference variables, and arrays—and how some built-in types override the default behavior of equality.

NOTE   *The convention* equals-equals, *or* double-equals *as it's sometimes known, is used by several languages to distinguish the comparison for equality from the assignment operator* =, *which is just* equals. *JavaScript has a third variation,* equals-equals-equals, *to check that two variables have the same type* and *value.*

Because every type in C# inherits the Equals method from object, we can compare any two variables with that method. However, using == to compare variables of the built-in types is more efficient and may even result in different behavior than using Equals, as you'll soon see.

Equality comparisons using == are baked into the CLR for all the intrinsic types—that is, all the numeric types except decimal (which has built-in compiler support but isn't a native CLR type), the char and bool types, and references. The CLR has a built-in instruction to compare two intrinsic values, so we can always compare those values with ==, and it's as efficient as it could possibly be.

Whole Numbers

The built-in *integral* types—int, short, long, and byte—represent whole numbers, and the char type represents UTF-16 characters. They all have the same behavior for the purposes of equality comparison. Values of bool type, while not strictly speaking numeric values, are compared the same way too. Listing 5-1 compares two integer values by using the == operator.

```
int x = 10;
int y = x;

Assert.That(x == y, Is.True);
```

Listing 5-1: Built-in numeric comparison

Here, we copy the value of x and assign it to y so that the two variables have identical values. The result is that they compare equal. If we look at the CIL generated by the compiler, we see how these built-in types get special support at run time:

```
❶ L_0001: ldc.i4.s 10
  L_0003: stloc.0  // x

❷ L_0004: ldloc.0  // x
  L_0006: stloc.1  // y

❸ L_0007: ldloc.0  // x
  L_0008: ldloc.1  // y

❹ L_0009: ceq
```

CIL instructions all follow a similar low-level format. Each line has a label in the format L_0*XXX*, followed by the instruction itself and any arguments it needs. The first instruction, ldc.i4.s, pushes its argument, the value 10, onto the evaluation stack ❶. The next instruction, stloc.0, has no arguments but pops the value at the top of the evaluation stack into the variable at location 0, which, as the decompiler helpfully tells us in a comment, is the x variable. The outcome of these first two lines is that the x variable is assigned the value 10.

Next, the previously stored value of x is loaded and then stored in y ❷. Then, the values of both x and y are pushed back onto the evaluation stack so they can be interpreted by the next instruction ❸. Lastly, the built-in instruction ceq compares the two values on the top of the evaluation stack for equality ❹. The ceq instruction corresponds directly with the == comparison between two built-in values.

The way the comparison using ceq is performed is up to the JIT compiler, which translates CIL to machine code at run time, but we can think of it as a bitwise comparison between two numeric values. If they compare equal, the integer 1, interpreted as the Boolean value true, is pushed onto the evaluation stack; otherwise, a 0 is pushed and interpreted as false.

The Boolean result is passed as the first argument to the Assert.That method (not shown in the CIL listing). The test passes because x and y have the same numeric value.

Floating-Point Values

The same ceq instruction is used when we compare float and double values with the == operator. However, for floating-point numbers, this method of comparison doesn't necessarily behave as we might expect. In C#, float and double values are represented in a binary format defined by the Standard for Floating-Point Arithmetic published by the Institute of Electrical and Electronics Engineers (IEEE). The IEEE-754 standard specifies a fixed precision for those types, with the result that many numbers can't be represented exactly.

When a number has no exact representation, it's rounded to the nearest number that can be exactly represented. The next nearest representable number may be relatively larger or smaller than the original value. The difference between two neighboring exact representations is proportional to the magnitude of those numbers, so the rounding difference of a very large number will generally be much greater than that for a very small number. Calculations with multiple numbers that have been rounded will compound the resulting rounding error, a problem that isn't restricted to either very large or very small numbers. Listing 5-2 compares two double values that we might intuitively expect to be equal.

```
double x = 0.3;
double y = 0.1 + 0.2;

Assert.That(x == y, Is.True);
```

Listing 5-2: A simple floating-point calculation

This test fails because none of the constant values can be represented exactly in the format of a double. The values given to x and y will be rounded to the nearest representable value. On top of that, the result of the addition has an inexact representation and so is rounded again, producing a value that differs from the value assigned to x. The test for equality between x and y fails because the values differ in their least significant digits.

Subtracting one floating-point number from another can also produce unexpected results: if the two numbers are nearly equal, the result will have values only in those least significant places, which is exactly where rounding will be noticeable. The consequence is that some or all of the significant digits in the result may be lost, a problem sometimes called *cancellation*.

Rounding and cancellation issues are inherent in the IEEE-754 representation of floating-point values and not specific to C#. It's possible to alleviate some of the problems that arise from them, however, depending on exactly what we want to achieve.

Mitigating the Limitations of Rounding and Cancellation

The magnitude of rounding is predictable, as it's directly related to the precision of the binary representation. *Precision* here means the number of binary digits that can be stored in the type. Importantly, that means any number without an exact representation in a given type will always round the same way for the same type.

The compounded error caused by repeated calculations is harder to predict, and the order of operations in a calculation can significantly affect the result. Performing the same sequence of operations twice might even produce different results, depending on factors such as optimization and the location of the result being stored. A complete analysis of the different approaches to comparing floating-point numbers is far too large a topic to cover here, but in essence, rather than comparing floating-point numbers for exact equality, we can provide an implementation that determines whether two numbers are approximately equal.

One approach is to compare whether two numbers are equal within a certain number of decimal places, as shown in Listing 5-3.

```
public static bool ApproximatelyEqual(double x, double y)
    => Math.Round(Math.Abs(x - y), 7) == 0;
```

Listing 5-3: A simple approximate comparison of floating-point numbers

We use the `Math.Round` method to determine whether two values are equal within an absolute number of decimal places—seven digits, in this example. We might also consider passing the number of required decimal places as a parameter rather than relying on a hard-coded constant. Either way, this is a quick and simple method for comparing floating-point values. The disadvantage is that it's insensitive to differences smaller than the number of decimal places we've specified and inaccurate when comparing very large numbers.

A second approach is to find out whether the difference between two numbers is smaller than a certain tolerance, like this:

```
public static bool ApproximatelyEqual(double x, double y)
    => Math.Abs(x - y) < Tolerance;
```

This `ApproximatelyEqual` method returns true if the absolute difference between two floating-point numbers is smaller than a predefined tolerance, but we need to define a sensible value for the `Tolerance`. Doing so isn't straightforward, because the difference between two floating-point values can vary according to their magnitude. Listing 5-4 uses a value for tolerance that is weighted according to the magnitude of the smaller of the numbers being compared.

```
private const double Tolerance = 1E-15;

public static bool ApproximatelyEqual(double x, double y)
    => Math.Abs(x - y) <
        Math.Max(Tolerance, Math.Min(x, y)) * Tolerance;
```

Listing 5-4: Approximate comparison using a weighted tolerance

We've added a `Tolerance` constant to represent how sensitive we want our comparison to be, although we don't use its unqualified value in the comparison. The rounding error for very large values has a far greater magnitude than the error for very small numbers, and our tolerance needs to be sensitive to that. Instead, we scale the tolerance according to the numbers being compared. We use the smaller of the two values for scaling because that's probably where we're most sensitive to the rounding error. As a compromise to avoid multiplying by 0, if the smallest value is smaller than `Tolerance`, we scale `Tolerance` by itself, which might cost us some precision in comparing tiny values.

The value chosen for `Tolerance` here is sensitive enough to be able to distinguish differences within around 25 decimal places when the values are close to 0. When the values are closer to 1.0, the scaling means that differences can be detected within 15 or 16 decimal places, and the sensitivity decreases as the size of the values increases. This approach to determining equality between floating-point numbers isn't universally suitable, and specific applications may require a much more refined implementation.

Using Alternative Number Representations

We must always keep in mind that floating-point numbers aren't real numbers in the mathematical sense, inasmuch as many real numbers can't be expressed as a floating-point value. Real numbers have infinite precision, but computer memory is finite, so the fixed and limited precision of double and float values is a compromise.

Whether the imprecision of floating-point values matters will depend on our objective. One alternative is to use a different representation, such as the decimal type that's represented in *decimal* rather than binary and has a greater precision than a double. In practice, a decimal can represent more real numbers exactly, because it has a greater number of significant digits with which to represent them. This means decimal values are less prone to rounding. However, each type has its own trade-offs, and decimal isn't a general-purpose type: it's intended for calculations that are most naturally represented in decimal, such as financial calculations. The representation of a decimal has a smaller range than either float or double, so the largest positive and negative values are smaller than either float or double can represent. Another consideration is that a decimal value requires more memory than a double.

As an example of the practical implications of choosing between double and decimal, consider the trigonometry methods in the Math class, such as Sin and Cos, which take double as their parameter and don't provide overloads taking decimal values. If our code uses these methods, we can't substitute double for decimal, because the decimal type is specifically designed for monetary values and thus can't represent the results of trigonometric operations.

Handling Invalid Numbers

Another consequence of working with double and float values is that some operations can produce a NaN (not a number) result, which has *no* numerical representation. When we're using double or float values, we need to make sure we correctly identify when the result of a calculation is NaN, because NaN is viral: any calculation involving NaN produces NaN as its result. We would get a NaN, for example, if we tried to divide 0.0 by 0.0.

We might expect that we could identify a NaN with a direct comparison using ==, as in Listing 5-5.

```
var x = 0.0 / 0.0;

Assert.That(x == double.NaN, Is.True);
```

Listing 5-5: Comparing NaNs

Dividing 0.0 by 0.0 certainly produces a NaN, so many programmers would expect this equality test with NaN to pass, but it doesn't. The IEEE-754 standard states that two NaN values don't compare equal, so this test's failure is correct behavior. Instead, C# provides the IsNaN static method, which we use like this:

```
Assert.That(double.IsNaN(x), Is.True);
```

As of C# v8.0, we can use a constant pattern to make the comparison more naturally:

```
Assert.That(x is double.NaN, Is.True);
```

The compiler translates the pattern expression into double.IsNaN(x), so there's no comparison using either == or Equals. The IsNaN method will always give us the correct result. It also highlights one important difference between comparing floating-point values with == and using the double.Equals method: the Equals method compares floating-point values with ceq, but, unlike the == operator, Equals also calls IsNaN when the values are *not* equal. Consider the following test, where we compare two NaN values by using the Equals method:

```
var x = 0.0 / 0.0;

Assert.That(x.Equals(Double.NaN), Is.True);
```

This test passes because, according to the Equals method, double and float values compare equal when the values are exactly equal or are both NaN. The result of Equals for floating-point numbers may therefore differ from the result of using ==, which doesn't compare the results of IsNaN. Both Equals and == ultimately make a strict comparison of float and double values using ceq, so we shouldn't rely on using either approach to compare floating-point numbers, because the result might not be what we expect.

NOTE *Some calculations can result in positive or negative* infinity, *represented as* double.PositiveInfinity *and* double.NegativeInfinity, *respectively. While either value may be an incorrect result, infinite values aren't usually considered* invalid *in the same way as* NaN. *We can compare a value with* double.PositiveInfinity *or* double.NegativeInfinity *in a constant pattern by using the* is *keyword, but values can also be directly compared using* == *with either kind of infinity.*

Reference Equality

As Chapter 2 explained, a reference is either null or an opaque handle to an object on the heap. An object can have several references to it, and two references to the same object compare equal. Every object instance has a unique identity, and the value of a non-null reference is the identity of the object to which it refers. To tell whether two references refer to the same object or different instances, then, we use an identity comparison.

We might also be interested in whether a reference is null, so let's look at the mechanics of comparing one reference with either another reference or the null reference.

Comparing Two References

If x and y are both references to the same object, they have the same identity and so compare equal via either == or Equals. If they refer to different objects, even if those objects have the same state, x and y won't compare equal. In Listing 5-6 we use == to compare two reference variables.

```
public sealed class MusicTrack
{
}

var x = new MusicTrack();
var y = new MusicTrack();

Assert.That(x == y, Is.False);
```

Listing 5-6: Comparing references

These x and y reference variables aren't equal because they refer to different objects, even though both objects have the same state. Rather than assigning constant values to two variables as we did in Listing 5-1, we're creating new objects on the heap, and the variables are references to those objects. When we examine the generated CIL, on the last line we can see that the two references are compared for equality by using the same ceq instruction as in Listing 5-1:

```
IL_0001:  newobj    instance void MusicTrack::.ctor()
IL_0006:  stloc.0  // x
IL_0007:  newobj    instance void MusicTrack::.ctor()
IL_000c:  stloc.1  // y
IL_000d:  ldloc.0
IL_000e:  ldloc.1
IL_000f:  ceq
```

The newobj instruction creates a new instance of a type and stores a reference to it on the evaluation stack. We create two instances of MusicTrack on the heap, since MusicTrack is a class, and store references to them in the x and y variables, respectively. Since x and y refer to different instances, the variables have different *values* and thus aren't equal when compared using ceq.

As far as the ceq instruction is concerned, at run time a reference is just a sequence of bits, in much the same way as a number is represented as a sequence of bits. The ceq instruction merely compares two bit patterns to determine whether they match. Two references to different object instances on the heap have different bit patterns, so they don't compare equal.

Comparing with the null Reference

The value of a reference variable is either a reference to an object on the heap or null. We can use == to compare any reference with null to determine whether it refers to an object. If the reference refers to an object, as in Listing 5-7, the reference isn't equal to null.

```
var x = new MusicTrack();

Assert.That(x == null, Is.False);
```

Listing 5-7: Comparing a reference with null

This comparison also uses the built-in ceq instruction:

```
IL_0016: newobj    instance void MusicTrack::.ctor()
IL_001c: ldloc.1   // x
IL_001d: ldnull
IL_001e: ceq
```

The null reference is a constant value pushed onto the evaluation stack by the ldnull instruction; null doesn't have a type of its own but can be implicitly converted to *any* reference type. When we assign null to a reference variable or pass it as an argument to a method, it's converted automatically to the type of the target variable. Here we can compare x with null because the null reference is compatible with the MusicTrack reference type.

Comparing Array Variables

C# arrays are always reference types, so comparing array variables works the same way as comparing references. C# arrays are the built-in syntax for declaring and using a sequence of elements that are always allocated on the heap. An array variable is a reference to the elements of the array. In Listing 5-8, we create two arrays with identical elements and use == to compare them.

```
int[] x = { 10, 20 };
int[] y = { 10, 20 };

Assert.That(x == y, Is.False);
```

Listing 5-8: Implicitly initializing and comparing two arrays

The compiler deduces the size of each array based on the values we use to initialize them. The two arrays have identical elements but compare unequal because comparing two arrays with == performs a reference comparison using the intrinsic ceq instruction. The x and y variables in Listing 5-8 are references to different arrays and thus don't compare equal, so the test passes.

When we compare two array variables, the comparison doesn't consider the array elements; it uses only the identity of the two array variables, so two array references compare equal only if they refer to the *same* array instance. To check whether two arrays have the same elements, we must manually compare each individual element or use a library facility such as `System.Enumerable.SequenceEqual`.

Strings and Value Equality

Although string variables are references, when we compare them we're usually more concerned with whether their contents are the same rather than whether they refer to the same string instance.

The string class overloads the default behavior of `==` and `Equals` to give strings value-like semantics. Comparing strings with either `==` or `Equals` performs a value-based rather than reference-based comparison. It's possible to have more than one reference to a single string instance on the heap, and those references will still compare equal. However, it's also possible to have two independent string instances that have the same content, and those instances also compare equal.

For example, in Listing 5-9, the x and y variables don't refer to the same string instance but do have the same *value* at run time.

```
var monarch = "Henry";
var number = "IV";

var x = $"{monarch} the {number}";
var y = $"{monarch} the {number}";

Assert.That(x == y, Is.True);
Assert.That(x.Equals(y), Is.True);

Assert.That(ReferenceEquals(x, y), Is.False);
```

Listing 5-9: Comparing string values

The string class customizes the behavior of both `==` and the `Equals` method, so the x and y variables compare equal because they both have the same content, although they're references to distinct instances. Since string overrides the behavior of `==`, we use the `ReferenceEquals` method here to perform a reference comparison. `ReferenceEquals` is a static method defined on object and performs an identity comparison between any two reference type variables. In this example, `ReferenceEquals` returns false because its arguments are references to different objects on the heap.

The x and y variables in Listing 5-9 both use string interpolation to insert the values of named variables within the string, ensuring that x and y really are distinct instances—at least in debug mode. If we use two simple string literals, as we do in Listing 5-10, `ReferenceEquals` gives us a different result.

```
var x = "Henry the IV";
var y = "Henry the IV";

Assert.That(ReferenceEquals(x, y), Is.True);
```

Listing 5-10: Comparing string literal values

This test shows that x and y really are the same instance in memory, even though they were independently assigned to two apparently separate strings. The reason for the different behavior is that the compiler conserves memory by using *string interning*, whereby it maintains an *intern pool* containing a single instance of each unique string literal used in a program. This way, even if the same string literal appears more than once in the code, only one instance is in memory. Strings are immutable, so having multiple references to one instance can never cause aliasing issues.

We can use the intern pool ourselves at run time, although we have other memory considerations to take into account. We might save memory on individual string values, but the intern pool itself isn't routinely garbage collected and will most likely stay in memory until the program terminates.

We can determine whether two string variables refer to separate instances with ReferenceEquals or another method, but it rarely matters. Whether two string variables are references to one string instance or two separate instances with the same contents, they still compare equal.

Custom Equality for Classes

If we want value-based rather than reference-based equality for our own class types, we override the Equals method and define operator== for the class to customize the behavior of equality comparisons. There are several aspects to a complete implementation of equality comparisons in a class, so we'll build it up in stages and implement each part in turn so you can better understand how all the components fit together.

Our first task is to customize the virtual Equals method for the class. The MusicTrack class in Listing 5-11 has two string properties, and we define Equals so that two instances of MusicTrack compare equal if the values for both fields compare equal.

```
public sealed class MusicTrack
{
    public MusicTrack(string artist, string name)
        => (Artist, Name) = (artist, name);

    public string Artist { get; }
    public string Name { get; }

    public override bool Equals(object? obj)
        => obj is MusicTrack other &&
            this.Artist == other.Artist &&
            this.Name == other.Name;
}
```

Listing 5-11: Overriding the Equals method

Because we're customizing the implementation of an inherited virtual method, we use the override keyword, and the method's signature must match the signature of the base class method being overridden. Note that compiling this code will issue a warning that we haven't overridden GetHashCode. We'll address that shortly.

The virtual Equals method takes a single nullable object reference, which we need to cast to our implementing type in order to compare it with the current instance. Here we use a *declaration pattern* to declare the other variable if the obj parameter is non-null and there's an identity conversion or implicit reference conversion from the type of obj to MusicTrack. An *identity conversion* simply means a type can be converted to itself. An *implicit reference conversion* can take several forms, but for simplicity here it means that MusicTrack is a base type of the run-time type of obj. In this example, since MusicTrack is a sealed class, the type will match exactly (an identity conversion) or not match at all.

If the obj variable's type matches the pattern, obj is cast to the specified type and assigned to the other variable. The other variable is therefore a MusicTrack reference, and we use it to compare its properties with those of the current instance to see if they're equal.

Defining Equality Operators

The Equals method is seldom used directly, because most programmers find using == more natural than calling Equals. It's generally desirable that == and Equals have identical behavior, and we achieve that most simply by implementing operator== for the MusicTrack class to call the Equals method we've already defined.

Operator definitions such as operator== are static methods. The operator== definition takes two parameters, at least one of which must be of the type implementing the operator. The return type is most often bool, although that's not a strict requirement. The usual implementation has both parameters of the same type, allowing us to use == to compare two instances, as shown in Listing 5-12.

```
public static bool operator==(MusicTrack? left, MusicTrack? right)
{
    if(left is null)
    {
        return right is null;
    }
    else
    {
        return left.Equals(right);
    }
}

public static bool operator!=(MusicTrack? left, MusicTrack? right)
    => !(left == right);
```

Listing 5-12: Defining operator== for the MusicTrack class

If we provide operator==, we must also implement a matching operator!=, which we do simply by inverting the result of calling the == operator method.

Since `MusicTrack` is a class, either or both of the arguments to the operators could be null, so we make that expectation explicit by using the nullable reference syntax for the parameters. If both arguments are null, they compare equal. If `left` is non-null, we call the `Equals` method, passing `right` as the argument even where `right` is a null reference. Our implementation of `Equals` already handles null being passed to its parameter.

Handling Comparisons with null

In Listing 5-12, we used the constant pattern and the is keyword to compare the `left` and `right` parameters with null. If we compared them with `==` instead, `operator==` would call itself recursively because null is implicitly converted to `MusicTrack` in those comparisons. Applying the constant pattern here avoids that pitfall because the `is null` expression never calls a user-defined `operator==` implementation. The compiler translates all such comparisons to use the intrinsic `ceq` instruction.

Since the contents of the `if` and `else` blocks are simple expressions, we make the implementation of `operator==` more compact in Listing 5-13 by using the ternary operator, which has the form *expression ? result if true : result if false*.

```
public static bool operator==(MusicTrack? left, MusicTrack? right)
{
    return left is null ? right is null : left.Equals(right);
}
```

Listing 5-13: A more compact implementation of `operator==`

We can further simplify the code for `operator==` by employing the null-conditional operator `?.`, which invokes an instance method only if the variable used to make the call is non-null. In the expression *x?.y*, if *x* is null, the result of the whole expression is null; otherwise, the result is *x.y*. Using the null-conditional operator to implement `operator==` makes the implementation much more compact, especially if we also make the operator an expression-bodied method, like so:

```
public static bool operator==(MusicTrack? left, MusicTrack? right)
    => left?.Equals(right) ?? right is null;
```

Here, the `Equals` method is called only if the `left` parameter is not null, since we've used the null-conditional operator on the `left` variable. We combine the null-conditional operator with the null-coalescing operator `??`, which evaluates its right-hand expression only if the whole left expression is null. If `left` is null, then `left` and `right` are equal if `right` is also null.

The null constant pattern, the null-conditional operator, and the null-coalescing operator are all different ways of testing whether a reference is equal to null without invoking an `Equals` method or ever calling a user-defined `operator==` implementation. While we can customize both `Equals` and operator==, we can't change the behavior of comparisons made with the is keyword or the null-conditional and null-coalescing operators.

Making Type-Safe Comparisons

When we compare values for equality, we're most commonly comparing two values of the same type, which is why the usual implementation of operator== has two matching parameters. Our Equals method, however, takes an object parameter, which must be cast back to MusicTrack so we can compare its individual property values. We can avoid this cast by writing an overload of Equals that takes a MusicTrack parameter, shown in Listing 5-14.

```
public bool Equals(MusicTrack? other)
    => other is not null &&
        this.Artist == other.Artist &&
        this.Name == other.Name;
```

Listing 5-14: A type-safe Equals method

We still need to compare the argument with null, and, as we did for operator==, we use the constant pattern to make that comparison as efficient as possible. To avoid duplicating the code for comparing the property values, we alter the Equals(object?) method to call the type-safe overload like this:

```
public override bool Equals(object? obj)
    => Equals(obj as MusicTrack);
```

Although we're employing a run-time cast using the as keyword, Listing 5-14's overload of Equals taking a MusicTrack? parameter is much more likely to be called than this overridden method with an object? parameter. In particular, our implementation of operator== will always call the type-specific overload because the parameters to the operator are both MusicTrack variables.

Since we've overridden Equals for the MusicTrack class, the compiler will warn us that we should override GetHashCode too.

Working with Hash Codes

The Equals and GetHashCode methods are closely associated. Like Equals, GetHashCode is defined on object and is virtual. The GetHashCode method is used by collection types like Dictionary and HashSet to efficiently store and look up keys. Essentially, a data structure such as a hash table uses an object's *hash code* to identify its location within the data structure. When we add a new key or try to locate an existing one, the lookup algorithm quickly identifies the correct place in the table by using a hash code.

However, a particular hash code in the table may identify several different keys, because although the items in a hash table are usually unique, hash codes don't have to be. When we add a new item to a hash table and the item's hash code already exists in the table—a scenario known as a *collision*—the `Equals` method is used on each key with a matching hash code to verify whether the table already contains the new item. This is why `Equals` and `GetHashCode` are so closely related.

A key can be any object, as long as these two rules are followed:

- Objects that are equal according to `Equals` have the same hash code.
- The hash code for an object being used as a key doesn't change.

Ideally, each unique hash code will identify a single key—meaning we avoid the need to compare several objects via `Equals`—and so searching for a key is much faster. When we search for a key in the table, if the hash code is matched by only a single key, it *must* be the required key as long as the two rules have been followed. Ensuring that hash codes are widely distributed is recommended to increase the likelihood that each hash code uniquely identifies one key.

For class types, the default implementation of `GetHashCode` uses an object's identity rather than its value to create a hash code, just as the default implementation of `Equals` compares object identities, not their state. If two references are equal, they must also have the same hash value, because they refer to the same *instance*. The default hash code for an instance also never changes. However, if we accept the default behavior of `GetHashCode` for classes, we must take extra care when using class types as keys.

We can safely use any class type that doesn't override the `GetHashCode` method as a key, but when we search for an object in a hashing collection like a `Dictionary` or `HashSet`, we must make sure to use the exact same instance of the object that was originally inserted. If we try to look up an item with a different instance, the item won't be found. To demonstrate, consider Listing 5-15, where we use a new object instance to find a key in a `HashSet`.

```
public sealed class Character
{
    public Character(string name)
        => Name = name;

    public string Name { get; }
}

var cast = new HashSet<Character>
    {
        new Character("MacReady")
    };

var key = new Character("MacReady");

Assert.That(cast.Contains(key), Is.True);
```

Listing 5-15: Using a Character class identity as a key

The test in this example fails because we're searching for a different instance of the `Character` class than was added to the `HashSet`. Since `Character` doesn't override the `GetHashCode` method, the instance being looked up has a different hash code than the item contained in the `HashSet`, even though both instances have the same state.

Creating a Suitable Key

Failing to find a key in a collection has important consequences. Elements in a `HashSet` and keys in a `Dictionary` should be *unique*. When we attempt to insert a new key, it should be added only if it isn't already in the collection. However, if the key exists but can't be found, we'll get a *duplicated* key. The new object will be erroneously added to the table, effectively corrupting the collection.

Needing to rely on using a single object instance to both insert and search for any particular key in a hashing collection is usually overly restrictive. If, for example, the collection is populated from a file or user input, the original instances frequently aren't immediately at hand when we come to search for a specific item. It's much more convenient for objects used as keys to generate their hash codes according to their state, not their identity. That way, we can use any key with the same state to identify an object in the table.

As things stand, the `MusicTrack` class we defined in Listing 5-11 isn't suitable as a key for a `HashSet` or `Dictionary` because it breaks the first of the two cardinal rules—that equal objects produce identical hash codes—because we've customized equality to compare the objects' state. To make `MusicTrack` behave correctly, we must also override `GetHashCode` and ensure that two instances of `MusicTrack` that compare equal according to our customized `Equals` method produce identical hash codes. To do that, we'll generate a hash code using the same properties that determine whether two instances are equal. Listing 5-16 shows one way to implement `GetHashCode` for the `MusicTrack` class.

```
public override int GetHashCode()
    => HashCode.Combine(Artist, Name);
```

Listing 5-16: Overriding GetHashCode

We use the `HashCode` static class from the Standard Library, which combines multiple arguments to create reasonably well-distributed hash codes. Our implementation of `GetHashCode` uses the same properties of `MusicTrack` as the `Equals` method in Listing 5-14, so two objects that compare equal will always generate identical hash codes.

Using Floating-Point Numbers as Keys

Using a floating-point number as the key in a hash table can result in keys being lost, in much the same way as relying on the default object implementation of `GetHashCode` for class types. As you saw earlier, comparing floating-point numbers for strict equality isn't reliable. In Listing 5-17, we try to identify whether the collection has a specific double value.

```
var history = new HashSet<double>();

var rate = 0.1+0.2;
history.Add(rate);

Assert.That(history.Contains(0.3));
```

Listing 5-17: Using floating-point numbers as keys

This test fails because the value `0.3` doesn't exactly match the representation of `0.1 + 0.2`. Because calculations using `double` values are imprecise, they're generally a bad choice as keys in a hashed collection. By extension, the same reasoning applies to user-defined types that have floating-point field values; comparing objects of such a type for equality necessarily means comparing any floating-point fields, with the same potential for errors.

In a type with floating-point fields, we might be tempted to override its `Equals` method by using an approach similar to the `ApproximatelyEqual` implementations from Listings 5-3 and 5-4, but doing so would introduce two problems. First, equality is a transitive relationship between values: for three values x, y, and z, if x is equal to y, and y is equal to z, then x must be equal to z. Implementing `Equals` to mean *approximately* equal means the transitive relationship wouldn't necessarily hold, because the difference between x and z could be larger than any tolerance we define, even when `x.Equals(y)` and `y.Equals(z)` are both true.

The second issue is directly related to hash codes. Recall that objects that compare equal should have the same hash code. Using `ApproximatelyEqual` to implement `Equals` could easily break that rule, because two *almost* equal values will still produce different hash codes. We could implement `GetHashCode` to ignore any floating-point fields, but doing so would compromise how well our objects' hash codes are distributed. It also raises the question of what to do about types that have only a single field that's a floating-point value, such as the `Speed` and `Angle` types we developed in Chapter 1.

Floating-point numbers and types containing floating-point values, then, don't make good keys for hash tables, dictionaries, and other data structures that depend on the implementation of `GetHashCode`. Unfortunately, C# doesn't allow us to prevent a particular type from being used as a key in a hash table or similar data structure, because `GetHashCode` is defined on `object` and can't be hidden. It's up to us to make sure that the keys we use are suitable for that purpose.

Strings make excellent keys for hash tables, because the `string` class overrides `Equals` and `GetHashCode` to compare the string contents. This is the same behavior the compiler adds for us in record and record struct types. Both the `Equals` method and `GetHashCode` are synthesized by the compiler, so record and record struct instances use their *value* for equality comparisons and for generating their hash codes. Although records are reference types, like strings they work very well as keys, subject to the caveats we've just discussed regarding floating-point fields.

The compiler also generates operator== and its companion operator!= for records and record structs. They follow the same general pattern we've used for MusicTrack, where operator== uses the Equals method, and operator!= returns the inverse of the result of operator==. The compiler does *not* generate any of these methods for ordinary structs, which instead rely on the ValueType base class common to all struct types.

Structs and Equality

Since value type instances are copied by value, every value type variable is a distinct instance of the type, so two instances can never compare equal according to their identity. We need to compare their values, meaning that we compare their state instead. This usually involves comparing each field of one instance with the corresponding field of another.

Structs implicitly inherit from the System.ValueType class, which provides the value-based equality required for value types. By default, calling Equals on a struct will use the ValueType implementation, because Equals is a virtual method. As Chapter 2 explained, for its implementation, the ValueType.Equals method relies on reflection, which provides the correct behavior for any possible struct type at the expense of performance. While it might not be the most efficient comparison, the ValueType.Equals method uses each field's Equals method to compare the field with its companion, so it has the behavior we require. Similarly, ValueType also overrides GetHashCode to create hash codes based on a struct's fields, ensuring that any two struct instances that are equal according to Equals also generate identical hash codes.

Overriding Equals for Structs

Overriding the default Equals and GetHashCode methods for struct types is common in order to address that the ValueType implementations of those methods may not be optimal. Implementing efficient equality for structs follows a similar pattern as for classes, as shown in Listing 5-18, where we create a struct to represent color values.

```
public readonly struct Color
{
    public Color(int r, int g, int b)
        => (Red, Green, Blue) = (r, g, b);

    public int Red { get; }
    public int Green { get; }
    public int Blue { get; }

    public bool Equals(Color other)
        => Red == other.Red &&
           Green == other.Green &&
           Blue == other.Blue;
```

```
    public override bool Equals(object? obj)
        => obj is Color color && Equals(color);

    public override int GetHashCode()
        => HashCode.Combine(Red, Green, Blue);
}
```

Listing 5-18: Overriding equality for a Color struct

As we did with `MusicTrack` in the previous section, we override the base class `Equals` method and add a type-specific overload taking a `Color` parameter. There are subtle differences, related to `null`, from the `MusicTrack` implementations of those methods. As a struct type, `Color` instances can't be `null`, so the type-safe `Equals` method takes its `Color` parameters by value rather than nullable references, and we don't check for `null` in the implementation of `Equals(Color)`.

In the `Equals(object?)` override, we use a declaration pattern to cast the `obj` variable to the correct type. We used a declaration pattern in Listing 5-11 for `MusicTrack` but later switched it for the simpler as run-time cast. We can't use as in our struct implementation because if the cast fails, the result is `null`, which can't be assigned to a struct variable. As noted in Chapter 2, we *can* use as to cast to a nullable `Color`, but in that case the argument would match the `Equals` method with an `object?` parameter instead of our type-safe overload, making the method recursive. Applying the declaration pattern here avoids that issue.

The `GetHashCode` implementation is identical in principle to the `MusicTrack` implementation from Listing 5-16.

Struct types don't allow comparison with == by default. If we want to support such comparisons, we must define our own `operator==` for the type. The equality operator is straightforward to implement in terms of our `Equals` method, as shown here:

```
public static bool operator==(Color left, Color right)
    => left.Equals(right);

public static bool operator!=(Color left, Color right)
    => !left.Equals(right);
```

While `Equals` is a virtual instance method and is overridden by `ValueType`, `operator==` is a static method and therefore *can't* be virtual. Static methods are never inherited, so these operators couldn't usefully be implemented by the `ValueType` class.

Since a `Color` variable can't be `null`, we can simply use the `left` variable to call `Equals`, passing `right` as the argument to invoke our type-safe implementation that takes a `Color` parameter by value. The equality operators are therefore simpler than their equivalents for a class, and, more significantly, the `left` and `right` variables won't be boxed when calling `Equals`. Notice that rather than inverting the result of ==, we invert the result of calling `Equals`. The effect is identical in both cases, but this version of != avoids the extra indirection of also calling `operator==` and the additional copies of the arguments it would involve.

Another reason a default implementation for structs provided by `ValueType` would be useless is that, as discussed earlier, an operator overload requires the type of at least one of its parameters to match the implementing type. We can't, for instance, define our own `operator==` to compare two `object` variables because that would hijack the default behavior of `==` for `object` variables. Comparing two `object` variables with `==` *always* compares identities, since those variables are references. This has important consequences when an `object` variable refers to an instance of a value type like `Color` that's been boxed.

Boxing Values and Comparing by Identity

Values are implicitly boxed anytime we use a reference type variable to refer to a value type instance. Because value types have value-based equality and reference type variables have reference-based equality, boxing has implications for object identity and equality. We went to some effort to ensure that `Equals` and `==` have identical behavior when comparing `Color` instances, but when we compare `Color` values that have been boxed, `Equals` and `==` behave differently.

To illustrate how boxing affects equality, Listing 5-19 creates two instances of the `Color` struct, but instead of having the compiler deduce the variable types as `Color`, we explicitly declare them as `object`, causing the values to be boxed. The variables aren't equal when we use `==` to compare them.

```
object x = new Color(0xFF, 0xA0, 0);
object y = new Color(0xFF, 0xA0, 0);

Assert.That(x == y, Is.False);
```

Listing 5-19: Explicitly boxing values

This test passes because reference variables are compared by their identity. These x and y variables are references to different boxed `Color` values on the heap, approximately as shown in Figure 5-1.

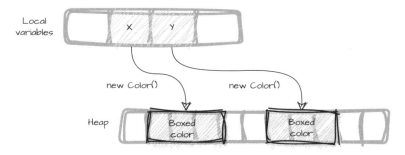

Figure 5-1: Boxed values in memory

The boxes for the two Color instances in Figure 5-1 could be anywhere on the heap; the way that memory is allocated is determined by the CLR. When we use == to compare the x and y variables, the instance values aren't considered. Even though Color has an overload of operator== to allow comparisons using == between two Color values, that custom equality implementation isn't invoked when we compare the two object references. This is because operator== is a *static* method that requires two Color arguments, not two object arguments. The comparison with == therefore correctly returns false, because the two object variables refer to independent instances.

If we make the comparison using the Equals method instead, the variables compare equal because the Equals method is virtual:

```
Assert.That(x.Equals(y), Is.True);
```

The x variable used to invoke Equals is an object reference but still refers to an instance of Color, so here it's our override of Equals that's called. If Color didn't override Equals, the ValueType implementation would be called instead. In either case, Equals returns true because the two instances of Color have exactly the same state.

We can think of a boxed value as an instance of a simple reference type on the heap that contains a copy of the value in a field with the same type as the original value. Since the box is on the heap, it can be referenced by more than one reference variable, as shown in Listing 5-20.

```
var color = new Color(0xFF, 0xA0, 0);

object x = color;
object y = x;

Assert.That(x == y, Is.True);
Assert.That(x.Equals(y), Is.True);
```

Listing 5-20: Two references to one boxed value

In this example, x is a reference to a boxed value, and y is a different reference to the *same box*, illustrated in Figure 5-2.

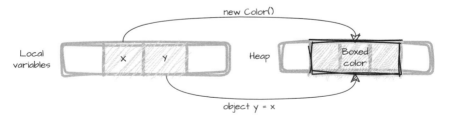

Figure 5-2: Adding a reference to an existing box

The x and y variables compare equal with == because both x and y are references to a single instance. The comparison with the virtual call to Equals also returns true because an instance will always compare equal with itself.

Boxed Method Parameters

A value will be automatically boxed when we pass it to a method that takes an object or other reference type parameter. The effects are the same as assigning directly to an object variable, as we did in Listing 5-19, but the box is less obvious in our code.

Consider Listing 5-21, where we pass the same value twice to the object .ReferenceEquals method, which takes two object parameters and compares them for identity equality.

```
Color x = new Color();

Assert.That(object.ReferenceEquals(x, x), Is.False);
```

Listing 5-21: Passing values as boxed arguments

This test asserts that the two arguments to ReferenceEquals are *not* equal. Should the test pass?

Yes, it should. The arguments to ReferenceEquals are different object variables. Passing a value type as an argument to an object parameter boxes the value. Even though the same value is passed to both parameters, each argument is boxed separately, resulting in two independent boxes. The outcome is identical to explicitly boxing the same value into separate object variables, like this:

```
object a = x;
object b = x;

Assert.That(object.ReferenceEquals(a, b), Is.False);
```

The value of x is explicitly boxed into two separate object references. The call to ReferenceEquals is equivalent to a == b, and they do *not* compare equal because they're different objects.

Compare Listing 5-21 with the following, where we explicitly box the value to an object variable *before* calling ReferenceEquals:

```
object x = new Color();

Assert.That(object.ReferenceEquals(x, x), Is.True);
```

We pass the same reference for both arguments to ReferenceEquals, so they compare equal. The call to ReferenceEquals in this instance is identical to the expression x == x, and the x variable is a reference to a boxed Color, as shown in Figure 5-3.

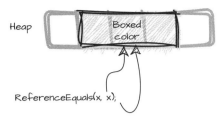

Figure 5-3: Passing an already-boxed value to a method

The ReferenceEquals method receives two arguments, but they're references to the same boxed value on the heap.

Quite apart from testing variables for equality, we need to be sure we understand where values are being boxed and whether our own code is using a boxed value. Boxing affects what *identity* means for a value—and while this is most apparent when we're comparing two values, it also has wider implications, such as whether we need to be concerned about aliasing or side effects.

Interface Boxes

We can refer to an object via any of the interfaces implemented by the type. To demonstrate, in Listing 5-22 the Angle value type implements IFormattable, one of the common system interfaces provided by the Standard Library. In this code snippet, we use the interface name to refer to two instances of Angle.

```
public readonly struct Angle : IFormattable
{
    --snip--
}

IFormattable x = new Angle();
IFormattable y = new Angle();

Assert.That(x == y, Is.False);
```

Listing 5-22: Referring to a value via interface name

An *interface type* is a reference type that defines the public operations guaranteed to be available for a type that implements it. Variables of interface type are always references, regardless of the implementing type. Referring to value type instances via interface variables must therefore box the value, with the result that the comparison in Listing 5-22 is effectively the same as when the values were boxed into object variables in Listing 5-19.

The x == y expression in this example, then, performs a reference check for equality that will compare object identities. The values returned from each of the new Angle expressions will be boxed so that the references x and y can refer to them, and each will refer to different boxes. The x and y variables will compare equal if we use x.Equals(y), owing to the virtual nature of the Equals method.

Comparing Generic Variables

We use a generic type or method to implement functionality that works for a range of other types, often for both reference types and value types transparently. In the context of a generic type or a generic method, a given variable might represent either a value or a reference at different times during a program's execution.

This poses an issue for equality comparisons of generic variables; in particular, using == to compare variables typed by a generic parameter will never invoke a user-defined operator== implementation. If a generic parameter is unconstrained, we can't even use == to compare two variables of the same generic type.

> **NOTE** *C# v11.0 introduces a preview feature named* static abstract interface members *that enables you to use user-defined operators, including* operator==, *in generic code. For more information on this feature, see* https://learn.microsoft.com/en-us/dotnet/csharp/whats-new/tutorials/static-virtual-interface-members.

Consider the simple generic class in Listing 5-23, which uses == to compare two variables declared using the generic type parameter T. As it stands, this class won't compile.

```
public class Playlist<T>
{
    public void PlayNow(T item)
    {
        if(item == current)
        {
            --snip--
        }
    }
    private T current;
}
```

Listing 5-23: Generic type parameter comparison

Playlist is a generic class with a type parameter that by convention is named T. We'd generally refer to this class as a *Playlist of T*.

We can't use == to compare the item parameter with the field current because when T is an unconstrained type parameter like this, the == and != operators can be used only to check instances of T for equality or inequality with null.

If we add a general class constraint, or a specific base class or interface type constraint for T, the comparison item == current will compile, but it will always represent a reference comparison. C# has no generic constraint we can add for T to allow the expression x == y to invoke an overloaded operator==, where x or y is typed by a generic parameter.

We *can* invoke the Equals method, which will call an overridden implementation if one exists on whatever type T represents at run time. The Equals method is defined on the object base class and so is available to any variable, regardless of its actual type. However, when the type of T is a value type, the argument may be boxed by calling the Equals method that takes object? as its parameter.

Generic Code and the Equals Method

In Listing 5-11, we implemented equality for our MusicTrack type so that instances of them compare by value rather than by identity. In Listing 5-18, we did the same for the Color struct to override the ValueType.Equals method. To make the comparison more efficient, we added a type-safe overload of Equals for both types by taking the parameter as MusicTrack and Color, respectively, rather than object, thereby preventing the argument from being boxed.

In the current implementations of MusicTrack and Color, however, their type-safe overloads of Equals won't be used if called using a generic type parameter variable. When Equals is called using a generic variable, the virtual method with an object? parameter is called by default. For the MusicTrack class, that merely results in an extra run-time cast, but for the Color struct, the parameter will be boxed to object and then unboxed again to compare Color's properties.

To demonstrate, Listing 5-24 uses Color as a type argument for the generic HashSet collection type. The HashSet<T>.Contains method uses a combination of GetHashCode and Equals to determine whether any item in the collection matches the orange argument.

```
var colors = new HashSet<Color>();
var orange = new Color(0xFF, 0xA0, 0);

colors.Add(orange);

Assert.That(colors.Contains(orange), Is.True);
```

Listing 5-24: Searching a collection of Color values

The test passes, but the Equals(object?) method will be used, because the HashSet.Contains implementation has no way of knowing that Color implements a type-safe overload of Equals that takes a Color parameter directly. This matters for Color because it's a struct, and so every comparison will box the argument to an object reference. If the HashSet contains a large number of elements, that boxing could well represent many unnecessary copies of Color.

The same would be true of a HashSet containing MusicTrack elements, and although the impact is a little less costly, it's still an unnecessary inefficiency.

To have generic code prefer our type-safe `Equals` over the more general implementation inherited from `object`, our types must implement the `IEquatable<T>` interface.

The IEquatable<T> Interface

When we implement the `IEquatable<T>` interface on any class or struct, we're signaling to generic code that the type has a public type-safe implementation of `Equals`. The `IEquatable<T>` interface specifies that the type represented by `T` contains an implementation of `Equals` taking a `T` as its parameter. Generic code such as `HashSet<T>` can detect that a generic type implements `IEquatable<T>` and will use the type-specific overload of `Equals` if it's available. Listing 5-25 shows how our `Color` struct would implement the `IEquatable<T>` interface.

```
public readonly struct Color : IEquatable<Color>
{
    --snip--
    public bool Equals(Color other)
        => other.Red == Red &&
            other.Green == Green &&
            other.Blue == Blue;

    --snip--
}
```

Listing 5-25: The IEquatable<T> interface

This `Equals` method is identical to the original type-safe method from Listing 5-18; the difference is that `Color` indicates the presence of that overload by explicitly implementing `IEquatable<Color>`. Now when we use a `Color` as the element type for a `HashSet` or other generic collection, any comparison using `Equals` will use our type-safe implementation and avoid the need to box the argument.

This works because generic collections like `HashSet` don't invoke `Equals` directly; instead, they defer the comparison to a helper class named `EqualityComparer<T>`, which internally selects a type-specific `Equals` method if `T` implements the `IEquatable<T>` interface. If `T` doesn't implement the interface, the virtual `Equals(object?)` is used instead.

We can use the `EqualityComparer` class in our own generic code to automatically select the best available implementation of the `Equals` method for a generic parameter type variable. Listing 5-26 shows the usual pattern for checking equality via an `EqualityComparer` object.

```
public void PlayNow(T item)
{
    var comparer = EqualityComparer<T>.Default;
    if(!comparer.Equals(Current, item))
        Current = item;
}
```

Listing 5-26: Equality using the EqualityComparer<T> class

The `EqualityComparer<T>.Default` static property returns an implementation of the standard `IEqualityComparer<T>` interface with the appropriate behavior for the T type parameter. When T implements `IEquatable<T>`, the `Default` property returns an implementation of `IEqualityComparer<T>` that uses the type-specific overload of the `Equals` method.

Besides `HashSet`, the `Dictionary` collection and some LINQ algorithms use `IEqualityComparer<T>` to define equality between elements. They can all be given a specific `IEqualityComparer<T>` implementation, so we can provide our own implementation of it to customize that behavior. We'll use this technique in Chapter 8 to modify the behavior of the `SequenceEqual` method.

The `EqualityComparer<T>` class is designed for generic code but can be useful when equality comparisons need to be made in the most general and efficient manner possible. One such situation is in code generated by the compiler.

Compiler-Generated Equality

The compiler itself is capable of synthesizing a correct and complete implementation of equality for some types. The code generated by the compiler uses the same techniques we've been exploring. In this section, we'll look at examples to better appreciate what the compiler is prepared to generate on our behalf, even for something as fundamental as equality comparison of variables.

Records and Record Structs

Records and record structs give us a compact way of creating a type that has value semantics built in. Records are syntactically different from both classes and structs, but in the CIL they're just classes with some compiler-generated features, including overrides of the `Equals` and `GetHashCode` methods. Similarly, record structs are structs in the compiled code and have most of the same compiler-provided features as records.

The notable exception is that the compiler implements a `Clone` method for records, but not for record structs. `Clone` emulates copying a record instance by value to support non-destructive mutation, which we examined in Chapter 4. Since record structs are natively copied by value, they have no need for a `Clone` method.

Both records and record structs implement `IEquatable<T>`, and the compiler-generated type-specific overload of the `Equals` method compares each field of the type, exactly as we did earlier in `MusicTrack` and `Color`. The `GetHashCode` method implementation uses all the fields to provide well-distributed hash codes. All this is in contrast to plain structs, where the default value-based equality behavior is provided by a common base class, `ValueType`.

This simple `Color` type is implemented as a positional record and demonstrates admirably how compact a record definition can be:

```
public sealed record Color(int Red, int Green, int Blue);
```

This positional syntax for a record causes the compiler to create three properties for Color, each with the same name and type as the respective positional parameters defined for the type. The compiler also provides a public constructor with those three parameters to initialize the three property values. This positional syntax can be used for records and record structs.

Inside Record Equality

All records are classes, but they have value-based equality semantics, courtesy of the implementation of the IEquatable<T> interface provided automatically by the compiler. The Equals methods shown in Listing 5-27 are almost—but not quite—the same as those generated for the Color record by the compiler.

```
public bool Equals(Color? other)
    => (object?)other != null &&
       GetType() == other.GetType() &&
       EqualityComparer<int>.Default.Equals(Red, other.Red) &&
       EqualityComparer<int>.Default.Equals(Green, other.Green) &&
       EqualityComparer<int>.Default.Equals(Blue, other.Blue);

public override bool Equals(object? obj)
    => Equals(obj as Color);
```

Listing 5-27: Equality implementation generated for a record

The compiler-generated type-safe Equals method can *directly* access the backing fields for the Red, Green, and Blue properties and thus avoids the extra method calls shown here for reading the property values. Note how the Equals method uses the EqualityComparer<T> class to compare each value, so if the type of any property implements IEquatable<T>, the type-safe implementation of Equals will be used.

Records can, by default, inherit from other records, so equality isn't quite as simple as comparing each object's fields. The other parameter for Equals could in that case refer to an instance of a more derived record. Checking for equality of objects that could have different run-time types requires extra care. In most cases, objects of different types aren't equal, which is why we use GetType on the second line of the Equals(Color?) method in Listing 5-27.

Our Color record is sealed and doesn't inherit from another record. Therefore, checking the type is redundant because the other parameter can't refer to anything other than an instance of Color.

Since the Color record is sealed and has no base types, we should consider making it a record struct. Record structs compile down to struct definitions, which can't be inherited or have null values, making their internals simpler. The type-safe Equals method for a record struct type doesn't check for null or whether the types match but is otherwise the same as for a record.

In addition to implementations of the `Equals` and `GetHashCode` methods, the compiler generates `operator==` and a corresponding `operator!=` for records and record structs. The implementation of `operator==` invokes the `Equals` method, so record variables exhibit value-based equality when they're compared with `==`, rather than the default identity-based comparison that classes have. We confirm this behavior for our `Color` record in Listing 5-28.

```
var red1 = new Color(0xFF, 0, 0);
var red2 = new Color(0xFF, 0, 0);

Assert.That(red1 == red2, Is.True);

Assert.That(ReferenceEquals(red1, red2), Is.False);
```

Listing 5-28: Comparing records with ==

Here we see that two `Color` variables compare equal, because even though they're definitely not two references to a single instance, the state of the instances is the same.

Custom Implementations for Record Equality

The compiler will normally generate at least two versions of `Equals` for a record or a record struct: one taking an `object` parameter (or `object?` within a nullable context) and the other implementing the `IEquatable<T>` interface, which performs the comparison of each instance's fields. The version taking an `object` parameter casts its argument to the required type and invokes the type-specific overload if the cast is successful, as we did for the `Color` record in Listing 5-27. We can provide our own implementation of the type-safe `Equals` method for a record or record struct type, in which case the compiler uses our implementation instead of generating one. If we do so, we should implement our own `GetHashCode` to match, which will also replace the compiler-generated implementation.

However, we can't provide our own implementation of `operator==` or `operator!=` for comparing two record or record struct instances. If we attempt to do so, the compiler gives us an error:

```
[CS0111] Type 'Color' already defines a member called 'op_Equality' with the same parameter
types
```

`op_Equality` is the name of the static method to which the compiler translates `operator==`. The name for `operator!=` is `op_Inequality`, and the compiler always provides both methods, preventing us from defining our own.

We should almost always accept the default implementation of equality for records and record structs, as the compiler-generated code is both correct and efficient. However, if we need to customize the behavior of equality for a record or record struct, we need only override the type-safe `Equals` method. Each of the other equality methods, including the overridden `Equals` method taking an `object` parameter, ultimately calls the type-specific overload to perform the actual comparison. The compiler's implementation of the == operator is identical to that shown here for Color, so if we alter the behavior of the Equals method, that behavior is also reflected in the implementations of operator== and operator!= provided by the compiler:

```
public static bool operator==(Color left, Color right)
{
    if((object)left == (object)right) return true;
    return (object)left != null && left.Equals(right);
}

public static bool operator!=(Color left, Color right)
    => !(left == right);
```

When we define a positional record or positional record struct, the compiler synthesizes a complete type, along with methods to support equality comparisons. The compiler generates code to support equality for nullable value types, too, although in a very different way.

Equality for Nullable Values

We denote a nullable value type by using the special ? notation on a value type variable. The compiler translates a nullable value type to an instance of the system type Nullable<T>, where T is the declared type for the variable. Nullable<T> is a struct, instances of which may have a value of type T or no value (represented by null).

Comparing nullable value type variables differs from comparing references, which may be null, because for two nullable value type variables, we must always compare each underlying value if one exists. To illustrate, consider Listing 5-29, where we compare two nullable value type variables, one with a value and the other null.

```
public readonly struct Color
{
    --snip--

    public static bool operator==(Color left, Color right)
        => left.Equals(right);

    public static bool operator!=(Color left, Color right)
        => !left.Equals(right);
}

Color? fg = new Color(0xFF, 0xA0, 0);
Color? bg = null;

Assert.That(fg == bg, Is.False);
```

Listing 5-29: Comparing nullable values

Both fg and bg in this example are nullable, but while fg has a Color value, bg is null. The test passes because the values aren't equal. Two nullable value type variables are equal if both have no value, or if both have a value and those values are themselves equal. What's interesting about this example is that while `Color` has a custom `operator==` to compare two `Color` values, it accepts two *non*-nullable `Color` parameters. Since `Color` is a struct, `null` isn't a valid value for it, although `null` is a valid value for a *nullable* `Color`.

The `Nullable<T>` struct doesn't have an overloaded `operator==` of its own. When the compiler encounters code comparing two nullable value types, or a nullable value type and a normal value type instance, it rewrites the comparison by inserting the implementation from the corresponding operator definition for the underlying—non-nullable—value type. This process is known as *lifting* the operator. Since one or both of those arguments may have *no* value, the lifted operation makes the additional checks for the existence of a value before finally comparing those values by using the original, non-nullable comparison.

For this reason, if `T` has no `operator==` defined, the comparison of two `T?` variables fails to compile, because the compiler has no operator implementation to lift. The `lifted_op_Equality` method in Listing 5-30 is fictional but demonstrates the basic algorithm for the lifted equality comparison operation.

```
bool lifted_op_Equality(Color? fg, Color? bg)
{
    if(fg.HasValue && bg.HasValue)
        return fg.Value == bg.Value; // uses Color.operator==
    else
        return !fg.HasValue && !bg.HasValue;
}
```

Listing 5-30: The lifted equality operator

The compiler doesn't generate a new method for this algorithm but simply inserts logic inline in our code, replacing the original comparison using `==` in Listing 5-29 with the equivalent of the following:

```
Assert.That(
    fg.HasValue == bg.HasValue &&
    (!fg.HasValue || fg.GetValueOrDefault() == bg.GetValueOrDefault()),
Is.False);
```

The logic of this code is essentially identical to that in Listing 5-30, but it's a single expression and thus easier for the compiler to inline. The reason for using `GetValueOrDefault` instead of the `Value` property is that the latter needs to check that a valid value exists and will throw an exception if it doesn't. `GetValueOrDefault` is therefore slightly more efficient.

Although nullable value types are instances of the special system type `Nullable<T>`, the same functionality couldn't be implemented by `Nullable<T>` simply having its own `operator==` to perform the comparison. The purpose of lifting the underlying type's `operator==` is to ensure that when both variables have a value, they're compared exactly as if they were non-nullable types—that is, direct instances of the original value type. An `operator==`

implementation for `Nullable<T>` would need to use == to compare two instances of the generic type `T`, which, as we know, isn't allowed.

By lifting the underlying type's `operator==`, the compiler ensures that the correct behavior is maintained and that values compare the same way whether or not they're nullable types.

The compiler also generates code inline to support comparisons of value tuple variables, introduced in C# v7.0, although the process for value tuples is a little different.

Value Tuples and Equality

Tuples are a common feature of many modern programming languages to gather several related values together into a single lightweight data structure. A tuple in C# is similar to a struct with all public fields and no member methods, although the syntax for declaring and using a tuple is different from doing so for such a struct.

Compiler support for tuple types supersedes the `System.Tuple` class introduced in .NET v4.0. The more modern feature, available since C# v7.0, is known as a *value tuple*. Value tuples are underpinned by a system type named `ValueTuple`, but that type isn't intended to be used directly. Instead, when we want to relate several fields together without the overhead of adding a full user-defined class or struct, we use the value tuple syntax.

Value tuples enjoy sophisticated support from the compiler, both in how variables are declared and in how they can be used. Listing 5-31 shows an example of comparing value tuple variables for equality.

```
var x = (10, "October");
var y = (ShortMonth: 10, LongMonth: "October");

Assert.That(x == y, Is.True);
```

Listing 5-31: Comparing value tuple variables for equality

We're declaring two tuple variables, x and y, by surrounding multiple values with parentheses; this syntax is common in several languages with tuple support and probably familiar to many programmers. However, although the x and y variables have the same *values*, they look distinctly different from each other in their declarations. In particular, y gives names to its component parts, whereas x doesn't. The test determines that x and y are equal and passes.

NOTE   *Support for using == to compare value tuples was introduced in C# v7.3, shortly after value tuples were introduced.*

When we compare value tuple variables with ==, the compiler generates code to compare each element of the value tuple with the corresponding element in the other value tuple. The elements of a value tuple are public fields, not properties, meaning that reading or writing a value accesses the field directly. As with nullable values, the compiler rewrites our comparison expression by inserting the code to compare the fields of x and y directly.

The CIL extract in Listing 5-32 shows just the comparison of the tuples' first component in Listing 5-31.

```
IL_0021: ldloc.2    // V_2
IL_0022: ldfld      !0/*int32*/ valuetype System.ValueTuple`2<int32, string>::Item1
IL_0027: ldloc.3    // V_3
IL_0028: ldfld      !0/*int32*/ valuetype System.ValueTuple`2<int32, string>::Item1
IL_002d: bne.un.s   IL_0042
```

Listing 5-32: New-style value tuple comparison CIL

The compiler directly loads the fields by using the ldfld instruction and then compares those values by using the bne instruction, which stands for *break if not equal*. The bne instruction is a companion to the ceq instruction we encountered in Listing 5-1. Whereas ceq pushes its result onto the evaluation stack, bne jumps to the specified label (IL_0042 in this example) if the values being compared are *not* equal; otherwise, processing continues from the next instruction following bne.

The fact that we're attempting to compare a simple tuple with a tuple that has named elements is irrelevant. The generated code doesn't attempt to use the names we've given the fields. It's comparing only their values, so the result of x == y is true. We could compare x with a tuple using different names with the same result; only the types and values of the fields matter.

The names we give the tuple components are a purely compile-time construct for *our* convenience. In fact, the names we give the y variable's components never even make it into the compiled code.

As with the generated code for comparing Nullable<T> values, the compiler will inject code to call a user-defined operator== if needed. You can see this in Listing 5-33, which shows the CIL for the comparison of the second component of our tuples, a string field.

```
IL_002f: ldloc.2    // V_2
IL_0030: ldfld      !1/*string*/ valuetype System.ValueTuple`2<int32, string>::Item2
IL_0035: ldloc.3    // V_3
IL_0036: ldfld      !1/*string*/ valuetype System.ValueTuple`2<int32, string>::Item2
IL_003b: call       bool [System.Runtime] System.String::op_Equality(string, string)
```

Listing 5-33: The call to a user-defined equality operator inserted by the compiler

Instead of the bne instruction used for the int field, the compiler has synthesized a call to op_Equality, exactly as if we'd handwritten the code. Fields of a value tuple are compared in the order in which they appear, so the first field of one is compared with the first field of the corresponding variable, and so on.

This approach differs from records, which use the EqualityComparer protocol instead of == to compare their fields. For records, the compiler generates the right methods on the underlying class or struct type to implement equality. When we compare two records with ==, we're invoking the op_Equality method generated for the record type. That method compares each field of the record in turn by using its Equals method.

For value tuples, as with nullable value types, the compiler generates the comparison code *inline*, effectively replacing the comparison of two tuples with a direct comparison of the component fields of each tuple type. If a component field of the tuple has an operator== defined for it, that implementation is used, but like Nullable<T>, the ValueTuple type used to implement value tuples has no operator== of its own.

If the fields can't be compared using either ceq or operator==, our code using == to compare the value tuple fails to compile. The ValueTuple type does override the Equals method and also implements the IEquatable<T> interface. Therefore, if a field has no operator==, we can still compare value tuple variables with Equals, which in turn will call each field's Equals method, safe in the knowledge that Equals is always there, whatever type we're using.

Summary

All animals are equal, but some animals are more equal than others.
—George Orwell, *Animal Farm*

For such a simple expression, comparing two variables for equality can represent a wide variety of behavior, from using a simple built-in equality check with ceq in the compiled code all the way up to the compiler automatically generating the correct code to perform a comparison. We've looked at how references are compared, how overriding the Equals method and == operator can affect behavior, and how the compiler can generate code to make sure the "right thing" happens.

For many programmers, using == to compare variables comes more naturally than calling the Equals method. For the built-in numeric types, using == is always more efficient, although with the binary floating-point types float and double, we have to be cautious of using either approach. Notwithstanding that, the cost of calling a method is very small, but it can never be as fast as the intrinsic ceq instruction.

The purpose of examining these effects in such intricate detail is to demonstrate that we can't necessarily take for granted what such a simple expression does when a program runs. The run-time complexity of any expression may be hidden from view, perhaps masked by the compiler choosing an unexpected method overload or override instead of a direct comparison between two variables. Certainly the performance costs in such examples are small, but they might be significant in "hot" paths through a program.

Boxing value type instances can have a significant effect on performance, not only because boxing generates copies of the value, but also because those copies are put on the heap and add pressure to the garbage collector. The standard `IEquatable<T>` and `EqualityComparer<T>` types help us avoid many cases where boxing would otherwise be required, especially in generic code.

We should always be aware of those circumstances where the compiler generates code on our behalf, but in the case of equality comparisons, the compiler goes to quite a lot of trouble to make sure that code is as efficient as possible.

6

THE NATURE OF VALUES

C# gives special meaning to the term *value type*, but the concept of a value certainly isn't unique to C#. In this chapter, we'll revisit values more generally and identify some key characteristics that indicate whether we should implement something as a value type. We'll look at the unique and important role of values and value types in our programs, and how implementing a well-behaved value type requires more than just using a struct or a record struct.

We'll explore the following:

- How to improve our designs by employing value type objects to encapsulate behavior
- How overriding the native reference semantics for some types adversely affects their behavior

- What application roles are fulfilled by different object types, and what characteristics define those roles
- Why equality isn't the same as equivalence
- How to identify appropriate candidates for value types in our applications

Every application is different, and it's our responsibility to create solutions to problems that are specific to a particular program. Ultimately, that requires us to use our own judgment on how best to apply our chosen programming language. In C#, to some extent, that means selecting whether we want to use classes, structs, records, or record structs for the types we create.

It's not appropriate for *everything* to be a value type; sometimes value semantics isn't suitable for the functionality we need. When choosing among the different types, we need to decide when value semantics makes sense for a type—and, equally importantly, when it doesn't.

Value vs. Reference Semantics

The term *value semantics* is widely used to describe value types, usually in contrast with its counterpart, *reference semantics*. However, while reference semantics is easily defined in terms of indirect access to instances via reference variables (or similar mechanisms in other languages), value semantics is often ill-defined or superficially explained as something value types possess. In C#, value types are epitomized by the struct.

Structs differ from classes in C# most conspicuously in that struct instances are copied by value, meaning the copy is a whole new instance. As a result, structs are commonly referred to as having value semantics. We might infer, then, that value semantics means that an instance is copied by value, and the C# Language Specification certainly supports this definition (*https://docs.microsoft.com/en-gb/dotnet/csharp/language-reference/language -specification/structs*):

> [Structs] can be conveniently implemented using value semantics where assignment copies the value instead of the reference.

As we've discussed in earlier chapters, copying by value is a direct consequence of the way value type variables use memory. The value of every value type variable is a complete instance of the type. When the value is copied, the copy is necessarily a whole new instance of the type, including copies of each field's value from the original instance. This differs from copying reference variables, where the copy is a new reference to the same instance in memory as the original variable. The original object's field values aren't copied at all.

The difference in copying behavior is merely a result of how value types and reference types are represented. Reference variables may be copied frequently, but the instances they refer to are rarely copied, which is a convenient and efficient use of memory. Struct and record struct variables are copied by value because they can't be copied any other way. However, copying behavior is only one part of the difference between value and reference semantics.

Copying and Equality Comparison Behavior

Equality comparison behavior is closely related to the way variables are copied. When we make a copy of a variable, the copy should compare equal to the original variable. That may seem obvious, but it's the reason all structs inherit `Equals` from `ValueType` and why that default implementation of `Equals` for structs is so important. Without `ValueType`, a copy of a struct variable wouldn't compare equal with the original value, because struct variables are copied by value. The copy is a distinct instance in its own right, and the default reference comparison offered by `object.Equals` would never compare the copy and original values as equal. The `Equals` method inherited from `ValueType` performs a value-based comparison to ensure that when we copy a value type instance, the copy and original variable will compare equal.

When we compare references, we're checking to see whether they represent the same specific instance, not whether those instances look alike. The behavior of the `Equals` method inherited by class types from `object` matches the copying behavior of references, because copying a reference variable doesn't also copy the instance.

Being copied by value isn't, on its own, what endows a value type with value semantics; it's simply the mechanism defined in the language for copying variables of struct type. In fact, copy-by-value behavior isn't even a necessary ingredient of value semantics. Take, for example, the `string` class, which overrides the default behavior of `Equals` and `operator==` to perform a value-based comparison. As noted in Chapter 5, `string` is a class, and `string` variables are references, but when we compare two `string` variables, we're most often interested in whether they both have the same content—that is, whether their character sequences are the same.

For the purposes of equality comparisons, at least, a string's *value* is the sequence of characters, not the actual value of the reference. Whether the two variables refer to the same string in memory is almost always irrelevant. Since `string` variables are references, `string` instances aren't routinely copied by value, but they are *compared* by value.

When we're trying to define or understand value semantics, equality behavior is more significant than the way variables are copied. In the broader sense, a value type is any type that bases its equality comparisons on its state; that is, two value type objects are equal if they have the same value. By extension, there's more to value semantics than a type being implemented as a struct or record struct; having value semantics is what makes a type a *value* type, if we accept a wider interpretation of the term *value type* than the definition in the C# Language Specification.

We can override that behavior for any of our own class types too, but doing so is not always appropriate.

Reference-Based Comparisons

Most objects have some state, whether that's private instance fields or public property values. We might be tempted to override the default reference equality behavior for all our classes and always use that state as an object's value for comparisons. However, although we can model values by using a class, as C# does with string, *having* a value and *being* a value are very different. Most types aren't intended to be values, and the default reference comparison is more appropriate for the majority of the classes we create.

As an example of reference-based comparisons being important for an object, consider the Login class in Listing 6-1 for a system tracking logged-in users. Since Login is a class, the semantics of reference comparisons makes sense for it because we need to be able to distinguish between individual instances.

```
public sealed class Login
{
    public string   UserName { get; }
    public DateTime Established { get; }
    public bool     Active { get; private set; }
    --snip--

    public void Disconnect()
    {
        Active = false;
    }
}
```

Listing 6-1: Reference-based equality matters for class types.

Even though the public properties directly expose the state of a Login instance, using those properties to implement equality would be a mistake. Two instances of Login with the same property values might easily represent different connections. Even if we presume that the UserName property is unique across all users, we may still need to identify an individual login in systems that allow multiple connections by the same user. The same user might even log in twice at exactly the same moment, so distinguishing different connections by their Established property isn't sufficient.

If we overrode the Equals method for Login to compare its property values, we couldn't use Equals to distinguish between different instances with identical properties. If we needed to forcibly disconnect a specific connection by calling its Disconnect method, we'd want to be certain we were disconnecting the right one! We therefore need to be able to identify a specific *instance* of a login, regardless of the values of its public properties.

We could use a mechanism other than Equals to distinguish between different instances with identical state, but we'd be adding extra complexity to support functionality that a normal reference-based comparison already provides.

Reference Semantics and Side Effects

The difference between value semantics and reference semantics is also defined partly by the potential for side effects via aliasing references, which in turn is closely associated with mutability. If we change an object via one variable and expect the change to be visible via another variable, we need reference semantics.

The `Login` class from Listing 6-1 has a `Disconnect` method that alters the internal state of an instance. If we call the `Disconnect` method by using one reference variable, we expect every reference to that instance to become inactive. As Listing 6-2 demonstrates, we also expect no other instances to be affected.

```
var mac = new Login("macreadyrj");
var norris = new Login("norrisv");

Assert.That(mac.Active, Is.True);
Assert.That(norris.Active, Is.True);

var thing = norris;
thing.Disconnect();

Assert.That(norris.Active, Is.False);
Assert.That(mac.Active, Is.True);
```

Listing 6-2: Intentionally changing an instance via a shared reference

Here, we copy the `norris` reference variable and call the `Disconnect` method on the copy, setting its `Active` property to false. Although we never use the `norris` variable to call `Disconnect`, the state of the instance `norris` refers to is changed after `Disconnect` is called because that instance has been modified via a different reference. The `mac` variable refers to a separate instance of `Login`, so it's not affected by the change to `thing`.

We want reference semantics for the `Login` class because it means we can have many references to a specific `Login` instance. We can pass a reference as an argument to methods and arrange for those methods to intentionally modify that instance. We don't need to worry about searching for all other references to the modified instance to make sure they've been updated with our changes, because references have that behavior built in.

A slightly more subtle outcome of reference semantics is that if we change the state of a reference type instance via one reference, the variable will still compare equal to any other references to the same instance. Listing 6-3 checks that two references compare equal even after the instance has been modified by one of those variables.

```
var norris = new Login("norrisv");
var thing = norris;

Assert.That(norris.Equals(thing), Is.True);

thing.Disconnect();

Assert.That(norris.Equals(thing), Is.True);
```

Listing 6-3: Checking for reference equality

This example demonstrates that when we change an instance of a reference type, that change is visible via all other references that are *equal* to the reference used to make the change. The outcome is that if two reference variables compare equal once in a reference-based comparison, and neither variable is assigned to a different instance, they'll *always* compare equal because references are equal when they have the same identity.

Object Identity

The *identity* of an object is what distinguishes it from other objects of the same type. Two reference type instances have different identities—they're independent objects—regardless of whether they have fields containing the same values. We can think of the address of an object as its identity, although this is only an analogy: an object's address can change if it's moved in memory because of heap defragmentation or other memory management tasks, but the object retains its identity.

In Chapter 2, you saw how the lock statement relies on reference semantics; that's one example of an object's identity being more important than the state it contains, even though the underlying Monitor class doesn't attempt to mutate the object used as a lock in any way. The implementation of Monitor relies on knowing the identity of a specific object instance, and that the identity is valid across multiple threads of execution.

Reference semantics is an important element in our toolbox so that we can identify a specific object instance, not just an object that has the same state as another object. Two reference variables to different class instances with exactly the same state shouldn't usually compare equal.

The one exception occurs when we're using a class to model a value type. In this case, the identity isn't important, because we're deliberately giving the class *value* semantics. The string type is a classic example. This type isn't a struct for valid reasons that are mostly concerned with efficiency: as a class, a string's contents won't be copied frequently, and its values will never be boxed. Nevertheless, string variables are compared by value, and using them is intuitive and straightforward thanks to value semantics for equality. Most classes, however, aren't intended to model values.

For types intended to have value semantics, instance identity has little or no significance. Values should be *referentially transparent*: we can switch one instance of a value with a different instance without affecting the program's logic or behavior, provided both instances have identical state.

An object's identity is important when we can alter that object's state, because identity is the only characteristic that distinguishes one object instance from another. The native reference equality of reference types tells us *which* variables will reflect a change we make to a particular instance.

Value-Based Comparisons

If the Login type in Listing 6-1 were a struct or record struct instead of a class, the final assertions in Listings 6-2 and 6-3 would fail because the

`Disconnect` method would be changing a different instance from the variable used in the assertion. Value types are useful when we don't need the aliasing behavior of reference semantics or the ability to have multiple references to a single instance. Contrast the `Login` type in Listing 6-1 with the `Color` type in Listing 6-4.

```
public readonly struct Color
{
    public int Red { get; init; }
    public int Green { get; init; }
    public int Blue { get; init; }
}
var crayon = new Color { Red = 0xFF };
var pencil = new Color { Red = 0xFF };
```

Listing 6-4: Comparing the state of two Color values

This `Color` type is a struct, making it a value type. The two variables `crayon` and `pencil` are clearly different instances, but they have the same color value and thus should compare equal. The only interesting aspect of the `Color` type, at least as far as testing two instances for equality is concerned, is its state. Two `Color` instances should compare equal if—and only if—their externally visible property values match.

From one perspective, the value of a `Color` *is* its identity, because identity is what distinguishes one object from another. Values are transient in that we can make one at any time with a given state. If we create multiple instances of a value type with the same state at different times or in different methods, then for all intents and purposes, they're *the same* value because they're indistinguishable, although the mechanics of the language means they're necessarily separate instances.

It *is* legitimate to say that equal values can be substituted for one another. Take, for example, the archetypal value type in C#: the int. Two integers with the same value might as well be the same integer. That may sound obvious, but the important point is that we—and our programs—don't care whether they're the same int in memory or two independent variables. All that matters is whether they have the same value.

In a sense, values have lifetimes that are beyond the technical boundaries imposed by scope or memory management. If two value type instances have exactly the same contents, and *that's all that matters*, they're indistinguishable from each other. For this reason, as you'll see next, values are usually immutable.

Mutability

Values are sometimes characterized as being *eternal*: their lifetimes aren't bounded by a variable's scope within a program or even by the lifetime of the program itself. We can, in a sense, pluck values out of thin air to use them. When we need the number 100, we just "materialize" it as a constant value.

This characteristic isn't limited to the built-in value types. The same is true of other values, such as a monetary amount like $9.99, the string "To be, or not to be", and the date January 1st 2024. They're *just there* when we need them.

In practice, real variables certainly do have a measurable lifetime, and each instance requires storage, so we can't simply dismiss the technical needs of our environment. Nonetheless, the theoretical view of eternal, immutable values is a useful way to model the way our own value types should behave.

When we add two numbers, we don't change either of them; rather, we get a new number representing their sum. Similarly, adding a day to a DateTime or rounding an amount of money to the nearest whole dollar doesn't alter the original—it produces a new value.

We can't change the value of the number 100,[1] but we can produce a new number by using 100 in an expression with another number. If we add 1 to 100, the value of 100 doesn't go away, even though we have a new number as a result of the expression. The same holds true for dates, speeds, lengths, temperatures, and other natural values. Values are immutable by nature.

Immutability can seem like an unnecessary restriction when we're creating types that represent values. After all, if we increase a speed value, we might not care about the previous value. Isn't it usually more efficient to change a value in place than to create a new instance with a changed value? Well, perhaps—we'd have to measure that. However, immutability has other, more subtle consequences and benefits.

Two immutable values—and remember from Chapter 4 that read-only isn't always the same thing as immutable—that compare equal will *always* do so. This has important implications for keys in hashed containers such as Dictionary collections. Hashed containers depend on the invariance of their keys. If we change the value of a particular key after it's been added to a container, we can't subsequently use the value to look up an item because, in a sense, we've altered that key's identity by changing its value.

The difference between state and instance identity is largely about equality. Specifically, when we check to see if one value equals another, are we interested in whether they have the same state or whether they're the same object? If it's the latter, we need a class. If it's the former—we're interested in the content and don't care whether the variables are the same instance—we need a value type.

Mechanics vs. Semantics

The Microsoft documentation has a section entitled Framework Design Guidelines that includes advice on choosing between classes and structs but not much guidance on when value semantics are a positive choice for a type. Among other suggestions, the guidelines offer this (*https://docs.microsoft .com/en-us/dotnet/standard/design-guidelines/choosing-between-class-and-struct*):

---

[1] FORTRAN programmers, please remain silent on this (*https://softwareengineering.stackexchange .com/questions/254799/ever-change-the-value-of-4-how-did-this-come-into-hayes-thomas-quiz*).

Consider defining a struct instead of a class if instances of the type are small and commonly short-lived or are commonly embedded in other objects.

This doesn't seem unreasonable if we take it at face value. In particular, the rationale behind value types being small is directly related to memory usage and copy-by-value behavior: structs that have many fields take up more memory space, and the cost of copying a value from one location to another is correspondingly higher.

However, this advice is focused purely on memory use and performance implications, and it's silent on when we should use records or record structs. Other semantic differences between value types and other types exist that we should take into account. While recommendations like this can guide us, they tell only a small part of the story. Every application will have its own requirements, constraints, and behavior. We don't have one single rule to apply that will be appropriate universally.

Policies that insist, or at least suggest, that value types have few data members and be short-lived focus on the technical mechanisms of memory representation and use, rather than the more conceptual premise of what behavior the type should exhibit. Values might often be small, but that doesn't mean that all small types should be structs. A reference type might have only a single field, but that doesn't automatically indicate that it should be a struct or other value-like type.

Correspondingly, just because we require a type that has several fields doesn't mean that it can't be a value type. If value semantics make sense for our type, we should make it a value type, regardless of how much data it carries with it. The number of fields required by an object shouldn't be the main factor in our decision-making. If we're worried about the cost of copying large values, we might endow a reference type with value-like behavior to address those concerns, a topic we'll revisit in Chapter 8.

One way we can determine where we might use value types is to compare their characteristics with other types in a program. Although we can't consider every possible object type for any potential application, some common categories of object roles are shared by many programs, as we'll discuss next.

Object Relationships

Object-oriented applications comprise a variety of objects with different roles, responsibilities, and interactions. These roles are characterized by the relationships between objects and how those objects collaborate to form a coherent application.

When we're designing an application, it's easy to overlook the central role played by values and value types. If we recognize their importance, we can often simplify our designs and make our programs clearer and easier to reason about.

We might think of a value as simply the payload of a variable, whether that's the representation of an int or the properties of an object on the heap. It's tempting to view the values we use as incidental to an application's purpose. Doing so can lead us to unduly rely on the built-in types and to oversimplify our custom value type implementations, resulting in what Martin Fowler describes as an *anemic domain model*.

The types used in an anemic design are perfunctory representations for common concepts in the design, especially for the value types. Such types often consist only of public properties, all of which have public getters and setters. They have no other associated behavior, instead relying on the surrounding code to perform common tasks such as data validation, calculations, and even managing comparisons. In turn, this leads to duplicated code, scattered error handling, and fragmented responsibilities.

The antidote to anemic design is a *rich domain model*, in which different kinds of types have individual roles and well-defined responsibilities. Each type incorporates behavior specific to it, rather than the behavior being scattered around the rest of the code. To successfully identify the types our applications require, we must recognize that objects aren't all the same; however, objects in even the most complicated systems do fall into a few categories.

Kinds of Objects

If we don't take care to partition our application's roles, our design can end up becoming incoherent, making it difficult to manage and maintain. Once we recognize the main roles that different kinds of objects can play, we can classify the types we create by those roles, giving our designs more structure and making them easier to understand and work with. Objects fall broadly into one of four categories:

Values

Values are responsible for ensuring that an application's data is valid and consistent and for controlling access to that data. They don't usually outwardly collaborate with other objects in a system, except to contain other values. A value's properties commonly don't change over time, but new values with different properties occur frequently.

Services

Services are boundary objects that represent interfaces to systems that are external to the application. Services are often stateless; they can be used and accessed as they're needed. They may be perpetual, meaning they are static types or have a global instance, or they're ephemeral and instantiated as and when required. Services may be used by many objects but generally have few collaborations of their own.

Entities

Entities are the higher-order design elements in an application. Whereas values are the currency of information, entities represent the transactions that use or act upon that information. They are often persistent, in the sense that they remain in memory rather than being created and destroyed often. They may change their properties over time—perhaps frequently—according to the needs of the system, and they collaborate often with other entities. An entity's properties are generally either other entities or values.

Controllers

Controllers are the task objects in a system: they do things. Entities and controllers generally cooperate to perform activities. Controllers are often also persistent and may have some state, which is usually related to their collaborations with other objects. Controllers are frequently employed to mediate the interactions between entities and services.

These are the application roles that define the behavior of a specific design and solution domain. These four are common in most systems, although not all applications will use or need all of them. Other categories of objects—such as collections, lifetime managers, and exceptions—have supporting roles in an application rather than being design elements in a system.

Values in C# are usually represented by structs, records, or record structs, although they can be modeled using classes, as you've seen with string. Each of the other roles will almost always be fulfilled by a class. Up to this point, the term *object* has been reserved for reference type instances. If we consider a value to be another kind of object, we have a common and uniform basis for comparing the characteristics of all the objects in an application.

The characteristics of a particular object, then, suggest the role it's fulfilling. Put another way, we can identify an object's role by looking at the characteristics of that object's implementation.

Object Characteristics

The three non-value roles—service, entity, and controller—are strongly behavioral in the sense that we use them to perform operations or tasks. By contrast, values tend to have a passive role in a system and are generally used by other objects.

Behavior is one of three main characteristics shared by all objects in a system, as described by Grady Booch and his coauthors in *Object-Oriented Analysis and Design with Applications* (Addison-Wesley, 2007). The other two primary characteristics are state and identity (see Figure 6-1), and the importance of each relative to the others is different for every application role.

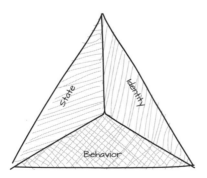

Figure 6-1: Characteristics of objects

Booch and his coauthors describe the three characteristics as follows:

Behavior

An object's behavior describes what it can do or its visible attributes. Those two aspects are frequently interrelated: when an object performs an action, the result may change its visible properties. The visible properties may form part or all of an object's state. A type's public interface defines the behavior of instances of that type; that is, the interface tells us what an object can do rather than how it's implemented.

State

The state of an object is defined by its member data, which may be persistent and immutable or may change over time. As just indicated, the state may be publicly visible in the interface or private and hidden, used only within the internal implementation of the type.

Identity

Every instance of a type has a distinct identity, which, as you've seen, allows us to distinguish one object from another. Identity is important when we need to know whether a variable represents a shared instance or a local value.

Each object role prioritizes different object characteristics, and in some cases, multiple characteristics are important for a given role. We can identify which role an object fulfills by looking at its profile in terms of these characteristics.

Values

Of all the application roles, values attach the most importance to their state; it is literally their distinguishing feature. Values always have some kind of behavior associated with the concept they represent, but that behavior doesn't alter the state. In most cases, the behavior is represented by properties to access the component parts of the state. A value might also have methods to return different representations of its state, or factory methods for creating new values. In any case, all of a value object's behavior is directly related to its state.

Values are strongly typified by their equality semantics, where one value is equal to any other with the same state. They're immutable and don't usually collaborate with other object types. Values frequently use other value types as fields, as demonstrated by the Product and Purchase types in Listing 6-5.

```
public readonly struct Product : IEquatable<Product>
{
    public Product(string desc, decimal amount)
        => (Description, Price) = (desc, amount);

    public string Description { get; }
    public decimal Price { get; }
```

```
    --snip--
}
public readonly struct Purchase : IEquatable<Purchase>
{
    public Purchase(DateTime time, Product product, int qty)
        => (Time, Product, Quantity) = (time, product, qty);

    public DateTime Time { get; }
    public Product Product{ get; }
    public int Quantity { get; }

    --snip--
}
```

Listing 6-5: Defining value objects

Both the `Product` and `Purchase` structs implement the `IEquatable<T>` interface, similar to the value types we examined in Chapter 5. Along with their properties, `Product` and `Purchase` both emphasize equality behavior, represented by the `IEquatable<T>` protocol, although that behavior is secondary to and entirely dependent on their state (see Figure 6-2).

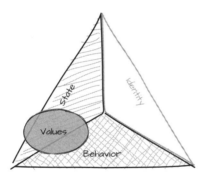

Figure 6-2: Value object characteristics

Here, you can see how the state of a value object is its primary feature; we distinguish different values by their state rather than identity, and values with identical state can be used interchangeably. The behavior characteristic for values is less prominent than the state, although equality semantics certainly make it important. However, the identity of a value is immaterial, so it's not shaded.

Services

Service objects often only encapsulate behavior and have no state. They generally provide some kind of façade or adaptation logic to interfaces that represent systems outside an application.

Identity usually isn't important for service objects. Services may be global and have a well-known instance available throughout the application, or they may be created as required, but each instance is indistinguishable from all the others, since none has any state. Services are sometimes implemented as purely static interfaces (as a static class with only static methods), like the InternetTime class in Listing 6-6.

```
public static class InternetTime
{
    public static async Task<DateTime> CurrentTime(Uri provider)
    {
        using var client = new HttpClient();
        var body = await client.GetStringAsync(provider);

        return Deserialize.DateAndTime(body);
    }
}
```

Listing 6-6: Implementing a static service

This InternetTime class is a service that merely exposes a static method; it has no identity because there is no object.

Figure 6-3 illustrates that the behavior of a service object isn't just its most important characteristic—it's frequently its *only* characteristic.

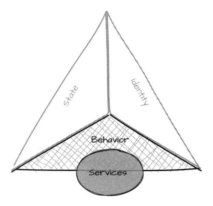

Figure 6-3: Service object characteristics

For services, like values, object identity is irrelevant, but for slightly different reasons. When a service object has an identity, such as when it's implemented as a globally accessible object, we can substitute that instance with a different object, as long as its public interface is the same. As we know, values are interchangeable if they have the same state. Unlike values, services rarely have any state, so state and identity are both unshaded in Figure 6-3.

Entities

Entities often do have some kind of state, which means we need to be able to distinguish one instance from another. An entity's state is usually observable only through its behavior, which may involve either reading or modifying the state. Entities commonly don't directly expose their state but instead provide methods to manipulate or access representations of it in different forms.

Consider the `Account` class in Listing 6-7, which has a method to add purchases to the account, affecting the account balance. The balance itself isn't represented directly as state in the `Account` class but is calculated from outstanding charges.

```
public class Account
{
    public virtual decimal ChargeToAccount(Purchase item)
    {
        activity.Add(item);
        return CalculateBalance();
    }

    public virtual decimal CalculateBalance()
        => activity.Sum(item => item.Product.Price * item.Quantity);

    public virtual IEnumerable<Purchase> Statement
        => activity.OrderBy(item => item.Time);

    private readonly List<Purchase> activity = new();
}
```

Listing 6-7: Creating an entity object

Entities may also have behavior that doesn't relate directly to their state but perhaps updates or modifies another entity object parameter. Abstract and virtual methods are a fairly common feature of entity types (as in the `Account` entity here), allowing them to be inherited, with derived types customizing the base class behavior.

We're usually interested in using a specific instance of an entity type, so object identity is critical, regardless of whether we have multiple instances with identical state.

As shown in Figure 6-4, then, entities place fairly high importance on all three object characteristics.

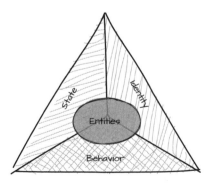

Figure 6-4: Entity object characteristics

Controllers

Controllers also often have some state, but they differ from entities in that the state affects the way controllers perform their task. One example is a database Command object whose state includes a connection to a data source and a representation of an SQL instruction. A controller may well expose its state publicly and even allow it to be directly changed, affecting the controller's behavior. For example, consider how the Command class's Execute method uses the Query property in Listing 6-8.

```
public class Command
{
    public Command(DatabaseConnection connection)
        => (this.connection, Query) = (connection, string.Empty);

    public string Query { get; set; }

    public QueryResult Execute()
    {
        connection.Open();
        var result = connection.ExecuteQuery(Query);
        connection.Close();

        return result;
    }

    private readonly DatabaseConnection connection;
}
```

Listing 6-8: Defining a controller

The Command object allows us to change its SQL instruction via the mutable Query property. We can repeatedly call the Execute method on one Command instance to obtain different results, rather than creating a new Command object for every query.

Controllers, as illustrated in Figure 6-5, are principally characterized by identity and behavior. They depend on their state to some degree but tend to rely on it less than entities do, because that data is used to support or modify the controller's behavior rather than being a hidden implementation detail.

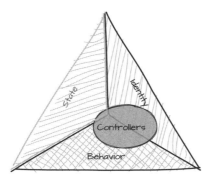

Figure 6-5: Controller object characteristics

Individual implementations of controller objects may attach more or less importance to their state or their behavior, depending on their specific requirements. However, as with entities, a controller object's identity is almost always significant, because we need to be able to distinguish between different instances. Reference semantics are often important for both entities and controllers so that any changes to an instance are reflected by all references to it.

Design Refinement to Model Object Roles

The three characteristics of identity, state, and behavior give us a relatively simple metric we can apply to determine whether an object most closely resembles a value, entity, controller, or service. We can use this information to refine a design or to refactor code. Looking at an object's characteristics might tell us that it has too much responsibility or represents a mixture of application roles, and we should adjust the code accordingly.

An object that's highly dependent on its state, and that has different instances with identical state that are considered equal, is a strong contender for being a value. If the identity of a specific instance is important, however, it most likely shouldn't be a value, so we'd look to the other characteristics to determine which of the non-value roles it best represents. If we can't clearly identify a specific role based on an object's characteristics, we should take the opportunity to decompose the type to better model individual roles with separate abstractions.

When designing a system, programmers often look for the main characters—that is, the service, entity, and controller roles. Identifying value type candidates isn't always so straightforward, which may be one reason they're often represented by the built-in types, such as int, double, or string.

An object should have a single responsibility and fulfill just one application role. By being mindful of the relative merits of identity, state, and behavior, we can more closely and clearly model our objects' roles. Because values place so much importance on their state, everything about a value is focused on that state, whether obtaining, reporting, or manipulating it. Identifying the value types in an application helps us simplify our design by partitioning responsibilities and encapsulating behavior.

Abstraction and Vocabulary

Some objects stand out as good candidates to be values—for example, simple measurements and quantities, such as speed, temperature, distance, length, and money. Such objects are often simple wrappers around primitive types like int and double. Each logically represents a single concept as an abstraction. We can't easily decompose them other than to revert to using primitive types.

We use the names of these types to form part of the *vocabulary* of a program. We write the program in terms of specific concepts like Speed and Length rather than more general-purpose types like double. More than that, when we talk to other people working on the same project, the names we use match the names in the code.

Using a specific named type instead of a built-in primitive type also prevents simple errors, such as mistakenly using a temperature value when we mean to use a length. If, for example, we pass an instance of a `Temperature` type to a method expecting a `Length`, the program won't compile. Such errors are easy to miss when we use built-in types like `double` to represent values for both length and temperature.

Other value candidates are less easily represented with primitive types because they consist of multiple components. Types to represent concepts such as currency rates of exchange, color spaces, Cartesian coordinates, and telephone numbers each have several related parts. Still, they all represent distinct abstractions to which we can give meaningful names like `FxRate`, `Color`, `Coordinate`, and `PhoneNumber`.

The names we give our types should provide vital information about their purpose. We could collect the red, green, and blue components of an RGB color space into a simple tuple type, but it would be hard to distinguish such a value from a tuple containing the x, y, and z components of a three-dimensional coordinate value. Creating separate user-defined types for `Color` and `Coordinate` makes our code easier for other programmers to understand.

When we use the name of an abstraction, we're implicitly referring to the behavior associated with that abstraction. The name becomes shorthand for the concept and is most easily understood when the type representing that abstraction is a single, cohesive idea and its behavior is well encapsulated. Value types are a rich vein for exploring those ideas, although the same principles apply for all types.

Encapsulation and Cohesion

When we're designing our own type, beyond giving it a name that conveys its purpose, it's also beneficial to collect the behavior that's appropriate for the abstraction we're modeling. This is what's commonly meant by *encapsulation*: assembling the object's data and the methods that support it. However, encapsulation is much more than just adding member methods; we also need to keep in mind a type's cohesion, which is a much less tangible concept.

A type is *cohesive* if the operations defined for it all work together to provide a well-defined and sensible interface for using instances of the type. In other words, cohesion means that the concept of the type makes sense as a whole. In this context, we're talking about whether other programmers find a type easy to comprehend. The compiler cares only about what's syntactically correct, but we'd likely be surprised to find a method for converting a string to uppercase on a type mostly concerned with money.

A type is more than just a place for defining methods; those methods should contribute to the abstraction we're trying to represent. Conversely, as mentioned earlier, a type with no behavior at all, such as the `Speed` type in Listing 6-9, is often simplistic.

```
public struct Speed
{
    public double InMetersPerSecond { get; set; }
}
```

Listing 6-9: Anemic type design

This Speed struct isn't encapsulating anything, and its InMetersPerSecond property might just as well be a public field. Although the name of the type gives us a clue as to its intended purpose and at least allows the compiler to catch many inappropriate uses, Speed is an example of an anemic type. Any behavior we add should support and contribute to the abstraction implied by the name Speed.

This advice applies equally to all types in a system, not just the value types. Whatever the purpose of the types we create, we need to capture individual abstractions in our designs. Good abstractions are well encapsulated; they don't leak their implementation details. A type that is cohesive is easier to comprehend than one that's just a collection of methods. Encapsulation and cohesion both contribute to the quality of the abstraction.

Many of the objects we create have some kind of state, but that's not the same as them representing values. For value types, the abstraction we're representing *is* that value. If we're defining a type to represent a speed, the operations we define for the type should present an interface consistent with a generally accepted notion of a Speed. The value is the core of the encapsulation and cohesion we want to achieve.

NOTE   *The term* encapsulation *is sometimes used to mean merely data hiding. While it's certainly true that exposing fields directly is usually a bad idea, as we'll talk about shortly, encapsulation involves more than making data private. Encapsulation has a close relationship with cohesion, and in concert they play an important role in designing types that are easy to use correctly and hard to use incorrectly.[2]*

Eliminating Duplication

Encapsulating behavior into a named type allows us to capture common code in one place. As you saw in Chapter 1, sensible values for a speed fall within a specific range, so attempting to use a speed with a value outside that range should be an error. If we use an overly simple type to represent a speed, we must duplicate those validation checks everywhere a speed value is used, which might be in multiple places. Consider the methods in Listing 6-10, which use the Speed struct from Listing 6-9. We must validate the value for every use of Speed.

---

[2] With thanks and apologies to Scott Meyers.

```
private const double C = 299792458;

public static double Distance(Speed speed, double time)
{
    if(speed.InMetersPerSecond > C ||
       speed.InMetersPerSecond < 0 ||
       speed.InMetersPerSecond is double.NaN)
    {
        throw new ArgumentOutOfRangeException(...
    --snip--
}
public static double Time(Speed speed, double distance)
{
    if(speed.InMetersPerSecond > C ||
       speed.InMetersPerSecond < 0 ||
       speed.InMetersPerSecond is double.NaN)
    {
        throw new ArgumentOutOfRangeException(...
    --snip--
}
```

Listing 6-10: Duplicated validation code

To protect these methods from invalid speed values being passed as arguments, we must validate the parameter to ensure that it's not larger than the maximum allowed value, it's not negative, and it's a real number. The tests we use are the same for every method using a Speed, and we should also validate the values for the time and distance parameters. It would be easy to forget one of these checks when we write a new function that uses a speed, time, or distance, or to accidentally use the wrong value for the maximum allowable speed.

The duplication of the validation code is also a maintenance problem. If we need to alter the acceptable range of values for speeds, we have to make sure we change it everywhere it occurs. We also need to test the validation logic in every method where it's applied, so those tests will also be duplicated.

If we instead encapsulate the validation logic within a constructor for Speed, we can test its characteristics in only one place and in isolation from other tests we need. We won't need to worry that the values might be out of range for methods using Speed values. Any method using a Speed can rely on the validation it encapsulates. We can remove the duplicated validation code as well as any duplicated tests.

Establishing Class Invariants

Having a constructor that performs all the necessary validation for a type's value is an example of establishing a *class invariant* (where *class* has to do with type theory rather than the class keyword). This approach ensures that all instances have values that make sense for the type.

Listing 6-11 shows how we can combine a switch expression with pattern matching to efficiently perform numeric validation in a constructor.

```
public readonly struct Speed
{
    private const double C = 299792458;

    public Speed(double val)
        => amount = val switch
        {
          ❶ double.NaN => throw new ArgumentException(
                            message: "Must be a number",
                            paramName: nameof(val)),

          ❷ < 0 or > C => throw new ArgumentOutOfRangeException(
                            paramName: nameof(val),
                            message: $"Must be between 0 and {C}"),

          ❸ _          => val
        };
    --snip--

    private readonly double amount;
}
```

Listing 6-11: Defining a simple value type with validation

The constructor for Speed ensures that we'll never have a value that is not a number, is negative, or is greater than the speed of light.

The patterns within the switch expression are matched from top to bottom, and wherever the value being tested—the val parameter in this case—matches the pattern, the associated expression is evaluated to produce a result. The first two patterns here are the error conditions and throw exceptions instead of producing a value.

The first pattern is a constant pattern matching NaN, as you saw in Chapter 5 ❶. The second pattern throws an ArgumentOutOfRange exception if val is either less than 0 or greater than the constant C ❷. This pattern uses a combination of facilities available since C# v9.0: a relational pattern and a disjunctive pattern.

The *relational pattern*, which is appropriate for any of the built-in numeric types, uses the relational operators <, >, <=, or >= to determine whether a number is within a given range. The *disjunctive pattern* combines other patterns by using the or keyword, and the pattern matches if any of its expressions match. The similar *conjunctive pattern* (not used here) uses the and keyword and matches if all of its component expressions match.

If the val value doesn't match either of the first two patterns, it matches the final discard pattern, whose expression is simply the value of val ❸. This becomes the result of the whole switch expression and is assigned to the amount field. Since the discard is always a match, it must be the final pattern in the switch expression.

In addition to encapsulating validation logic within the Speed type, we've made Speed immutable to ensure that an instance, once successfully validated, can never become invalid. If the state can't be changed, the class invariant needs to be checked only once—in the constructor.

Clarifying with Symmetry

The role of symmetry in an interface is often underestimated, but it can be important in making our types easy to use and understand. For instance, you saw in Chapter 1 how class factory methods can help us represent units for a type like Speed. We use such methods instead of directly accessing a public constructor, and each method encapsulates the name of the units it represents. Listing 6-12 shows how we can couple the class factory methods with their corresponding properties to obtain a value in different units.

```
public static Speed FromMetersPerSecond(double value) => new Speed(value);
public        double InMetersPerSecond => amount;

public static Speed FromKmh(double value) => new Speed(value * 1000 / 3600);
public        double InKmh => amount * 3600 / 1000;
```

Listing 6-12: Applying symmetry by pairing class factory methods with their respective properties

We'd probably expect that if we can create a Speed by using a value in kilometers per hour, we could get the value in the same unit at a later stage. We emphasize the symmetry between each class factory method and its corresponding property by declaring each pair for a particular unit together.

The methods and properties in Listing 6-12 don't prevent us from using the wrong units. We could still pass a value in kmh to the FromMetersPerSecond factory method. However, by encoding the units that we're using in the names of the class factory methods and properties, we make them more explicit and more expressive than using a plain constructor.

Being explicit helps to make the interface to Speed consistent and easier to use correctly than incorrectly. Our Speed type has become much more than a simple wrapper around a primitive value.

Using explicit names like FromKmh and InKmh to represent the available conversions for a Speed instance helps maintain the encapsulation of the internal representation. A constructor taking a double parameter, along with a vaguely named property to simply return that value, leaks the detail that Speed has a particular underlying representation. The class factory methods and properties shown here hide these implementation details and add value for users in the form of some common conversions.

We can easily imagine using similar class factory methods and properties to convert between units for other types, such as between Celsius and Fahrenheit for temperature, or meters and feet for length.

Encapsulation and the Public Interface

While it involves more than making data private, encapsulation is built on the premise that a type's internal data can't be directly accessed—and especially can't be changed—by code other than the type's methods. Access to private data is controlled by the type's public interface.

Well-encapsulated types aid us in reasoning about code because we can always be sure that private fields have consistent values, and that those values can never change without our knowing about it. More than that, it means that, as designers, we can change the underlying representation without changing the interface. If we never directly expose a type's data, no code other than that type's member instance methods can ever depend on its representation.

By encapsulating the `double amount` field of `Speed` as private and exposing or operating on it only under the controlled conditions afforded by member methods and properties, we limit the scope and impact of changing the representation to just those members.

Correspondingly, if we limit the number of members with direct access to a field, we reduce the scope of the change even further. If we write methods that depend only on the public interface of `Speed`, they'll continue to work even if we change the underlying data type.

Extending the Interface

If we add too many instance methods to any type, we risk cluttering its interface. The core interface of a type is harder to discover when the type has methods that are only occasionally useful. By contrast, keeping the methods of a type to a reasonable minimum makes the code easier to understand.

One alternative to instance member methods is to use extension methods, which are defined outside the type they extend. An example extension method for `Speed` is shown in Listing 6-13, where the `WithPercentAdded` method uses the public methods and properties defined in `Speed` to create a new `Speed` with a different value.

```
public static class SpeedExtensions
{
    public static Speed WithPercentAdded(this Speed speed, double percent)
        => Speed.FromMetersPerSecond(speed.InMetersPerSecond +
                    percent / 100 * speed.InMetersPerSecond);
}

var start = Speed.FromMetersPerSecond(100);
var end = start.WithPercentAdded(25);

Assert.That(end.InMetersPerSecond, Is.EqualTo(125));
```

Listing 6-13: Extending the interface of Speed

The `WithPercentAdded` method doesn't modify the instance of `Speed` passed to it—it can't, because `Speed` is a read-only struct. Instead, we return a new instance of `Speed` with the desired value. An extension method must be defined in a static class, so it's always a static method. It's common to group methods that extend a particular type together in one static class definition, so the `SpeedExtensions` class might include several methods to extend the interface of `Speed`.

Extension methods are useful for adding utility methods to a type without overburdening its principal internal interface.

Reducing the Internal Interface

A type's interface defines the collaborations that objects of that type can have with other objects in a system. The public methods, constructors, and properties defined within the type form the *internal*, or *intrinsic*, interface and define what other objects can do with instances of the type. A type also has an *external*, or *incidental*, interface comprising methods that take parameters of the type but are defined outside it. The external interface defines which other objects depend on the type. Those external methods can't access the type's internals, so they're unaffected by any changes to the underlying representation.

The essential characteristics of a type with many public members can be difficult to discern because the physical definition of the class becomes large. If we restrict the internal interface members to those that require access to the type's private implementation details, the type definition becomes shorter and thereby easier to comprehend. Methods that can be implemented entirely in terms of the internal public interface can be factored out into separate classes. Whether to make them extension methods or plain static methods depends on which is the most natural usage.

The logical conclusion is that, where possible, we should actively try to reduce the internal interface as much as we can without breaking the type's encapsulation or reducing its cohesion. This approach has two competing perspectives. On one hand, by extracting methods like WithPercentAdded that are implemented in terms of Speed's other public methods, we make Speed smaller and easier to comprehend. We also reduce the potential impact of any changes we might make to Speed's internal representation. On the other hand, WithPercentAdded is still part of the overall accessible interface of Speed, and by extracting that method out separately, we make it harder to discover.

We must find the balance between the internal and external interfaces of Speed. Although the WithPercentAdded method may be a useful utility for Speed values, it isn't really intrinsic to the concept of Speed. Extracting it as an extension method doesn't reduce Speed's cohesion or break its encapsulation by requiring us to introduce a new property that would otherwise be unneeded or change a private member to be public. Collecting extension methods like WithPercentAdded in one place is one way to make the external interface easier to discover.

The FromKmh class factory method, on the other hand, is much better suited as a member of Speed. We could implement it as a static method on a different type and in terms of FromMetersPerSecond. However, doing so would reduce the cohesion of Speed because FromKmh and FromMetersPerSecond naturally go together. If we extracted both of those methods to a separate type, we'd need to make Speed's constructor public, reducing its encapsulation. The FromKmh method is intrinsic to the interface of Speed because it represents a way to create a Speed in specific units and has a natural affinity with other intrinsic methods.

Some methods *must* be members of their type, even if they could conceivably be implemented in terms of other public properties and methods. The `Equals(object?)` method overrides a base class implementation and must be an instance method. Overloaded operators must all also be static member methods. An operator overload takes at least one parameter of the type of which it's a member, so we can't implement it in a separate type.

Composing Abstractions

Values can be more than simple wrappers around primitive types such as `double`. A struct can contain other user-defined types as fields, so we can create new abstractions by composing existing ones. We might, for instance, create our own type to represent a `Velocity`, which combines a `Speed` type with an `Angle` type. Although the `Velocity` type in Listing 6-14 has no behavior of its own, it can take advantage of the richer abstractions represented by `Angle` and `Speed`.

```
public readonly struct Velocity
{
    public Velocity(Speed speed, Angle angle)
        => (Speed, Angle) = (speed, angle);

    public Speed Speed { get; }
    public Angle Angle { get; }
}

var velocity = new Velocity(100.Kmh(), 45.Degrees());
```

Listing 6-14: Composing a new abstraction for Velocity

The `Velocity` type benefits from the validated constraints on the possible values of `Speed` and `Angle` and can use any of their public operations and properties, including any extension methods. Building on those contained types, we can add to `Velocity` any behavior that's specific to it, such as arithmetic operations or conversions to and from different representations.

`Velocity` represents a specific single concept, even though it's a kind of container for values of other types. The `Speed` and `Angle` properties of `Velocity` aren't arbitrary; they define what it means to be a measurement of velocity. The `Velocity` abstraction forms part of the vocabulary of a program, along with `Speed` and `Angle`.

`Velocity` is a good candidate for implementation as a record or record struct, particularly using the compact positional syntax available for those types. However, the positional syntax is less well suited for the `Speed` and `Angle` types. To explain why, in the next section we'll look at some of the trade-offs and compromises among the different ways of defining types.

Choosing Between Value and Reference Semantics

In most programs, the majority of user-defined types will be classes, which support the widest array of features offered by C#. Classes are the most general-purpose way in C# of creating our own types because they support all the object-oriented facilities of the language, such as inheritance and virtual methods. Class instances also benefit from the automatic memory management afforded to objects allocated on the heap. Generally, only when we need the behavior associated with value semantics should we define a type differently.

We have a few indicators that value semantics are appropriate for a type we're defining. Values shouldn't support changes to their state, which is why it's recommended that value types contain only other values. When all value types are immutable, regardless of whether they're implemented using classes, records, structs, or record structs, we don't have to worry about the state of an object changing unexpectedly, because the behavior of our code is more predictable. A type that requires unrestricted write access to its state is usually a poor candidate for being a value.

A related indicator is needing the type to support a full deep copy of its state. We need a *deep copy*, also known as a *clone*, to copy mutable state when we want to avoid the side effects associated with aliasing references. Most commonly, the state needs to be written only immediately after cloning so that the new object can have different properties than the original. The non-destructive mutation facility we examined in Chapters 2 and 4 is a good example of providing limited mutability for value-like types.

Anytime we customize equality behavior for a class so that two instances can be compared according to their state, it's another strong indicator that the type should be implemented as a full-fledged value. Cloning is often accompanied by an overridden Equals method.

State-based equality behavior and support for deep copies to avoid aliasing problems are two of the strongest signs that value semantics are needed. Although it's possible to use a class to implement a value (as we've seen with string), the other kinds of type definition are usually preferable.

Records, structs, and record structs are all facilities for creating types that represent values—that is, for defining types that have *value semantics*. The choice between them isn't necessarily obvious, as each has different advantages and disadvantages.

Avoiding the Pitfalls of Default Variables

For struct and record struct types, we need to remember that instances can always be default-initialized, so the default value must be considered valid both by the type's implementation and by code using the type. For simple numeric types like Speed or Length, this isn't a problem. The default value for such types is 0, which is a perfectly acceptable state no matter the unit: 0 meters is precisely the same value as 0 miles or 0 inches.

The same is not universally true for all values. In temperature measurements, for example, the unit of the stored value matters: 0°C is 32°F, and 0°F is approximately –17.78°C. We might establish the convention that the default unit for Temperature is Celsius, but it's hard to make that explicit without having a separate type for each unit, which seems unnecessary.

If we use a class or record instead of a struct or record struct, we can prevent default values and force our users to specify the correct units when creating instances. However, classes and records are both reference types, meaning that variables can have a null value. We can mitigate that in C# v8.0 and later by taking as much advantage of non-nullable references as we can, although that might not prevent every possible misuse.

Notwithstanding that, when we're deciding between a class or record to model a type that has value-like characteristics, a record is almost always preferable. Records are specifically intended to define types that have value semantics, and the compiler provides the default equality behavior for records based on the state of the instances being compared.

Implementing Custom vs. Generated Behavior

If we want a class to have value-based equality, we must define it ourselves. As a minimum, we should override the Equals(object?) and GetHashCode methods, but, as you saw in Chapter 5, a more complete definition includes implementing the IEquatable<T> interface and overloading operator==, and its companion operator!=, to make equality comparisons natural and easy.

For most value-like types, implementing those methods is straightforward as long as we're careful to avoid common mistakes. However, if we use record instead of class, the compiler generates implementations for all those methods. This makes a record type definition smaller and easier to comprehend and saves us from having to remember all the potential pitfalls.

For our prospective Temperature type, we might consider a positional record, saving us the trouble of a complete definition. A provisional implementation of Temperature as a positional record might look like the definition in Listing 6-15, but positional records have limitations to take into account.

```
public sealed record Temperature(double InCelsius)
{
    public static Temperature FromCelsius(double val)
        => new Temperature(val);

    public double InFahrenheit => InCelsius * 1.8 + 32;
    public static Temperature FromFahrenheit(double val)
        => new Temperature((val - 32) / 1.8);
};
```

Listing 6-15: A positional Temperature record

The compiler uses the parameters of Temperature's definition to automatically generate a property named InCelsius, but we must write our own InFahrenheit property so we can add the code to perform the conversion. Users can invoke the class factory methods to create Temperature instances with different units, but the constructor for Temperature generated by the compiler is *public*. The generated constructor also won't validate its parameters, and we might want to ensure that a Temperature can't be below absolute zero.

If we want users to be explicit about the units, we need to force them to use those class factory methods, so a positional record doesn't meet our needs. For the same reasons, the positional syntax isn't appropriate for the Speed and Angle types we used in Velocity in Listing 6-14.

Overriding Generated Methods

When the positional record syntax won't meet our needs, we can use a full record definition, which doesn't have the positional type arguments. We can then provide our own *private* constructor and use that to validate the initial value.

We sacrifice some of the convenience of using a positional record for Temperature because we have to write our own InCelsius property, since the compiler generates properties only for positional records. The record definition in Listing 6-16 shows how we can customize behavior for a record type while still enjoying the benefits of the other code provided by the compiler.

```
public sealed record Temperature
{
    private const double ZeroKelvin = -273.15;

    private Temperature(double celsius)
        => value = celsius switch
            {
                Double.PositiveInfinity or < ZeroKelvin
                    => throw new ArgumentOutOfRangeException( --snip-- ),

                double.NaN =>  throw new ArgumentException( --snip-- ),

                _            => celsius
            };

    public double          InCelsius => value;
    public static Temperature FromCelsius(double val)
        => new Temperature(val);

    public double          InFahrenheit => value * 1.8 + 32;
    public static Temperature FromFahrenheit(double val)
        => new Temperature((val - 32) / 1.8);

    public static Temperature AbsoluteZero
        => new Temperature(ZeroKelvin);

    private readonly double value;
}
```

Listing 6-16: A full record definition for Temperature

The compiler will still generate the methods to implement value-based equality for a nonpositional record, leaving us to concentrate on correctly implementing any other behavior specific to a record type like Temperature.

Records and record structs offer the greatest benefit over classes and structs, respectively, when we can accept all the default behavior of the positional syntax. A good example is the Color type from Listing 6-4, which as a positional record struct would look like this:

```
public readonly record struct Color(int Red, int Green, int Blue);
```

For Color, a default-initialized instance is a valid Color and compares equal to an instance with properties that are all 0, as shown in this example:

```
var background = new Color();
var black = new Color(0, 0, 0);

Assert.That(background == black, Is.True);
```

We don't have to add any of our own methods or properties, so the positional syntax is compact and does exactly what we need.

Records and record structs can be convenient for defining simple value types like Color, although the compiler might not provide everything required by a type. In particular, if we need to compare two values to see if one is less than the other, we must always provide our own implementation of that comparison.

Comparison for Ordering

The principle of value-based equality is the *one thing* that defines what it means to be a value. When we talk about whether something is a value type, that's really shorthand for whether two instances compare equal according to their state or according to their identity. Using state as the basis for equality is intrinsic to all values. However, some values may be equivalent but not necessarily equal.

Normally, two values are equal if they have exactly the same state. Two instances of the LogEntry record struct in Listing 6-17 are equal if all the properties are also equal, whereas the identity of individual LogEntry instances isn't important.

```
public enum Severity { Debug, Info, Warning, Error }

public readonly record struct LogEntry(DateTime stamp,
                                       Severity Level,
                                       string Message);
```

Listing 6-17: Value type equality

Some, but not all, values have a natural ordering, which enables us to sort collections of them. Many sorting algorithms exist, but all generally work by comparing each item in a collection with the others in turn to determine whether one is less than the other. If the left-hand value is less than the right, the items are considered to be in order.

We can customize the meaning of *less than*, and therefore *in order*, for our own purposes. In C#, the protocol for defining *less than* is the `IComparable<T>` interface, which requires us to implement a single method named `CompareTo` for a type. If the left argument is less than the right, `CompareTo` returns a negative integer; if the right is less than the left, the result is positive. Otherwise, the result is 0.

When we compare two `LogEntry` values to see if they're equal, we use all the properties. For ordering, however, we might care only about the `TimeStamp` property, because we merely want to put the entries in the order in which they were logged. Ordering `LogEntry` values by message makes little sense, and ordering them by severity isn't necessary for our use case.

The `TimeStamp` property of `LogEntry` is a `DateTime` instance, which itself implements the `IComparable` interface, so Listing 6-18 implements `CompareTo` for `LogEntry` simply by comparing only the `TimeStamp` properties.

```
public readonly record struct LogEntry(DateTime TimeStamp,
                                       Severity Level,
                                       string Message)
    : IComparable<LogEntry>
{
    public int CompareTo(LogEntry other)
        => TimeStamp.CompareTo(other.TimeStamp);
}
```

Listing 6-18: Defining ordering by `TimeStamp` for a `LogEntry` value

We normally wouldn't call `CompareTo` on a `LogEntry` instance directly; it would usually be invoked indirectly when we sort a collection of `LogEntry` values. Unless we explicitly specify a different comparison to be used for sorting, our `CompareTo` method will be used to determine how to order `LogEntry` elements, so the default ordering for `LogEntry` values is based solely on the `TimeStamp` property.

Values have *extensionality*: two instances are equal if they have the same observable properties. This isn't necessarily the same as having the same structural definition, called *intentionality*. It's possible, although relatively rare, to need extra data that doesn't contribute to the value in a meaningful way and thus isn't used in a test for equality. Such data is usually also a private detail of the implementation.

The distinction between intentionality and extensionality becomes more important when we want not only to compare values for equality but also to order them. Putting values in order requires a different but closely related comparison, which may result in two unequal values being equivalent for the purposes of sorting them.

Equivalence vs. Equality

For most value types, if `CompareTo` returns 0, then the two values are indeed equal, and calling `Equals` will return true. This is the case for the `DateTime` value underlying our `TimeStamp` property. However, while this result is what we'd normally expect, it's not a strict requirement. The `CompareTo` method should return 0 when neither value is less than the other, although those values may not actually be equal. Rather, the values are *equivalent* for the purposes of ordering.

With our `LogEntry` value, two values are equivalent when their `TimeStamp` properties exactly match. Even so, the two values might very well be *un*equal because their `Severity` or `Message` properties might be different, as the simple test in Listing 6-19 demonstrates.

```
var logTime = new DateTime(year:2020, month:5, day:31, 15, 35, 01, 12);

var log1 = new LogEntry(logTime, Severity.Debug, "Debug Message");
var log2 = new LogEntry(logTime, Severity.Info, "Info Message");

Assert.That(log1.Equals(log2), Is.False);
Assert.That(log1.CompareTo(log2), Is.Zero);
```

Listing 6-19: Equality versus equivalence for LogEntry

This code shows no contradiction: the two entries have clearly different values, but for the purpose of sorting `LogEntry` instances, they're nevertheless equivalent because it doesn't matter whether one goes before or after the other. Equivalence doesn't necessarily imply equality, and we should avoid the temptation to implement equality in terms of `CompareTo`.

A fairly common example demonstrating the difference between equivalence and equality is comparing string values. Sometimes we want to use a case-insensitive string comparison for ordering but not for equality. The two string values `"September"` and `"september"` might be considered equivalent for sorting, but they're clearly not equal.

The Contract for Comparisons

We must meet certain expectations for the `CompareTo` method. In particular, comparing a single value with itself should report equivalence; that is, `x.CompareTo(x)` must be 0. More generally, for two objects that are equal according to the `Equals` method, `CompareTo` should return 0. The `IComparable` interface is a contract, and the semantics of comparing one object with itself is just one aspect of that contract.

We can use the `CompareTo` implementation to define the comparison operator `<` for LogEntry, which gives us a natural way to see if `log1 < log2` and a more compact way of expressing the rest of the contract. The contract for the less-than relationship specifies that it has the following characteristics:

Irreflexive

x < x is always false.

Antisymmetric

If x < y is true, then y < x must be false.

Transitive

If x < y and y < z are true, then x < z must also be true.

Stable

The result of x < y remains the same as long as neither value is changed.

Safe

Comparing values of the same type does not throw exceptions.

We can define `CompareTo` and `operator<` for reference types in a similar way, although we also need to consider the `null` reference, which should always compare less than any non-`null` value.

Other Kinds of Ordering

Ordering by `DateTime` or `number` is an example of ordering by magnitude, but other orderings are possible. Strings commonly use a *lexicographical* ordering, which broadly means that one string is less than another if it would appear before the other in a lexicon, better known as a dictionary.

Other values are ordinal in nature, such as months of the year. Ordinal comparisons sometimes need a bit of care. Take days of the week in English as an example: should Sunday come before Monday? The answer to that question depends on how we define the first day of the week.

Some values aren't intrinsically less than another. The `Color` type is an example: red comes before blue when we enumerate the colors in a rainbow—a property of their relative wavelengths—but blue certainly comes before red in an English dictionary. We might apply one of several orderings to `Color` objects under different circumstances, but those definitions of ordering are external to the concept of a color.

We can customize the ordering of elements in a sequence on a case-by-case basis by creating our own comparer, or even multiple comparers to address different scenarios. The `IComparer<T>` interface complements the `IEqualityComparer<T>` interface from Chapter 5. Just as `IEqualityComparer<T>` establishes an equality comparison that's external to the types being compared, an implementation of `IComparer<T>` is an externally defined ordering comparison. Listing 6-20 shows a custom comparer type for ordering `LogEntry` objects by their `Message` property rather than by time.

```
public sealed class LogEntryComparer : IComparer<LogEntry>
{
    public int Compare(LogEntry x, LogEntry y)
        => string.Compare(x.Message, y.Message, StringComparison.Ordinal);
}
```

Listing 6-20: Defining an external comparer for LogEntry objects

The semantics of the `Compare` method match those of `IComparable.CompareTo`, returning a negative integer when x is less than y, a positive integer when y is less than x, and 0 otherwise. Several of the sorting algorithms in the Standard Library have overloads that accept an explicit comparer object as an argument, including the `Order` method shown here:

```
var log = new List<LogEntry>();

--snip--

var comparer = new LogEntryComparer();
var alphabeticalLog = log.Order(comparer).ToList();
```

This `alphabeticalLog` is a new list of `LogEntry` elements sorted alphabetically by using the `LogEntryComparer.Compare` comparison. Similar overloads are provided for `List<T>.Sort` and `List<T>.BinarySearch` and the constructor for `SortedList`.

Ordering is a common characteristic of values, but not an essential one in the same way that value-based equality is. When a value has a natural ordering, implementing the `CompareTo` method makes sense. Reference types, on the other hand, generally don't override `CompareTo` unless they also override `Equals`. Mixing identity-based equality with value-based ordering, or vice versa, will likely lead to confusion and probably errors that are hard to track down. In particular, references have no natural ordering; saying that the value of one reference is less than another makes no sense.

The Perils of Uniformity and Consistency

Sometimes coding guidelines advise that we should override `Equals` and implement `CompareTo` for every type. The thinking behind such rules is usually to try to remove restrictions on the use of objects. Types that don't implement `IComparable` can't be used as keys in a `SortedList`. Types that don't override `Equals` and `GetHashCode` can't be used reliably as keys in a `Dictionary`. While we can use an implementation of `IComparer<T>` to address the former, and a custom `IEqualityComparer<T>` for the latter, we must remember to explicitly use those implementations.

Such guidelines aim to improve consistency and remove the barriers to commonplace requirements. The goal is usually to enable *any* object to be used as a key in a hashing container, or collections of them to be sorted according to their state, without needing explicitly defined external comparers.

Guidelines that suggest this kind of uniformity ignore the fact that values and non-values are semantically and conceptually different, and the differences go far beyond the technical characteristics of reference types and value types. Reference semantics have their own desirable characteristics, especially when we actively need multiple aliasing references to a single, mutable instance. Those characteristics don't lend themselves well to being used as keys in collections, and they often cause conflict with ordering too. A sorted collection of mutable objects can easily become *unordered* by altering the state of its elements, which gives us one more reason for all our value types to be immutable. A collection of values that has been sorted should remain sorted.

As we've discussed, some types have no natural ordering. Let's revisit the example of `Color`. Insisting that a `Color` type implement the `IComparable` interface would leave us with a problem: how should `CompareTo` behave for two `Color` values? We could choose one plausible implementation, but that might not satisfy every use case, leading to difficulties in other aspects of our code. This is why, while records and record structs provide a default implementation of the `IEquatable<T>` interface, they don't also implement `IComparable<T>`. Even when the individual fields can be compared with `CompareTo`, it doesn't always mean that the whole type can be compared that way. All the fields for `Color` are `int` values that implement `IComparable<int>`, after all, but *less than* isn't a meaningful comparison for `Color` values.

The purpose of overriding the `Equals` method for value types isn't primarily to allow them to be used as keys. Values have no use for referential equality, because one value is as good as any other value with the same properties. Value-based equality is the single, natural way to compare those variables that are values.

Reference types, by contrast, often depend on identity-based equality. Any type not specifically intended to have value semantics probably shouldn't be used as a key in a `Dictionary`.

Arithmetic and Nonarithmetic Types

Just as not all values have a natural ordering, some values are arithmetic by nature, and some are not. We might, for example, define operations to allow instances of the `Speed` type from Listing 6-11 to be added together. Operations like addition have a natural representation with arithmetic operators, such as in an expression like `startingSpeed + Speed.FromKmh(10)`.

Introducing support for arithmetic operations, or indeed any operation, requires a certain amount of discretion on our part as designers. We need to be mindful of both the common use cases for the types we create and the wider expectation from, for example, being able to add two instances together with a + operator.

Unlike `Speed`, the `LogEntry` type in Listing 6-17 isn't arithmetic in nature, so we should avoid overloading the arithmetic operators for it. Adding two `LogEntry` instances makes no sense.

It does make sense for `LogEntry` to overload `operator==` and its counterpart `operator!=` for equality comparisons. The `LogEntry` type is a record struct, so the compiler will provide the equality operator definitions automatically. Since we've implemented `IComparable<LogEntry>` for `LogEntry`, we should also consider overloading `operator<` and `operator>`, which the compiler won't provide. Listing 6-21 shows that implementing these operators in terms of the `CompareTo` method is straightforward.

```
public static bool operator<(LogEntry left, LogEntry right)
    => left.CompareTo(right) < 0;

public static bool operator>(LogEntry left, LogEntry right)
    => left.CompareTo(right) > 0;
```

Listing 6-21: Equivalence comparison operator definitions

These operator definitions make handling equality and comparisons much more natural for LogEntry instances.

Nonstandard Operator Behavior

Occasionally, arithmetic operators are useful beyond truly arithmetic operations. For example, string instances can be "added" together, and most programmers understand that adding two strings concatenates them, so "key" + "board" becomes "keyboard". In arithmetic, addition is commutative, so a + b gives the same result as b + a. This clearly isn't true when used with string instances, but concatenating two strings with + is a widely used and accepted convention.

When we bend the rules this way, it's especially important that we're mindful of conventions, natural usage, and expectations. For instance, in arithmetic the ability to add numbers together goes hand in hand with the facility for subtraction. Consider what subtracting one string from another might mean. Would it remove all instances of the right-hand argument from the left-hand string? Only if it appeared at the end of the string? String subtraction doesn't have the natural and conventional appeal that string addition/concatenation does.

We'd normally expect to find a symmetry between + and -, and symmetry is usually a desirable quality. When we overload ==, the compiler insists that we also implement the != operator. Coupling addition with subtraction for string values is one example where symmetry is undesirable, because it introduces conflicting expectations.

Symmetry is inappropriate in other situations too. For example, matching every property get accessor with a corresponding set is superficially attractive but contradicts the recommendation that value types are immutable. This is another instance where we need to apply our own judgment on whether symmetry is a positive characteristic.

Summary

> *It's not hard to make decisions when you know what your values are.*
> —Roy Disney, American film writer and producer

Although C# has its own definition of ValueType, the broader concept of a value isn't specific to C#. That more general idea of a value type has commonalities with the C# definition, but notable differences exist.

The language definition of a value type focuses mainly on the memory requirements and behavior associated with structs. We need to take other factors into account, however, in order to decide when and how to introduce values into our programs. In this chapter, we've explored some of those considerations by contrasting values with reference types—in particular, by examining how values fulfill specific and important roles in a program.

Object-oriented systems are made up of several kinds of objects with varying emphasis on the characteristics of identity, state, and behavior.

When an object's role places a high importance on instance identity, it's a strong indicator that the type shouldn't be a value type. When the priority is an object's state and identity is unimportant, the type is almost certainly best modeled as a value.

Whether a type has a single field or many fields isn't necessarily the best metric for choosing whether to make it a value. Sometimes we want value semantics, and sometimes reference semantics are more important. The phrases *value semantics* and *copy by value* are sometimes used interchangeably and even defined in terms of each other. However, value semantics has more to do with value-based equality than with copying.

Distinguishing value types from other kinds of types is an important first step in partitioning their responsibilities in an application. Identifying candidate value types helps us clarify our designs by introducing specialized types that encapsulate behavior and responsibilities. In turn, we benefit from a more modular system, both in its implementation and in the testing it requires. Having decided a type should be modeled as a value, we have more options for implementing it. C# has rich support for all user-defined types, but its facilities for value types are sometimes unappreciated.

7

VALUE TYPES AND POLYMORPHISM

As an object-oriented programming (OOP) language, C# has good support for features that allow us to capture complex ideas and express them intuitively, such as classes, virtual methods, and inheritance. However, the language support for inheritance doesn't extend to value types. Structs and record structs implicitly derive from the `ValueType` class, which is derived directly from `object`, but they can't inherit any other type and can't themselves be inherited; that is, structs and record structs are implicitly sealed. Inheritance is a central feature of OOP that enables us to treat a reference to a derived class as though it refers to the base class, overriding the base class's properties and methods to have new behavior as needed. These features don't apply to value types, but that doesn't mean value types are inferior.

Using the term *polymorphism* interchangeably with *inheritance* is common, but polymorphism is a more general concept; it relates to writing code that works uniformly for a variety of types to reduce duplication. As this chapter discusses, inheritance is just one kind of polymorphism, and while there are sound technical and semantic reasons for why value types can't employ inheritance relationships, they can take advantage of other kinds of polymorphism.

We'll explore the following:

- Why value types are sealed and why value-like types in general shouldn't use inheritance

- How subtyping differs from subclassing and why it matters

- What *type substitutability* means and how it relates to inheritance

- Where to use other kinds of polymorphism, rather than inheritance, to model relationships between objects

Why Value Types Are Sealed

The principal technical reason for prohibiting inheritance for structs, and by extension record structs, is that they have different lifetime and storage characteristics than reference types. The restriction is more than an arbitrary rule: it results directly from how value type variables behave in memory, and how that behavior differs from reference types.

Inheritance between classes allows us to use a reference to a base class type to refer to an instance of a derived class, so the static, compile-time type of a reference variable isn't necessarily the same as the dynamic, run-time instance type. This characteristic permits *virtual dispatch* for method calls—the mechanism whereby the appropriate method implementation will be called based on the actual type of the object at run time—and relies on the extra level of indirection afforded by references; therefore, inheritance is appropriate only for reference types.

Value type variables directly contain their data, so we can't declare a variable as one type to represent an instance of a different type, other than via boxing. Inheriting from a struct thus makes no sense, and the compiler forbids it.

Remember, though, that we can use classes to model value-like behavior. As you saw in Chapter 6, string behaves like a value but is implemented as a reference type. The string type uses a value-based (rather than identity-based) equality comparison, is immutable, and has various other characteristics that identify it as a value. Being a class, string could support virtual method dispatch, but we can't derive from the string class because it's explicitly sealed. This means we can't create our own augmented subclass of string any more than we could inherit from DateTime, Guid, or any other value type.

Like the string class, records are reference types but have value-like equality behavior. Records can derive from other records and can also have virtual methods, so they seemingly unify the ideas of values and inheritance. However, using records is not that straightforward. We need to note the subtleties and avoid the pitfalls when using any inheritance, whether between classes or records.

When we allow our types to participate in inheritance relationships, we need to be mindful of what deriving from those types might entail. There's a difference between *implementation* and *interface* inheritance. Inheriting an implementation presents some of the same difficulties as deriving from a value type. To explore why doing so is ill-advised, let's look at a class with value-like characteristics and use implementation inheritance to demonstrate some of the problems that can result.

Implementation Inheritance

Anytime we inherit from a concrete class—that is, one that's not fully abstract—we are, by definition, inheriting its implementation. Listing 7-1 shows a simple inheritance relationship: a `TranslucentColor` class derives from a `Color` base class and adds a new feature of its own.

```
public class Color
{
    public Color(int red, int green, int blue)
        => (Red, Green, Blue) = (red, green, blue);

    public int Red    { get; }
    public int Green  { get; }
    public int Blue   { get; }
}

public class TranslucentColor : Color
{
    public TranslucentColor(int red, int green, int blue, int alpha)
        : base(red, green, blue) => Alpha = alpha;

    public int Alpha { get; }
}
```

Listing 7-1: Creating a derived class, `TranslucentColor`, that inherits the implementation of `Color`

This `TranslucentColor` class subclasses the `Color` class and inherits all of `Color`'s structural representation, along with its methods and properties. Both classes have automatic properties, which are each given a backing field of the same type as the property—int in this example—and every field of `Color` is inherited by `TranslucentColor`.

Even if we'd used private fields in `Color` and returned their values via the properties, those fields would be inherited by the `TranslucentColor` class, although they'd still be accessible only via the inherited *public* properties.

The implementation inherited by `TranslucentColor` from `Color` depends on those private fields. An instance of `TranslucentColor` requires its own copies of all the fields declared by its base class so that the properties inherited from `Color` work correctly. We can use `Color`'s properties via a `TranslucentColor` variable as if they were declared as members of `TranslucentColor`, as shown here:

```
var foreground = new TranslucentColor(red: 0xFF, green: 0, blue: 0, alpha: 0x77);

Assert.That(foreground.Red, Is.EqualTo(0xFF));
Assert.That(foreground.Alpha, Is.EqualTo(0x77));
```

In this simple test, we use the `Red` property of a `TranslucentColor` variable, which inherited that property from `Color`. We can also use the `Alpha` property, which was declared as a member of `TranslucentColor`.

Using inheritance like this—to reuse the implementation of `Color` in `TranslucentColor`—is attractive, because it means that the `TranslucentColor` type definition doesn't duplicate `Color`'s properties. By deriving from `Color`, the `TranslucentColor` class gets those properties for free.

Both `Color` and `TranslucentColor` look like good candidates to be value types because an equality comparison should compare each instance's state. However, making value-based equality behave correctly in an inheritance hierarchy hides complexity that can easily result in undesirable behavior. To demonstrate that, let's give `Color` and `TranslucentColor` value semantics by following the recommendations from Chapter 5 to override `Equals` and its companions for both classes.

Value-Based Equality for Classes

We begin with the base class, `Color`. With the implementation in Listing 7-2, we can compare two `Color` instances to see whether their properties are equal.

```
public class Color : IEquatable<Color>
{
    public int Red   { get; }
    public int Green { get; }
    public int Blue  { get; }

    public bool Equals(Color? other)
        => (object?)this == (object?)other ||
           other is not null &&
           GetType() == other.GetType() &&
           Red == other.Red && Green == other.Green && Blue == other.Blue;

    public override bool Equals(object? obj)
        => Equals(obj as Color);

    public override int GetHashCode()
        => HashCode.Combine(Red, Green, Blue);

    public static bool operator==(Color? left, Color? right)
        => left?.Equals(right) ?? right is null;
```

```
    public static bool operator!=(Color? left, Color? right)
        => !left?.Equals(right) ?? right is not null;
}
```

Listing 7-2: Defining value equality in the base class, Color

This implementation of equality follows common practice for implementing value-based equality for classes, including the guidelines given in the Microsoft documentation. The Color class implements the IEquatable<Color> interface, which requires an overload of the Equals method specifically for Color. We use this overload to provide the full implementation, which we can call from any other method, including the Equals method overridden from the object base class. Since we've overridden Equals(object?), we also override GetHashCode to ensure that two instances of Color produce the same hash code if they compare equal. Finally, we provide implementations for the == and != equality operators.

Let's examine each step in detail.

The Canonical Form of Equals

First we have to override the virtual Equals method inherited from object, as shown in Listing 7-3. Since Color is a class, by default Equals compares object identities, so we need to override that behavior to give Color a value-based implementation.

```
public override bool Equals(object? obj)
    => Equals(obj as Color);
```

Listing 7-3: Overriding Equals

The override of Equals must match the base-class signature. In this example, we declare the types within a nullable context, so we use object? as the parameter type for Equals, indicating that we know the parameter could be null and can handle that circumstance safely. Here we use the as operator to cast obj to Color in order to call the type-safe Equals method. If obj isn't a Color or is null, the argument passed will be null, which is explicitly handled by the type-safe overload in Listing 7-4.

```
public bool Equals(Color? other)
    => (object?)this == (object?)other ||
       other is not null &&
       GetType() == other.GetType() &&
       Red == other.Red && Green == other.Green && Blue == other.Blue;
```

Listing 7-4: Implementing IEquatable<Color>

The type-safe Equals implementation of the IEquatable<Color> interface takes a nullable Color parameter. This overload will always be preferred over the method taking an object? parameter when we're comparing two variables whose static type is Color, including when we call it from the operator== or operator!= methods.

One implication of `Color` being a reference type is that it's possible for the `other` parameter to refer to the same instance as `this`. To handle this scenario, Listing 7-4 casts both `this` and `other` to `object` to make it clear that we intend a reference comparison. While the cast we used in Listing 7-3 from `object` to a more derived type is a relatively costly run-time conversion, the conversion from `Color` to its `object` base class is very efficient and allows the comparison to be made with the intrinsic `ceq` instruction introduced in Chapter 5. One alternative would be to use `ReferenceEquals(this, other)` here, making the reference-based comparison explicit.

Comparing the two variables to see whether they reference the same object is a simple but not mandatory optimization. The logical || operator short-circuits if its left-hand expression is true, so the rest of the comparisons are attempted only if `this` and `other` are references to different instances. Note that the order of comparisons in this code relies on operator precedence; the logical AND operator (&&) has a higher precedence than logical OR (||), so the comparisons on the right side of || all bind together as if they were explicitly grouped within a pair of parentheses. Although redundant, the extra parentheses don't affect the behavior in any way, and some programmers prefer to add them to avoid having to remember the operator precedence rules.

Because `Color` is a reference type, the argument passed could be `null`, so we use the `is not` constant pattern to compare `other` with `null` and avoid the common trap of calling our own `Equals` method recursively.

The `Color` class is intentionally not sealed, so we also check that the `other` value is exactly the same type as `this` by using the `GetType` method, defined on the `object` base class. This method returns the run-time type of an instance, and the types won't match if `other` is a reference to a more derived type such as `TranslucentColor`. Objects of different types don't normally compare equal, even if their types are related by inheritance.

Finally, if the types match, we compare each property's value in turn. If they all match, our `Equals` method returns true. We use == rather than `Equals` here because all the properties of a `Color` are simple `int` values. Built-in values such as these can be compared intrinsically, and much more compactly than calling the `Equals` method for each of them.

To make comparing `Color` instances natural, we also implement `operator==` and `operator!=`, which both defer to the type-safe `Equals` method, like this:

```
public static bool operator==(Color? left, Color? right)
    => left?.Equals(right) ?? right is null;

public static bool operator!=(Color? left, Color? right)
    => !left?.Equals(right) ?? right is not null;
```

The == operator will return the result of Equals if the left parameter is not null; otherwise, it returns true if both the parameters are null. The != operator returns the opposite of == by inverting the comparisons.

The Contract for Equality

Implementing equality in a way that is self-consistent is critical. It would be a strange state of affairs if we had two references to the same instance of Color that did *not* compare equal, and stranger still if Equals could return false when comparing a value with itself. Equality has a contract similar to the one you saw for less-than comparisons in Chapter 6. Namely, equality has the following characteristics:

Reflexive

x == x is always true.

Symmetric

If x == y, then y == x.

Transitive

If x == y *and* y == z, then it follows that x == z.

Safe

Non-null values are never equal to null.

Stable

The result of x == y doesn't change as long as x and y don't change.

In Listing 7-5, we write some tests to prove that we've met the requirements of the equality contract.

NOTE *These tests are presented this way for emphasis, not to demonstrate a good style of assertion writing.*

The first test also ensures that we're comparing the variables by value, not merely comparing references.

```
var pencil = new Color(0xFF, 0, 0);
var crayon = new Color(0xFF, 0, 0);
var brush =  new Color(0xFF, 0, 0);

// Reflexive, value-based equality
Assert.That(pencil == pencil, Is.True);
Assert.That(pencil == new Color(0xFF, 0, 0), Is.True);

// Symmetric
Assert.That(pencil == crayon, Is.True);
Assert.That(crayon == pencil, Is.True);

// Transitive
Assert.That(pencil == crayon, Is.True);
```

```
Assert.That(crayon == brush, Is.True);
Assert.That(pencil == brush, Is.True);

// Safe with null
Assert.That(pencil != null, Is.True);
Assert.That(null != pencil, Is.True);
```

Listing 7-5: Testing the contract for equality for Color

Writing a test for comparison stability is more difficult, so in Listing 7-6 we test the opposite: that if one of the values changes, the instances are no longer equal.

```
var pencil = new Color(0xFF, 0, 0);
var crayon = new Color(0xFF, 0, 0);

Assert.That(pencil == crayon, Is.True);

pencil = new Color(0, 0xFF, 0);

Assert.That(pencil != crayon, Is.True);
```

Listing 7-6: Testing that equality is stable

Since Color's properties are immutable, we can change the value of pencil only by assigning it to a new instance. However, the effect is the same as if we had mutated one or more of the properties, because we have arranged for Color instances to be compared by value.

We have one other requirement for the Equals method and its operator counterparts: they must never throw an exception. Our implementation has no danger of that, since we have already tested that it is safe with null.

Equality Behavior in Derived Classes

The next step is to implement equality for the derived TranslucentColor class, which, as we know, inherits all the methods and properties from Color. Since TranslucentColor is a value-like type, it should implement the IEquatable<T> interface for itself, substituting the T for TranslucentColor. As Listing 7-7 shows, implementing IEquatable<TranslucentColor> is a little simpler than the Color base class, which already does most of the work.

```
public class TranslucentColor : Color, IEquatable<TranslucentColor>
{
    public int Alpha { get; }

    public bool Equals(TranslucentColor? other) ❶
        => base.Equals(other) && Alpha == other.Alpha;

    public override bool Equals(object? obj)
        => Equals(obj as TranslucentColor);
```

```
    public override int GetHashCode()
        => HashCode.Combine(Alpha, base.GetHashCode());

    public static bool operator==(TranslucentColor? left, TranslucentColor? right) ❷
        => left?.Equals(right) ?? right is null;

    public static bool operator!=(TranslucentColor? left, TranslucentColor? right)
        => !left?.Equals(right) ?? right is not null;
}
```

Listing 7-7: Behavior inheritance in the derived class, `TranslucentColor`

As with the `Color` implementation, `TranslucentColor` overrides the `Equals(object?)` method, converting the object parameter to `TranslucentColor` in order to call the `Equals(TranslucentColor?)` method ❶. That method also checks whether we're comparing two references to a single instance and ensures that the `other` parameter isn't `null`.

Since `Color` already performs the check for identical references, the comparison with `null`, and the type check, as well as comparing the `Red`, `Green`, and `Blue` properties, we don't need to duplicate those comparisons and can simply invoke the base class's `Equals` method before finally comparing the `Alpha` properties that are specific to `TranslucentColor`. Passing other to `base.Equals` is fine because a `TranslucentColor` reference will convert implicitly to its `Color` base class type.

We also give `TranslucentColor` its own implementations of `operator==` and `operator!=`, and they, too, follow the same pattern as in `Color`, except that they take two `TranslucentColor` parameters ❷.

The contract for equality applies not only to `Color` but also to `TranslucentColor`. We can use a test similar to the one from Listing 7-5 to ensure that `TranslucentColor` meets the contract's requirements. Listing 7-8 shows a variation on Listing 7-6's stability check for `Color` as we test that differences in the `TranslucentColor` class's `Alpha` property value will cause instances of `TranslucentColor` to compare unequal.

```
var pencil = new TranslucentColor(0xFF, 0, 0xFF, 0x77);
var crayon = new TranslucentColor(0xFF, 0, 0xFF, 0x77);

Assert.That(pencil == crayon, Is.True);

pencil = new TranslucentColor(0xFF, 0, 0xFF, 0);

Assert.That(pencil != crayon, Is.True);
```

Listing 7-8: Testing the equality contract for `TranslucentColor`

In this example, the two `TranslucentColor` instances differ only in their `Alpha` property and correctly compare *not* equal. We might conclude, then, that all is right with the world—but we'd be wrong.

Equality Comparisons and Type Substitution

We've used a suite of tests to reassure us that the equality contract is intact for both Color and TranslucentColor when we're using variables whose dynamic (run-time) instance type is the same as their static (compile-time) variable type. However, the types might not always match. The compiler allows us to pass a reference to a TranslucentColor anywhere a Color reference is required because Color is a direct base class of TranslucentColor. In other words, the Color type can be *substituted* by a TranslucentColor. At run time, any Color reference may, in fact, refer to a TranslucentColor instance.

To illustrate the effect on equality of using a base class reference to a derived class instance, Listing 7-9 explicitly uses a Color base class reference to declare two TranslucentColor values that aren't equal because their Alpha properties differ.

```
Color pencil = new TranslucentColor(0xFF, 0, 0xFF, 0x77);
Color crayon = new TranslucentColor(0xFF, 0, 0xFF, 0);

Assert.That(pencil == crayon, Is.False);
```

Listing 7-9: Testing equality from the base class

This test fails: the pencil and crayon variables compare equal even though the instances have different values. It makes no difference whether we compare the variables with == or call the Equals method; the outcome is the same.

The static types being compared are Color variables, so what's invoked here is the base class implementation of operator==, which in turn calls the Equals method. The Equals method in Color knows nothing about the Alpha property of TranslucentColor, so Equals determines equality by using only the Red, Green, and Blue properties. Those properties are all identical, so according to Color.Equals, the two objects are equal.

Those are the mechanics that explain why our pencil and crayon variables incorrectly compare equal, but type substitution isn't always so easy to spot, and its consequences are far-reaching.

The Effects of Type Substitution

We would rarely explicitly use a Color reference for a TranslucentColor object, but we can use a TranslucentColor reference as an argument to a method with a Color parameter. We can substitute a TranslucentColor when a Color is expected.

Listing 7-10 shows that if we pass two references to TranslucentColor objects that differ only in their Alpha values to a method with Color parameters, those parameter variables compare equal within the method. If we pass the same two references to a method that takes TranslucentColor parameters, the values won't compare equal even though they haven't changed.

```
bool EqualViaBase(Color left, Color right)
    => left.Equals(right);

bool EqualViaDerived(TranslucentColor left, TranslucentColor right)
    => left.Equals(right);
```

```
var pencil = new TranslucentColor(0xFF, 0, 0xFF, 0x77);
var crayon = new TranslucentColor(0xFF, 0, 0xFF, 0);

Assert.That(EqualViaBase(pencil, crayon), Is.True);

Assert.That(EqualViaDerived(pencil, crayon), Is.False);
```

Listing 7-10: Testing the stability promise

In the first assertion, the `pencil` and `crayon` references are automatically converted to `Color` references when we call the `EqualViaBase` method because a reference to a derived class is implicitly convertible to a reference to any of its base classes. The call to `Equals` within `EqualViaBase` invokes `Color`'s implementation, which incorrectly determines the parameter variables to be equal. The `EqualViaDerived` method calls `TranslucentColor.Equals` directly, which correctly reports that the parameter variables are not equal.

The equality implementation for `TranslucentColor` isn't stable: it can produce a different result for the same two instances depending on the static type of the variable used to refer to those instances, even when their underlying state remains unchanged.

Breach of Contract

The behavior of the tests in Listing 7-10 demonstrates that `TranslucentColor` breaks the promise of stability established by the contract for equality—namely, that the result of `Equals` doesn't change if the values being compared don't change. When we compare two variables that have different values, they should compare not equal, and as long as no changes are made to either variable's state, the result of the comparison shouldn't change.

One problem with our `Equals` implementation is that the type-specific overload of `Equals` in the `Color` class isn't virtual, and therefore it can't be overridden in `TranslucentColor`. The virtual version of `Equals`, which takes an `object` parameter, isn't considered in overload resolution because the overload with a `Color` parameter is a much better match, even when the run-time type is derived from `Color`.

To get the test in Listing 7-9 to pass, we could make the type-specific `Equals` method virtual in `Color` and add an override for it in `TranslucentColor`. Another possibility would be to remove the implementation of the `IEquatable<T>` interface for `Color` so that the only `Equals` method would be virtual. We'd lose the facility for type-specific comparisons, with a small performance cost, but this option would address the problem of stability. However, either approach would be solving the wrong problem.

The real underlying problem is that we've used inheritance inappropriately, not that our implementation of equality is incorrect. To fully appreciate why, we need to be clear on the difference between subclasses and subtypes.

Inclusion Polymorphism and Subtyping

We think of the classes, structs, records, and record structs we write as being user-defined types. By extension, then, it's natural to think that the definition of a class is its type. That perception is partially true, but a more formal distinction between *type* and *class* exists.

The polymorphism afforded by using inheritance is known as *inclusion* polymorphism. If we were to group all the objects in a system by type, each group of any specific type would *include* all the types that inherit from it, known as *subtypes*. In our example, the group for the Color type includes both the Color and TranslucentColor types.

An object's type is a contract for its interface and describes the allowable operations on the object. The operations defined by a type are, therefore, valid for any subtypes in its group. Practically speaking, if we derive from a given type, all the operations that are valid for an object of the base type must be valid—and behave correctly—for an object of the derived type.

In our example, a TranslucentColor object is an instance of a Color type as well as being a TranslucentColor. This relationship means we can invoke any Color operation on a TranslucentColor, which in turn means we can pass a TranslucentColor instance to a method taking a Color parameter. As far as the compiler is concerned, a TranslucentColor must be able to support all the operations of its base type, so it allows the substitution.

The type of an object establishes which operations a subtype must support, but it doesn't specify any structural details or specific implementation. We're free to implement the same interface in different ways, using various classes. However, while the contract for a type doesn't mandate a specific implementation, it does define the expected behavior of any of its operations. When we inherit from a concrete class, we inherit its implementation, and this sets an expectation for that behavior. When implementing a type as a class or record, we must be mindful of the distinction between subtyping and subclassing, since we can inherit from reference types unless they're explicitly sealed. For value types in C#, this isn't an issue, because they're implicitly sealed and so can't have derived types.

As noted earlier in this chapter, implementation and interface inheritance differ. In other words, simply inheriting from a class isn't the same as actually respecting its behavioral characteristics. Code written in terms of the more general *type*, which defines the interface, may well depend on the specific characteristics of the *class*, which represents a particular implementation. If the derived class doesn't respect the behavioral aspect of the type's contract, when we use an instance of the derived class in code written for the base type, that code will very likely have unexpected behavior.

When we inherit from a class, we inherit its behavior, characteristics, and expectations. A class that inherits from another concrete class is, then, a subclass, and only a true subtype if code using the base class *type* can use the derived class transparently with no change in observable behavior. When we inherit only the type, we have no implementation behavior to consider.

Mechanically speaking, we can substitute a reference to a TranslucentColor where a Color is required because we can use a reference to the derived type as an argument to a method expecting the base type. However, as you've seen with the behavior of Equals, using Color and TranslucentColor instances interchangeably is not really possible.

The lack of substitutability between Color and TranslucentColor arises because TranslucentColor is a *subclass* but not a true *subtype* of Color.

Working with Input and Output Types of Virtual Methods

The difference between a subtype and a subclass has implications that go beyond how an inherited Equals method is implemented. We can override any virtual method with an implementation that is appropriate for the derived class. If the observable effects, including any side effects, of calling the more derived method are identical to the effects of the base class, then the derived type is a good substitute for its base type—that is, the derived type is a proper subtype. Side effects might include writing to a file or to the screen, or perhaps updating the value of a variable visible outside the method. If a derived class does any of these things when its base class doesn't, it's not a true subtype.

A method's behavior includes what the method considers to be valid inputs and outputs—that is, what parameters a method accepts and what it may return—each of which directly affects the method caller. To illustrate, suppose we add a virtual method to the Color class like the one in Listing 7-11 to subtract one Color value from another.

```
public virtual Color Subtract(Color? other)
{
    --snip--
}
```

Listing 7-11: Adding a virtual Subtract method to Color

Since the Subtract method is virtual, we can specialize its implementation in TranslucentColor to handle subtraction appropriately for TranslucentColor instances. Regardless of the actual algorithm used to implement Subtract, its return value is the observable behavior of the method, as long as it has no side effects.

If the Subtract implementation in Color never returns a null reference but the overridden version in TranslucentColor might, then the TranslucentColor method has a weaker behavioral contract than the base class method. Allowing the TranslucentColor implementation to return a null value requires extra checking in the calling code to avoid null-reference exceptions. The calling code, knowing only about the Color type, might reasonably expect only non-null values. The weaker requirements on the return type mean that TranslucentColor isn't substitutable for Color.

A corresponding situation arises when we *strengthen* requirements on the parameters in an overridden method. If we insist on non-null values in the derived type but the base class accepts null references, we break the contract established by the base class method. Once again, code written in terms of the base class has no notion of those requirements in derived classes and can easily violate them.

The Subtract method shown in Listing 7-11 mitigates both of these potential problems by using the nullable reference type feature available since C# v8.0. The return type of the base Subtract method is non-nullable, and the compiler will warn us if we override it with a method having a nullable reference type or if that method attempts to return a null reference. Similarly, the parameter to the Color.Subtract method is a nullable reference, indicating that null is an acceptable argument. If we override the method with a non-nullable reference type, the compiler will warn us that the method signature doesn't match the base declaration.

Note that if the base method returns a nullable reference and we override it to return a non-nullable reference, the compiler won't give a warning. That is because in this case we're strengthening the behavioral contract in the derived method, and it's entirely reasonable for the more derived method to prohibit null, even if the base method allows it. The requirements on any code calling the method from a base type reference aren't affected.

Likewise, the compiler is silent if the base method has a non-nullable parameter and we override it to allow a null reference to be passed to the derived method, because weakening the parameter's contract in the more derived type is safe and reasonable. The change is visible only to code using the more derived type *directly* rather than via a base type reference.

Upholding a Type's Contract

Our test for equality using base class references in Listing 7-9 fails because the contract for Color.Equals isn't properly fulfilled by the derived class. The expectations set out by Color aren't met by TranslucentColor, which imposes a new requirement on Equals because equality between TranslucentColor instances must also compare the Alpha property. Our test fails as a direct result of our using implementation inheritance and expecting type substitutability, when in fact TranslucentColor isn't substitutable for a Color. The implications of implementation inheritance apply to all inheritance relationships, not just when we're modeling value semantics.

Upholding a type's contract matters in practical ways. The behavior of an inherited method is part of that contract, and failing to uphold it can result in extremely hard-to-diagnose errors. If we fail to meet the *interface* contract of a base class—for instance, by using a different signature in an overridden method—the compiler will inform us with an error. However, the compiler can't check that we've also kept the behavioral promises of a base class. Here we must use our own judgment, and that's not necessarily as straightforward as it might seem.

One rule of thumb is to avoid implementation inheritance whenever we use inheritance. The simplest way to be certain of that is to never derive from a class that has any concrete behavior—including abstract classes with any nonabstract methods. Types defined with the interface keyword can't have any implementation, and any class implementing an interface is a true subtype.

Another rule is that value types implemented as classes shouldn't inherit from anything and should be sealed. In fact, this second rule arises as a result of the first: it makes little sense for a value type to be fully abstract, since a defining feature of value and value-like types is that we compare them according to the value they represent. It follows, then, that value types are concrete types. The built-in value-like class string leads the way with this advice, which is why string is intentionally a sealed class.

Similar to strings, records are reference types that have value semantics for the purpose of comparisons with Equals. Unlike strings, records can inherit from other records, but just as when we derive from a concrete class, a derived record inherits all the base record's behavior. Therefore, we must still take care to uphold the base record's promises in a derived record; however, as with classes, doing so isn't always as simple as it might seem. Even though records permit inheritance, they're specifically intended to model value types, so the advice to seal value types applies equally to them.

Inheriting Record Types

When compiled, a record type is a class with some compiler-generated methods, including everything required for value-based equality. Moreover, records defined using the positional syntax are immutable by default. Using records instead of classes for creating value-like types, then, saves us from having to write a lot of boilerplate code.

Records, unlike structs, can inherit from other records, although they can't be part of an inheritance relationship with a class. We might therefore recast our Color and TranslucentColor types as records, as in Listing 7-12.

```
public record Color(int Red, int Green, int Blue);

public record TranslucentColor(int Red, int Green, int Blue, int Alpha)
        : Color(Red, Green, Blue);
```

Listing 7-12: Inheriting record types

Here we define Color and TranslucentColor as positional records with positional parameters that represent read-only properties with those names, and a constructor taking parameters of the same type. The inheritance syntax for records differs slightly from that for classes because we need to initialize the positional parameters in the base record. The TranslucentColor record derives from Color and passes its Red, Green, and Blue parameter values to the respective positional parameters of Color.

As we explored in Chapter 5, the compiler generates the implementations of the constructor and properties for us, along with implementations for various overrides of Equals and a few methods, including a value-based implementation of GetHashCode, ToString, and others. Equality comparisons between record variables compare the value of each property, so two record variables are equal if all their properties are equal.

We can write our own implementation of the type-safe Equals method created by the compiler if we wish. However, the implementation of Equals provided by the compiler is specially crafted to take inheritance into account.

Records and the Equality Contract

The contract for equality applies to records just as for any other type, and the code provided by the compiler ensures that every aspect of the contract is respected, including the stability of comparisons via base class references. The test in Listing 7-13 differs from the test in Listing 7-10 in that the Color and TranslucentColor types are records rather than classes. Here we compare two TranslucentColor record values with different Alpha properties and assert that they compare unequal whether we compare them directly using their concrete type or indirectly via a base class reference.

```
bool EqualViaBase(Color left, Color right)
    => left.Equals(right);

bool EqualViaDerived(TranslucentColor left, TranslucentColor right)
    => left.Equals(right);

var pencil = new TranslucentColor(0xFF, 0, 0xFF, 0x77);
var crayon = new TranslucentColor(0xFF, 0, 0xFF, 0);

Assert.That(EqualViaBase(pencil, crayon), Is.False);

Assert.That(EqualViaDerived(pencil, crayon), Is.False);
```

Listing 7-13: Equality between record types

This test passes, and the pencil and crayon variables compare not equal whichever method we call, EqualViaDerived or EqualViaBase.

Because the compiler-generated implementation of equality pays particular attention to the equality contract, the variables compare not equal whether we use a base Color record reference or the derived TranslucentColor reference. In particular, the type-safe implementation of Color.Equals(Color) is virtual in a record implementation and is overridden in the derived TranslucentColor record. As mentioned, doing this for our class implementations would make the test behave correctly. With records, the compiler injects those implementations for us.

We can override the Equals methods ourselves, in which case the compiler won't synthesize methods whose signature matches our own custom implementations. However, if we do so, we must pay the same attention to the equality contract as the compiler would in its generated version.

In nonsealed records, the compiler creates a virtual property named EqualityContract, which uses typeof to report the static (compile-time) type of its containing record. The implementation of Equals for the Color record shown in Listing 7-14 is equivalent to the one generated by the compiler, although, as you saw in Chapter 5, some implementation details differ.

```
public class Color : IEquatable<Color>
{
    --snip--
    protected virtual Type EqualityContract
        => typeof(Color);
```

```
    public virtual bool Equals(Color? other)
        => (object?)this == (object?)other ||
           other is not null &&
           EqualityContract == other.EqualityContract &&
           Red == other.Red && Green == other.Green && Blue == other.Blue;
}
```

Listing 7-14: Using the equality contract in a nonsealed record

When one record derives from another, as TranslucentColor does from
Color, the compiler adds an override of EqualityContract in the derived
record to report its static type. The compiler-generated implementation of
Equals in the base class checks that the EqualityContract properties match for
both objects. If they don't, Equals returns false.

Notwithstanding the EqualityContract property, the implementation of Equals follows the canonical form shown in Listing 7-4. Since
TranslucentColor derives from Color, the other parameter could refer to an
instance of TranslucentColor. If we attempt to compare a Color record with
a TranslucentColor, the EqualityContract properties won't match, and the
objects will (correctly) compare not equal. Checking the EqualityContract
property is analogous to our original Color class in Listing 7-4 checking that
GetType returned the same type for both objects. Using the static type as
EqualityContract does has a slight benefit over GetType because typeof is evaluated at compile time, whereas GetType is evaluated at run time.

The EqualityContract property is protected so that it can be overridden
by the derived type, but it can't be called publicly. As Listing 7-15 shows, the
virtual EqualityContract property is overridden in the TranslucentColor record
to return the type of TranslucentColor.

```
public class TranslucentColor : Color, IEquatable<TranslucentColor>
{
    --snip--
    protected override Type EqualityContract
        => typeof(TranslucentColor);

    public override bool Equals(Color? obj)
        => Equals(obj as TranslucentColor);

    public virtual bool Equals(TranslucentColor? other)
        => base.Equals(other) && Alpha == other.Alpha;
}
```

Listing 7-15: Overriding the equality contract in the TranslucentColor record

The implementation of Equals in TranslucentColor calls the base class
implementation before comparing the local properties of each object,
ensuring that the contract properties are always compared. Crucially, the
virtual Equals(Color?) method is overridden in TranslucentColor and casts
its argument to a TranslucentColor. If that cast fails, the argument passed
will be null. When we compare two TranslucentColor instances using Color

reference variables, as when we call the `EqualViaBase` method in Listing 7-13, it's this override of `Equals` that's executed via virtual dispatch.

If we write our own `Equals` method, it must also compare the `EqualityContract` properties because it rarely makes sense for instances of different types to compare equal.

The `EqualityContract` property alone doesn't solve the problem of comparing two `TranslucentColor` instances using `Color` references. Our test in Listing 7-13 passes because the compiler generates a virtual type-safe `Equals` method for `Color` and overrides it in the derived record. When we call `Equals` on a `Color` variable, if the run-time instance is a `TranslucentColor`, we call the more derived implementation. Note that the `Equals(TranslucentColor?)` method is also virtual, because `TranslucentColor` can itself be inherited. A record deriving from `TranslucentColor` will have compiler-generated overrides of both `Equals(TranslucentColor?)` and `Equals(Color?)` alongside its own type-safe `Equals` method.

However, equality isn't the only implementation we can inherit from a class or a record. We can define our own virtual and nonvirtual methods for a record exactly as we do for a class.

Contracts Other Than Equality

The behavioral contract established by a base class or record applies to all its methods, not just `Equals`. The compiler generates the right implementations to compare two record instances for equality, but we have to supply any other implementations for ourselves. One common interface implemented by value types is `IComparable<T>`, which, as you saw in Chapter 6, allows us to sort collections of value types. The `Area` and `Volume` records in Listing 7-16 are related by inheritance, and each implements the `IComparable<T>` interface by defining a `CompareTo` method.

```
public record Area(double Width, double Height)
    : IComparable<Area>
{
    public int CompareTo(Area? other)
    {
        if(other is null) return 1;
        return (int)(Width * Height - other.Width * other.Height);
    }

    public static bool operator<(Area left, Area right)
        => left.CompareTo(right) < 0;

    public static bool operator>(Area left, Area right)
        => left.CompareTo(right) > 0;
}

public record Volume(double Width, double Height, double Depth)
    : Area(Width, Height), IComparable<Volume>
{
    public int CompareTo(Volume? other)
    {
```

```
            if(other is null) return 1;
            return (int)(Width * Height * Depth -
                        other.Width * other.Height * other.Depth);
        }

    public static bool operator<(Volume left, Volume right)
        => left.CompareTo(right) < 0;

    public static bool operator>(Volume left, Volume right)
        => left.CompareTo(right) > 0;
}
```

Listing 7-16: Sorting Area and Volume records with IComparable<T>

The compiler will generate the code to implement IEquatable<T> for both Area and Volume, although we should keep in mind that Equals is comparing double values in each case, leading to possible problems, as we discovered in Chapter 5. However, the compiler doesn't provide the implementation for IComparable<T>, so we must write our own. Here, we define the ordering for Area so that one object is less than another if its total area is smaller. Similarly, for Volume, one is less than another if its total volume is smaller. We also add operator< and operator> for both Area and Volume, implemented in terms of the CompareTo method.

As we explored in Chapter 6, ordering comparisons have their own contract, and the implementations of IComparable<T> in Listing 7-16 effectively suffer the same problems as our original implementation of the IEquatable<T> interface in the Color and TranslucentColor classes.

Although we're using record instead of class in the declarations, we're still employing implementation inheritance. Subclassing is as much an issue for records as it is for classes. We can demonstrate this with a new test in the same vein as checking whether two TranslucentColor instances compare not equal when their Alpha properties differ. In Listing 7-17, two Volume instances differ only in their Depth property, but we compare them with < by using references to the base record type.

```
Area door =   new Volume(Width: 100, Height: 200, Depth: 25);
Area window = new Volume(Width: 100, Height: 200, Depth: 5);

Assert.That(window < door, Is.True);
```

Listing 7-17: Testing the contract for CompareTo in two Volume instances

This test *fails* because the static, compile-time types of the door and window variables differ from their dynamic, run-time types. When we compare them using the base class static type, the Depth property of the derived record is ignored, giving an incorrect result.

As with the compiler implementation of IEquatable<T>, we could make the implementation of CompareTo virtual in the Area record and override it in the Volume type. While doing so would address the immediate problem of this failing test, it wouldn't solve every problem with our implementation. For example, when we compare an Area with a Volume, what should CompareTo return? An equality comparison between instances that aren't the same type simply returns `false`, but it's not so straightforward for `CompareTo`. We might choose to compare any `Area` as less than any `Volume`, but that too may lead to confusion.

The question of whether an `Area` is less than a `Volume` is not a meaningful one, but disallowing ordering comparisons for the `Area` and `Volume` types individually would be extremely prohibitive; it makes perfect sense to see if one `Area` is less than another, and likewise for `Volume`. We can arrange for `CompareTo` to throw an exception if the objects being compared have different run-time types, but this will add complexity to the calling code and may surprise some users.

This demonstrates first that records are not a "silver bullet," and second—and more importantly—that we might still be trying to solve the wrong problem.

Avoiding Implementation Inheritance

Our problems with inheriting `Equals` and `CompareTo` demonstrate why value types don't make good base types, regardless of whether we use `class` or `record` to define them.

More generally, inheriting any implemented behavior makes it challenging to ensure that code written for the base type will work correctly if we substitute an inherited type. Even if we don't override the base type's methods, we can't easily guarantee that those methods will work correctly for any derived type. While inheritance is a popular mechanism for reusing a base type's implementation, fulfilling the base type behavioral contract in a derived type is often much more difficult than it appears.

One way to ensure that one type can be substituted for another is to avoid implementation inheritance entirely. Remember, when we implement an interface, the implementing class is truly a subtype of the interface type; there's no behavioral contract to consider because interfaces have no implementation. An interface type defines what an implementing type must be able to do but doesn't prescribe any specific implementation. An interface, in effect, defines *only* a type, not a class.

An interface type can be substituted by any implementing type, so we can use different implementations under different circumstances. Code that depends only on an interface type—whether as a parameter in a method or a field in a type—is completely decoupled from the way that interface is implemented. This means that interfaces are *seams*—customization points in our code where we can swap one implementation for another.

Code that's written in terms of interface types rather than concrete implementations is more flexible because it doesn't depend on a particular implementation. It's also easier to test because we can switch out concrete implementations of an interface with our own *test double*, sometimes known as a *stub*, *fake*, or *mock object*.

It's common to see interface types represent the controllers and services described in Chapter 6, sometimes with several implementations. A specific concrete implementation may be selected at run time, perhaps according to configuration parameters or the run-time environment. However, code *using* the controller or service—frequently in the entity types—doesn't need to change because its behavior depends only on the interface, not the specific concrete type. The controllers and services are also where we're most likely to want a fake implementation during testing so that the testing doesn't need access to an external or expensive resource, such as a real database.

When value types implement one or more interfaces, it's to define specific protocols, such as IEquatable<T> and IComparable<T>, rather than to allow client code to use different implementations. Value types, no matter the mechanism we use to implement them, should stand alone and be largely, if not wholly, independent of other types in an application.

The advice to avoid implementation inheritance leads to the recommendation that records should *always* be sealed, because they're specifically designed for modeling value types. Classes should also be sealed by default, whether or not we're using them to model values, and inheritance enabled only when we have a specific design rationale for it.

Although this advice might seem to limit the flexibility of our designs, we can use other ways to define relationships in our code without deriving new types from existing ones. Inheritance isn't the only option for reusing the implementation of an existing type to extend its capabilities.

Containing Instead of Inheriting Types

One way we can use the behavior of one concrete type to implement another is to simply *contain* (or *compose*) an instance of the type as a field or property. This is especially true when we need a value type, like TranslucentColor, that's easily implemented in terms of a simpler type, like Color, but without implying any type substitutability between them. While value types should generally be stand-alone, containing another value as a field is one exception that's frequently beneficial.

We implemented Color as a class and then as a record so we could take advantage of inheritance. Modeling values with a class is not unreasonable—and, as we know, records are specifically provided for that purpose. But if we contain a Color in TranslucentColor instead of deriving from Color, using struct to implement both types is much simpler. Using record struct is even simpler still, as we do in Listing 7-18, where a TranslucentColor contains an instance of Color.

```
public readonly record struct Color(int Red, int Green, int Blue);

public readonly record struct TranslucentColor(Color Color, int Alpha)
{
    public TranslucentColor(int red, int green, int blue, int alpha)
        : this(new Color(red, green, blue), alpha)
    {
    }
```

```
    public int Red => Color.Red;
    public int Green => Color.Green;
    public int Blue => Color.Blue;
}
```

Listing 7-18: Containing Color rather than inheriting from it

Here, the compiler provides the implementation for IEquatable<T> for each type, leaving us to define just the properties and behavior for them. The TranslucentColor type contains a read-only Color instance, and we add a new constructor as a convenience for our users, who can either create a new Color value to pass to TranslucentColor's generated constructor or call our new constructor with each component part separately. We also mirror Color's properties in TranslucentColor and forward them to the contained Color value. We don't get those properties for free, but they afford users of TranslucentColor a much more natural interface, like this:

```
var bg = new TranslucentColor(0xFF, 0xA0, 0, 0x77);

Assert.That(bg.Red,   Is.EqualTo(0xFF));
Assert.That(bg.Green, Is.EqualTo(0xA0));
Assert.That(bg.Blue,  Is.EqualTo(0));
Assert.That(bg.Alpha, Is.EqualTo(0x77));
--snip--
```

The alternative would force users to explicitly obtain the Color property in order to access its properties, like so:

```
Assert.That(bg.Color.Red,   Is.EqualTo(0xFF));
Assert.That(bg.Color.Green, Is.EqualTo(0xA0));
Assert.That(bg.Color.Blue,  Is.EqualTo(0));

Assert.That(bg.Alpha,       Is.EqualTo(0x77));
--snip--
```

Whether we use structs or define our value types with sealed records or classes, or record structs, testing our new types is much simpler to reason about now, as we don't need to consider cases where TranslucentColor instances are referred to by Color references. That in itself is a large consideration because those tests will be not only easier to write but also easier to read by the next programmers who visit the code.

Composing types isn't a perfect match for the version that employed inheritance, because we can't use a TranslucentColor instance as an argument to a method expecting a Color. As you've seen, sometimes that substitutability isn't appropriate.

Inheritance isn't the only form of polymorphism nor the only mechanism that exhibits type substitutability, but other approaches allow the compiler to inform us when we incorrectly substitute one type for another. Let's take a look at some of them.

Parametric Polymorphism with Generics

C# generics offer *parametric polymorphism*, a form of polymorphism that allows us to write code once that works for multiple types by using generic type parameters instead of actual types. This approach provides a common form and purpose for all the types that can be substituted for those parameters.

This is most clearly demonstrated by the generic collection classes in the Standard Library, such as List<T>, where T is a generic parameter type that can be substituted by *any* run-time type, including any types we define ourselves. For example, in Listing 7-19 we declare two List<T> variables parameterized with different, unrelated types.

```
var colors = new List<Color>();
var names = new List<string>();
```

Listing 7-19: Using a generic type

Although the List implementation's behavior doesn't change, a List<Color> is a distinct type from List<string>, and there's no relationship between the two types. The generic List<T> code is written in terms of the T generic parameter, and since List<T> doesn't need to know anything about the structural or behavioral characteristics of T, it can be used with any type.

To put that another way, in the context of List<T>, any type can be substituted for the T parameter without implying any subtype relationship. We have no behavioral contract to take into account, because List<T> makes no assumptions about T.

If we need to be more selective about the types that are suitable for a generic parameter type in our own generic code, or if we require the generic code to use methods and properties beyond those provided by object, we can constrain the parameter to allow only types having specific behavior.

Generic Constraints and Protocol Interfaces

Since object is the base class of every type, generics can use its methods via a variable of type T, but to access anything else, the compiler needs more information on what T can be. We provide that information through generic type constraints. One example is an interface constraint, which restricts T to a type that implements the specified interface, ensuring that all interface operations are legal for a variable of that generic type. Consider, for instance, the interface shown in Listing 7-20.

```
public interface IParser<T>
{
    public T Parse(string input);
}
```

Listing 7-20: A contract interface

The generic IParser<T> interface defines a single Parse method for turning a string value into an object instance of type T. The T parameter in IParser<T> is unconstrained, so this interface can be implemented by any type. In Listing 7-21, we use the IParser<T> interface to constrain the TParser parameter of the DataAdapter generic class.

```
public sealed class DataAdapter<TParser, TResult>
    where TParser : IParser<TResult>
{
    public DataAdapter(TParser parser, IEnumerable<string> source)
        => (this.parser, items) = (parser, source);

    public IEnumerable<TResult> Read()
    {
        foreach (var item in items)
        {
            yield return parser.Parse(item);
        }
    }

    private readonly TParser parser;
    private readonly IEnumerable<string> items;
}
```

Listing 7-21: Constraining a type for its API

The DataAdapter class has two generic parameters. The TParser parameter is constrained to the IParser<T> interface in the where clause following the type definition. TParser is constrained using the second generic parameter TResult, which also corresponds to the return type from the Read method, meaning that TParser can be substituted by an implementation of IParser<TResult>. The constructor for DataAdapter takes a TParser parameter, so the argument passed must be an implementation of IParser<T>, with the T substituted by the same type as the TResult parameter for DataAdapter.

For simplicity, the DataAdapter constructor takes a sequence of string values to represent the input values, but in a real application, DataAdapter might be obtaining its data from a database or more elaborate source.

The interface type constraint on the TParser generic type parameter enables us to call parser.Parse in the Read method, which returns a sequence of TResult elements. Without the where constraint for TParser, the Read method would fail to compile because object has no Parse method.

The IParser<T> interface in Listing 7-20 isn't intended to be used as the type of a variable; rather, it's a contract interface whose purpose is to describe the *protocol* for parsing a string into an object. We even use TParser as the type of a field in the DataAdapter class rather than declaring the field as IParser<T>.

The presence of the constraint on the TParser generic parameter of DataAdapter means that we can create a DataAdapter only by providing an implementation of the IParser<T> protocol. The constraint guarantees that whatever type is substituted for TParser at run time will have a Parse method whose signature matches the operation defined in the IParser<T> interface.

Implementing the IParser<T> Protocol

The IParser<T> interface is itself generic, allowing an implementing type to specify the return type from the Parse method. The ColorParser class in Listing 7-22 implements IParser<Color> to convert a string to a Color object. In this example, the input string represents each color component as a two-digit hexadecimal value, so the entire value is in the format "RRGGBB".

```
public interface IParser<T>
{
    public T Parse(string input);
}

public sealed class ColorParser : IParser<Color>
{
    public static int FromHex(string part)
        => int.Parse(part, NumberStyles.HexNumber);

    public Color Parse(string input)
        => new(Red:   FromHex(input[0..2]),
               Green: FromHex(input[2..4]),
               Blue:  FromHex(input[4..6]));
}
```

Listing 7-22: Implementing a contract interface

The Parse method of the ColorParser class uses the range operator syntax, introduced in C# v8.0, on the input parameter to split the string into three parts of two characters each. A range like [begin..end], also called a *slice*, specifies a substring from the begin index up to but not including the end index. Ranges can also be used with arrays to specify a subrange of the array.

NOTE *A range is a half-open interval of indices and would more properly be written [begin..end), but C# syntax doesn't allow nonmatching brackets or parentheses. Be careful not to confuse this syntax with the Enumerable.Range method, which takes the starting index and a count of items to include as its parameters.*

Parameterizing the DataAdapter Class

Since ColorParser implements the IParser<T> interface, we can use a ColorParser with the DataAdapter class, as shown in Listing 7-23.

```
string messages = "FFA000 A0FF00 00F0F0"; ...

var provider = new DataAdapter<ColorParser, Color>
                   (new ColorParser(), messages.Split(' '));

foreach(Color color in provider.Read())
```

```
{
    --snip--
    // Do something with a color
}
```

Listing 7-23: Using the generic type

While the DataAdapter class itself is written in a polymorphic way (inasmuch as it works on any type implementing the required IParser<T> protocol), using it requires us to explicitly indicate the concrete type we're substituting for both the TParser parameter and the TResult parameter type to be returned by the Read method.

This prevents us from accidentally using TranslucentColor for the TResult parameter of DataAdapter along with a ColorParser class like this:

```
var other = new DataAdapter<ColorParser, TranslucentColor>
                    (new ColorParser(), messages.Split(' '));
```

The ColorParser class is specific to Color types because it implements the IParser<Color> interface. The compiler will catch such transgressions and report an error:

```
[CS0311] The type 'ColorParser' cannot be used as type parameter 'TParser' in the generic
type or method 'DataAdapter<TParser, T>'. There is no implicit reference conversion from
'ColorParser' to 'IParser<TranslucentColor>'.
```

However, the TResult generic parameter of DataAdapter is already implied by the concrete type of the IParser<T> implementation we provide, as it must be the same type that's returned by IParser<T>.Parse. The type constraint we used for the TParser generic parameter for DataAdapter in Listing 7-21 makes this relationship explicit:

```
public sealed class DataAdapter<TParser, TResult>
    where TParser : IParser<TResult>
--snip--
```

Since we've gone to the trouble of ensuring that the DataAdapter class can work with any IParser<T> implementation, having to specify which implementation we mean seems superfluous. Instead, we can have the compiler deduce the correct type for the TParser parameter based on the actual type we use.

Generic Method Parameters and Type Deduction

Although the compiler doesn't infer the actual type for any parameters of a generic class, it may do so for a generic method if a generic parameter type is used in the method's formal parameters. Since the TParser type parameter is used only by the DataAdapter.Read method, we can move it from the DataAdapter class and add it instead to the Read method, making Read a generic method, as shown in Listing 7-24.

```
public sealed class DataAdapter<TResult>
{
    public DataAdapter(IEnumerable<string> source)
        => items = source;

    public IEnumerable<TResult> Read<TParser>(TParser parser)
        where TParser : IParser<TResult>
    {
        foreach (var item in items)
        {
            yield return parser.Parse(item);
        }
    }

    private readonly IEnumerable<string> items;
}
```

Listing 7-24: Defining DataAdapter.Read as a generic method

The DataAdapter no longer needs a field to store a TParser object since it's passed to the Read method. The generic method still requires the interface constraint so that we can call the Parse method via the parser variable, but we don't need to specify the type of the parser argument when passing it; the compiler infers the type of TParser based on the argument we pass to Read, as shown in Listing 7-25.

```
var provider = new DataAdapter<Color>(messages);

foreach (Color color in provider.Read(new ColorParser()))
{
    --snip--
}
```

Listing 7-25: Parameter type inference

We mention the ColorParser type just once, when we create an instance of it to pass to the Read method. Compare this with Listing 7-23, where we not only required an instance of ColorParser but also needed to specify its type for the TParser parameter of DataAdapter. By taking advantage of the type inference afforded by a generic method, we avoid the redundant code.

Parameterized Types

We still need to specify Color for the TResult parameter of DataAdapter in Listing 7-25, even though TResult is used only by the Read method. The compiler can only infer the real type of a generic parameter from the arguments we pass to a method, and TResult isn't used as the type for any parameter in Read. If a method has generic parameters, they must all be either explicitly specified or deduced from the arguments; the compiler won't partially deduce the types just from available arguments.

However, this is a benefit of the DataAdapter class, because it ensures that the T parameter of IParser<T> matches the TResult parameter of DataAdapter.

If we want a different type to stand in for TResult, we need a different parser implementation. In Listing 7-26, we implement the IParser<T> interface in a TranslucentColor type and create a DataAdapter for the new type.

```
public sealed class TranslucentColorParser : IParser<TranslucentColor>
{
    public TranslucentColor Parse(string input)
        => new(Color: color.Parse(input[0..6]),
               Alpha: ColorParser.FromHex(input[6..8]));

    private readonly ColorParser color = new();
}

--snip--
var provider = new DataAdapter<TranslucentColor>(messages);

var colors = provider.Read(new TranslucentColorParser()).ToList();
```

Listing 7-26: Parameterizing DataAdapter with a different type

We specify TranslucentColor instead of Color to implement IParser<T> in the TranslucentColorParser class, and we specify TranslucentColor as the type for the TResult parameter of DataAdapter. The TranslucentColorParser implementation uses a ColorParser object to parse the Color portion of TranslucentColor as a convenience, but otherwise it's an entirely new type. Similarly, the DataAdapter<TranslucentColor> type is unrelated to DataAdapter<Color>.

The DataAdapter class is polymorphic according to the type we provide as an argument for its TResult parameter because that type affects what the Read method returns. The Read method is itself polymorphic, as it has its own generic parameter. We need to write the Read method only once, and it works for any type that implements IParser<T>, where T matches the TResult type of DataAdapter.

We can think of a generic method as representing multiple method overloads, each with different parameter types but all having an identical implementation. Even without generics, overloaded methods represent their own kind of polymorphism, known as *ad hoc polymorphism.*

Ad Hoc Polymorphism with Overloading

Ad hoc polymorphism, or *method overloading*, is how we define a family of operations that have the same name but differ in the type or number of their parameters. The compiler selects the correct method overload based on the method name and the arguments we use to call it. Each method can have a different implementation, so the method *name* is polymorphic with respect to its parameters.

You've seen a few examples of overloading instance methods in this and other chapters, where we've overridden the virtual Equals method and then overloaded it with a type-safe implementation. The compiler will select the type-safe overload of `Equals` if the static type of the argument matches the implementing type rather than being an `object` or another type. In a record struct, the compiler provides implementations for both methods, although we can provide our own type-safe `Equals` if we wish. Listing 7-27 shows how using different arguments changes which method is called when the variables being compared are value types.

```
public readonly record struct Color(int Red, int Green, int Blue);

var plum = new Color(0xDD, 0xA0, 0xDD);
var other = new Color(0xDD, 0xA0, 0xDD);

Assert.That(plum.Equals(null), Is.False);
Assert.That(plum.Equals(other), Is.True);
```

Listing 7-27: Selecting method overloads

The first assertion, which compares the `plum` variable with `null`, will call the `Equals` method override with an `object?` parameter because `object` is a reference type, and `null` will automatically convert to a reference parameter. In the second assertion, the method taking a `Color` as its parameter is a better match for the `other` argument because the types match exactly, so the type-specific overload is called. If `Color` were a record instead of a record struct, both assertions would directly invoke the `Equals(Color)` overload, since in that case `Color` would be a reference type but a more specific one than `object`, making it a better conversion target for overload resolution when the argument is `null`.

When we call an overloaded instance method, the compiler identifies the candidate methods by using the static type of the variable used to invoke the method. The candidate methods may include extension methods with the same name if they're in scope where the method is called. It's always the invoking variable that determines how the list of possible overloads is selected, and the arguments passed determine the specific overload from that candidate list. In Listing 7-28, we change the static type of the `plum` variable to be `object` instead of `Color` before calling its `Equals` method.

```
object plum = new Color(0xDD, 0xA0, 0xDD);
Color other = new Color(0xDD, 0xA0, 0xDD);

Assert.That(plum.Equals(other), Is.True);
```

Listing 7-28: Argument type versus invoking type

The candidates for `Equals` are selected from the methods defined on `object` because that's the compile-time type of the `plum` variable. We have only one such method, which takes a parameter of `object?`, so that's automatically a match, even though the `other` argument is a `Color`, and `plum` is still a reference to a `Color` that has an overloaded `Equals` method taking a `Color` parameter. The same would be true if `Color` were a reference type: the type-specific overload isn't even considered during overload resolution because it's not a member of the type of the variable used to call the method.

Static methods can be overloaded too, although the candidate overloads are identified from the type name used by the caller. In either case, from this list of candidates, called a *method group*, the compiler chooses the best match according to the arguments being passed.

If no match is found—that is, the arguments aren't implicitly convertible to any of the parameter types—or there are multiple equally good candidates with no single best match, our program fails to compile.

Symbolic Polymorphism with Overloaded Operators

Overloading can be especially powerful in conjunction with custom operators. It's common for value types to overload `operator==` to correspond with the `Equals` method. Not only is this more compact, but it also looks more natural to compare values with `==` than to compare them by calling a method.

We have to write our own operator implementations for structs, but the compiler provides `operator==` and `operator!=` for records and record structs, making it convenient to compare two variables of the same type like this:

```
var plum = new Color(0xDD, 0xA0, 0xDD);
var pink = new Color(0xFF, 0xCC, 0xCC);

Assert.That(plum != pink, Is.True);
```

We're not permitted to alter the implementations of `operator==` or `operator!=` synthesized by the compiler for records and record structs, but we can add overloads of them to accept different types, just as we can with other methods. For instance, in Listing 7-29, we overload `operator==` for `Color` to permit comparisons between a `Color` and an `int`.

```
public static bool operator==(Color left, int right)
    => left.Equals(new (right));

public static bool operator==(int left, Color right)
    => right.Equals(new (left));
```

Listing 7-29: Overloading operators

We need to add a corresponding `operator!=` for each overload (not shown here). These overloads are a convenience for users, who don't need to explicitly construct `Color` instances in order to compare them with their raw RGB value and who can compare values like this:

```
var plum = new Color(Red: 0xDD, Green: 0xA0, Blue: 0xDD);

Assert.That(plum == 0xDDA0DD, Is.True);
Assert.That(0xDDA0DD == plum, Is.True);
```

Overloading operators isn't essentially different from overloading other methods, but rather than using named methods, we're overloading *symbols* to behave in a polymorphic way with our types. A good example of symbolic polymorphism is embodied in the string class, which defines the + symbol to mean concatenation rather than addition. This is a widely accepted convention familiar to most programmers.

We should be cautious of introducing our own operations that don't follow the usual rules. Overloading methods, and especially operators, requires careful thought and a hefty dose of what we might call "good taste." Families of methods overloaded for different types give the impression of type substitutability by giving one common name to an operation that may be implemented differently for each type.

The string class doesn't, for example, allow us to add a number with a string, for the simple reason that the type of the result may be misinterpreted: should "5" + 0.5 be the same as 0.5 + "5"? The designers of the string class decided to disallow either use to avoid any potential confusion.

Generic Delegates for Polymorphism

A *delegate* is a type that represents a method with a specific signature—the type and number of parameters—and a delegate object can be constructed from different methods as long as the signature matches the delegate type. Delegates are a central feature of the LINQ libraries; for example, the Select method takes a delegate parameter to represent the method for transforming one element of a sequence into a different type. We most commonly see lambdas being used as the arguments for methods with delegate type parameters, as shown in Listing 7-30.

```
var colors = new List<Color>
    {
        --snip--
    };

var formatted = colors.Select(
    color => $"{color.Red:X2}{color.Green:X2}{color.Blue:X2}");
```

Listing 7-30: Passing a lambda for a delegate parameter

Select is an extension method for IEnumerable<T>, and here we call it via the colors variable, passing a lambda to represent a method taking a Color parameter, since that's the element type of the colors sequence. The lambda is invoked for each element in the sequence and returns a hexadecimal representation of the value as a string formatted to "RRGGBB"—the reverse operation of the Parse method defined in Listing 7-22.

Inline lambdas like the one in Listing 7-30 are convenient but generally lack the flexibility offered by method overloads. For example, if we change the element type of colors to be TranslucentColor instead of Color, our code still compiles, and the lambda implementation will continue to work with the TranslucentColor type defined in Listing 7-18, but the result won't have the extra 2 bytes for the Alpha property. We have to write a new lambda for

TranslucentColor, and if we need to support both Color and TranslucentColor elements, we have to handle them separately.

Overloaded methods are a perfect way to capture the common purpose we need while simultaneously enabling us to encapsulate the different implementations required. Consider the two static methods in Listing 7-31.

```
public static class Formatter
{
    public static string Format(Color color)
        => $"{color.Red:X2}{color.Green:X2}{color.Blue:X2}";

    public static string Format(TranslucentColor color)
        => $"{Format(color.Color)}{color.Alpha:X2}";
}
```

Listing 7-31: Overloaded methods for different types

Notice that the Format(TranslucentColor) method's implementation calls the Format(Color) overload—something we couldn't do with separate anonymous lambda expressions.

Rather than passing a lambda as the argument for Select, we can pass the Format method group, as shown in Listing 7-32.

```
var colors = new List<TranslucentColor>
{
    --snip--
};


var formatted = colors.Select(Formatter.Format);
```

Listing 7-32: A method group as an argument

Here, Formatter.Format is the common name for two method overloads and represents a method group. The compiler selects the correct overload in the group based on the element type of the sequence used to call Select. The delegate parameter for Select is a generic delegate—that is, one that has its own generic type parameters. Like generic methods, the compiler will infer the actual types based on the arguments passed to the delegate.

The Formatter.Format method group is polymorphic according to the arguments that are passed by the Select method internally. Here, the Format(TranslucentColor) method from Listing 7-31 is called because the element type of the colors sequence is TranslucentColor. If we changed the colors variable to be a List<Color> instead, the Select method would call Format(Color), but without us needing to change the Select expression in any way.

Coercion Polymorphism Using Conversions

As you've seen, inheritance allows us to use a reference to an instance of one type when a different type is expected, as long as the first type inherits from the second type. A derived class is syntactically substitutable for its base class because there's a natural implicit conversion from a specific type to any of its parent types.

We can implement our own type conversions to mimic substitutability between two otherwise unrelated types. Casting—or *coercing*—a variable to a different type can be convenient, whether via implicit or explicit conversions, but doing so may mask problems beneath the surface. However, applied carefully, conversions between unrelated types can be an effective and concise way to express a design.

To demonstrate some of the problems with implicit conversions that we haven't yet explored, Listing 7-33 implements an implicit conversion operator in `TranslucentColor` to convert an instance to a `Color` type.

```
public readonly record struct TranslucentColor(Color Color, int Alpha)
{
    --snip--
    public static implicit operator Color(TranslucentColor color)
        => color.Color;
}
```

Listing 7-33: Implicit conversion operator

The conversion operator in `TranslucentColor` is an *outward* conversion: we're converting from an instance of the implementing type to something else. It will allow us to call a method expecting a `Color` value when we have a `TranslucentColor` at hand, as we do when we call the `EqualViaColor` method in Listing 7-34.

```
public bool EqualViaColor(Color left, Color right)
    => left.Equals(right);

var red = new TranslucentColor(0xFF, 0, 0, 0);
var blue = new TranslucentColor(0, 0, 0xFF, 0);

Assert.That(EqualViaColor(red, blue), Is.False);
```

Listing 7-34: Implicit conversions in action

Owing to the implicit conversion operator, the red and blue variables are converted to `Color` instances when we pass them as arguments to the `EqualViaColor` method. The conversion happens invisibly because the conversion operator is defined as `implicit`.

We could achieve the same effect by defining an inward conversion operator on the `Color` type taking a `TranslucentColor` parameter. The difference is merely about where we choose to define the operator. Since `TranslucentColor` already depends on the `Color` type, and `Color` otherwise has no knowledge of `TranslucentColor`, the outward conversion defined in `TranslucentColor` makes better sense here.

However, we must be careful with all conversions, especially implicit ones. As you saw in Chapter 1, implicit conversions may hide complexity and can even lead to undesired behavior. A user-defined coercion is not quite the same as the implicit reference conversion from a derived type to its base type.

Widening vs. Narrowing Conversions

When `TranslucentColor` inherited from `Color`, we could pass a `TranslucentColor` reference to a method expecting a `Color`, but it was still a reference to the same instance of a `TranslucentColor`, and only a copy of the reference would be made. In Listing 7-33, `TranslucentColor` and `Color` are record structs and therefore value types. When we invoke the conversion operator of `TranslucentColor`, we're simply creating a new `Color` instance, so the copy has lost some of the information specific to `TranslucentColor`—namely, the `Alpha` property.

A conversion from a derived class reference to a base class reference is a *widening* conversion. We can refer to a specific instance by using a more general (base) type, but no loss of information occurs. We're still able to explicitly cast the base class reference back to the original derived instance, although that's a relatively expensive run-time operation. Our implicit conversion from a `TranslucentColor` struct to a `Color` via our own operator method is *narrowing*: neither type is really more specific or general than the other, and they're independent values, but the act of conversion loses information.

While we've replicated the behavior of converting from a derived class to a base class, it doesn't give us the same flexibility. The converted value really *is* just a `Color`, and we need other means of capturing the extra properties of a `TranslucentColor` if we need to reinstate them.

Conversions aren't appropriate for trying to replicate the characteristics of inheritance, but they can be useful for other scenarios.

For Representation

Conversions between unrelated types make more sense when the types have a common meaning with different representation. For instance, we might need to use an external API that uses the common `int` representation of the hexadecimal RGB value of colors. Changing a value's representation is usually better implemented as an explicit rather than implicit conversion, as shown in Listing 7-35. However, any conversions—whether explicit or implicit—require careful consideration of alternate approaches.

```
public readonly struct Color
{
    --snip--
    public static explicit operator int(Color color)
        => color.Red << 16 | color.Green << 8 | color.Blue;
}
```

Listing 7-35: Converting to a different type representation

In Listing 7-36, we test the explicit conversion operator's implementation by casting the `plum` value to `int` in order to pass it as an argument for a method taking an `int` parameter.

```
int Converted(int color)
{
    return color;
}

var plum = new Color(0xDD, 0xA0, 0xDD);

Assert.That(Converted((int)plum), Is.EqualTo(0xDDA0DD));
```

Listing 7-36: Testing an explicit conversion

This local `Converted` function takes an `int` parameter and, for the purposes of the test, simply returns its parameter value. Since the conversion operator is explicit, we must cast the `Color` value when we call the `Converted` method; the compiler will complain if we try to use a `Color` value directly as an argument for `Converted`. The compiler will also catch any unintentionally inappropriate expressions like this:

```
var blue = new Color(0, 0, 0xFF);
var green = new Color(0, 0xFF, 0);

Assert.That(blue < green, Is.True);
```

If we had made the conversion operator implicit in `Color`, this code would compile but would compare two `int` values, probably with unexpected results.

The cast to `int` in Listing 7-36, while explicit and obvious in the code, doesn't say much about the intention behind the conversion, which is implied to some extent by the use. We might consider replacing an explicit outward conversion like this with a method or property that more definitively describes the intent of the conversion, perhaps by calling it `ToWebColor`.

Naming the conversion allows us to better express what we mean and why, making the code more self-documenting without being overly intrusive or syntax-heavy compared to an explicit cast. One frequently overlooked consequence of using a named property instead of a cast is that the property name is easier to search for, should we need to find everywhere it's used.

For Purpose

Conversion operators, even implicit conversions, aren't exclusively a bad choice. Conversions are commonly used to allow a value to be represented by unrelated types that support different operations, although the value itself has a common representation. For example, `Color` is an immutable value type, but we might want to build up its value incrementally. A `Color` has multiple properties, and sometimes setting them individually might be more convenient than setting them all at once in a constructor.

Rather than compromising the immutable nature of Color by adding set accessors for its properties, we introduce a new companion type that looks very much like Color, except that it allows its properties to be changed. When the values are in their final state, we can then materialize an instance of the mutable type into an immutable Color. Key to this is that we can easily convert from the companion type to the target value type. Listing 7-37 shows such a *mutable companion* type for Color that allows an implicit conversion to the immutable target value.

```
public class ColorBuilder
{
    public int Red { get; set; }
    public int Green { get; set; }
    public int Blue { get; set; }

    public static implicit operator Color(ColorBuilder color)
        => new Color(color.Red, color.Green, color.Blue);
}
```

Listing 7-37: A mutable companion for Color

The ColorBuilder type isn't itself a value type; its sole purpose is to provide a kind of factory for Color values.

Applications of the *Mutable Companion* pattern are fairly common, and we see it in the Standard Library with string and StringBuilder. The string type is immutable, and when we need to build up a string variable from several parts, using its mutable companion, StringBuilder, is efficient. When we've finished "building" the string, we turn it into its *immutable* state.

Unlike with ColorBuilder, we must call the ToString method of StringBuilder to turn it into a string, but an implicit conversion can be used to good effect here. Since ColorBuilder is implicitly convertible to a Color, we can call a method taking a Color parameter with a ColorBuilder value, as we see in Listing 7-38, where we call the RelativeLuminance method with both a ColorBuilder and Color value.

```
public static double RelativeLuminance(Color color)
    => 0.2126 * color.Red + 0.7152 * color.Green + 0.0722 * color.Blue;

var background = new Color(0, 0, 0);

var builder = new ColorBuilder();
builder.Red = 0xFF;
builder.Green = 0xFF;
builder.Blue = 0;

if(RelativeLuminance(builder) < RelativeLuminance(background))
    background = builder;
```

Listing 7-38: Converting a companion type

The implicit conversion operator we defined for ColorBuilder in Listing 7-37 permits us to pass the mutable builder variable as an argument to any method that expects a `Color`. Any code written for `Color` instances won't be expecting to be able to use the mutating properties of the companion class, so the conversion is safe and convenient.

The `ColorBuilder` can be substituted for `Color` courtesy of the implicit conversion. No information is lost because the two types share a common representation; however, a narrowing of the interface occurs, because the `Color` target type has no set accessors for its properties.

Conversions represent a form of polymorphism, as we explicitly allow a variable of one type to be coerced to a variable of a different but unrelated type. Like parametric polymorphism using generics, and ad hoc polymorphism with overloading, coercion polymorphism is a compile-time activity, in contrast to the dynamic, run-time characteristic of inclusion polymorphism using inheritance. Inclusion polymorphism is a powerful tool, but because the type relationships are resolved at run time, the compiler can't identify many of the errors that may occur. When we improperly use generics, overloading, or coercions, we can rely on the compiler to tell us about most errors in our code.

Summary

Trying to outsmart a compiler defeats much of the purpose of using one.
—Brian Kernighan and P.J. Plauger, *The Elements of Programming Style*

Asking how to make value types behave correctly when used polymorphically is the wrong question: polymorphism itself takes many forms! Combining value types and inheritance can cause hard-to-diagnose errors, but inheritance is only one kind of polymorphism. The dynamic nature of inclusion polymorphism with virtual dispatch brings an expectation of type substitutability and doesn't sit well with value-based equality.

Inheriting one type from another imposes a responsibility on the derived type to respect the contract established by the base class. Failing to uphold that contract can lead to undesirable behavior. One type is genuinely substitutable for another only if they share the same behavioral contract, which is something the compiler can't enforce. It's up to us, the programmers, to judge whether inheritance is appropriate. In the case of structs, it's not even permitted, freeing us from that particular responsibility.

With records, we need to pay just as much attention to the base class contract as we do with classes. Although the compiler carefully crafts its implementation of equality to ensure that `Equals` behaves correctly for records, it doesn't do the same for any of our own virtual and overridden methods in those types.

Records aren't necessarily appropriate for everything, and as noted earlier, making `Equals` "just work" for values using inheritance is an incomplete solution to the wrong problem. In particular, records are reference types and thus subject to garbage collection. The implementations of `Equals` are all virtual, as is the `EqualityContract` property, and they all carry an associated cost. Records are a very compact way of declaring immutable value-like types, but programming is more than the amount of typing required of us.

Value types do combine much better with the other ways of representing polymorphic behavior: coercion, overloading, and generic. These three forms of polymorphism are static in nature; that is, they are resolved by the compiler. Although type parameters in generic classes and methods are resolved at run time, we must still provide compile-time guarantees about which operations those parameters support.

It can be tempting to use inheritance in order to reuse code from a base class. This is a bad idea because inheriting a class implies that the base class can be substituted by the inheriting class, but it can be difficult to ensure that the base class's behavioral characteristics are properly met. We can still reuse another type's implementation by containing an instance of the type and using the contained instance privately to implement our new type.

Inheriting from concrete types—that is, nonabstract classes—in general presents us with the challenges of respecting the contracts established by those base classes. When we override an abstract method or implement an interface, we don't suffer from those issues because there is no base class implementation to respect. In those cases, we're inheriting only the interface contract, which is much easier to uphold.

The moral of the story is that if we always implement true interfaces or inherit from fully abstract classes, the problems we've encountered in this chapter will never cause us difficulties. Correspondingly, we should seal any class or record that models a value type and ensure that it has no user-defined base types. We can still write code that behaves polymorphically with the value types we use and create, but we should express it differently by employing generics, overloading methods, and permitting type conversions.

8

PERFORMANCE AND EFFICIENCY

Few programmers set out to write ineffi-
cient code, but we don't always have time to
fine-tune an algorithm to extract the maximum possible performance. Nevertheless, it's
important to understand how some coding practices
can hurt performance and how we can employ alternative approaches to make our code more efficient.
In this chapter, we'll put some common techniques
and practices under the microscope to examine their
performance and compare their characteristics with
potential alternatives.

We'll explore the following:

- Where default code behavior may not be optimally efficient
- Why some common performance concerns are misconceptions

- How to evaluate code performance and target its bottlenecks
- When making small optimizations may be worth the trouble

Measuring and Optimizing Performance

The term *optimization* is often used to mean altering code to make a program run more quickly, but we might want to optimize for many other outcomes: lower memory use, higher numeric calculation precision, increased data throughput, and ease of deployment, to name just a few. Sometimes we trade raw performance for code readability or even convenience. We may decide that making our code easy to test is more important than making the program run at maximum speed. However, optimizing for one area can often adversely affect one or more other areas of an application, so we must make sure that the potential benefits are worth the cost and that our efforts aren't actually leading to *pessimization*: writing or using code that prevents a program from running efficiently.

The easiest and most direct method for optimizing a program's performance is to enable optimizations in the build configuration. A release build configuration has optimizations enabled by default. When building the debug configuration, the compiler generates code that closely matches the source code's structure and logic, which allows for setting diagnostic features like breakpoints, step-by-step debugging, and inspecting variables. The optimizations enabled in a release build may change the code's logical structure in subtle ways, making debugging much more difficult but potentially improving the code's efficiency or reducing the program's size.

The C# compiler itself performs very little in the way of optimizing the code, leaving the majority of that work to the JIT compiler.

The JIT Compiler

The C# compiler translates our C# code into CIL format, which in turn is translated to native machine code either ahead of time (AOT) by a tool such as the CrossGen utility or at run time by the JIT compiler, the latter being the default. In normal operation, the JIT compiler translates the program piecemeal; rather than producing the machine code for the entire program all at once before running it (as AOT tools do), the JIT compiler translates portions of the CIL to native format *just in time*. A portion would generally be a method, but in principle it could be part of a method, such as a loop or if block.

Because JIT compiler optimizations occur during a program's execution, they'll vary among platforms and run-time environments. While AOT compilation may improve a program's startup time, the JIT compiler can take advantage of optimizations specific to a particular CPU, register set, operating system, and program state to produce efficient code on the fly.

One common optimization is to inline the code within a method, avoiding the overhead of a method call. The JIT compiler may also be able to replace some method calls with native intrinsic CPU instructions, further improving performance. Once a block has been translated by the JIT compiler, its native code remains in memory, so it usually doesn't need to be recompiled if the program runs it more than once.

In a debug build, the JIT compiler is much less aggressive in the optimizations it applies so that normal debugging operations are supported. When we're trying to assess our code's performance, it usually makes the most sense to base that assessment on a release build so it will account for all of the optimizations performed by the JIT compiler.

Performance Benchmarks

When our code runs more slowly than we expect, simply observing the running application may give us some insights, but measuring performance precisely will allow us to target our optimization efforts more effectively.

Recording the time it takes for code to run—whether it's a complete end-to-end run or just a portion of a program—is known as *benchmarking*. More generally, a *benchmark* is a standard against which something is measured. By timing our code, we establish a benchmark with which to compare a new version, to determine whether our changes have made the code faster or slower, or have had no discernible effect.

Many unit-testing frameworks report how long it takes for the tests to run, and even the elapsed time taken for individual tests. Keeping an eye on these numbers is certainly worthwhile because a sudden increase can indicate that an efficiency problem has been introduced somewhere. This approach can be particularly valuable in an automated *continuous integration (CI)* service, in which changes from multiple contributors are automatically integrated into a program; we can set up a CI service to alert us if the timing of the unit tests begins to change. If a particular test that usually runs in a few hundred milliseconds starts taking considerably longer, we can focus on the piece of code being tested to see if further investigation is warranted.

A more fine-grained and precise approach to measuring how fast a section of code runs is to instrument the code itself. The basic technique is simple in principle: just before running the code to be measured, we create a timer to record the elapsed time, and when the code has finished running, we record the timer's measurement. Listing 8-1 shows a simple but naïve benchmark using the Stopwatch class from the System.Diagnostics namespace.

```
// Start the clock
var clock = Stopwatch.StartNew();

// Run the code to be measured
var result = SomeTask();

// Stop the clock, and record elapsed time
clock.Stop();
var millisecs = clock.ElapsedTicks * 1000.0 / Stopwatch.Frequency;
```

Listing 8-1: A simple benchmarking approach

The Stopwatch class is a lightweight high-resolution timer that records elapsed time with very high precision. The Stopwatch.Frequency value is the number of ticks per second, so by multiplying the count of elapsed ticks by 1000.0 before dividing by the frequency, we can report the time taken with millisecond granularity. This technique simply measures the elapsed time since the clock was started, so it can't, for instance, determine whether the code being measured is actually running for all that time. The clock continues to tick even if the code is interrupted (for example, by switching to a different thread).

Instrumenting code with a timer and recording it in the log or another audit trail can be a useful way to measure code running in a live system. However, measuring and reporting the performance takes time too, so we must be sure to take the measurements at a relatively high level. For instance, measuring and reporting how long code takes to respond to an HTTP request or call a remote procedure probably wouldn't significantly impact the application's performance. On the other hand, using this technique in a tight loop might well introduce more overhead than the cost of the loop itself.

Benchmarking is also a useful way to explore performance in a test environment, perhaps to compare alternative approaches to solving a specific problem. The technique in Listing 8-1 is naïve in that it measures the code only once. A more accurate approach for measuring performance would run the code many times and report the average time. We could write our own framework based on Listing 8-1, although a few freely available libraries for C# will do the heavy lifting for us, producing a report of the recorded performance along with other useful statistics, such as margin for error.

The Profiler

Benchmarking will tell us overall how quickly a piece of code runs, but to determine what the code does in detail, we need a *profiler*. Using a benchmarking tool in combination with profiling will give us the most accurate measurements. Among the several kinds of profiler available, the two most common are performance profilers and memory profilers.

A *memory profiler* will show us where our program allocates memory, how much is being used, and when it's garbage collected. If we need to find out which parts of our code are using the most CPU time or which methods are being called most often, a *performance profiler* will give us precise measurements, allowing us to target specific hot spots in the code and optimize them if necessary. While optimizing memory usage is important, in this chapter we'll focus on discovering bottlenecks in our code by using a performance profiler.

Performance profilers usually operate on a release build of a program and so take into account any optimizations applied by the compiler and JIT compiler. Measuring a debug build for its performance usually makes little sense, although sometimes it can be useful: comparing the results of profiling both a debug build and a release build of the same code, for instance, can provide insights into some of the optimizations the JIT compiler performs.

While performance measurements can give us an idea of where bottle-necks may be slowing our code, it's vital to keep in mind that a program's performance is affected by many factors other than the code, including the version of the CLR or the version of the software development kit (SDK) we use. Even running the same program twice on the same machine can produce a different result, depending on how cache memory is allocated or how instructions are pipelined by the CPU's scheduler. The JIT compiler may also apply different optimizations for each run, possibly further affecting the result. We must therefore be cautious of attaching too much importance to the absolute times in a profiler's report, and instead look for trends or obvious anomalies, such as results differing by an order of magnitude or more.

We'll use a performance profiler to selectively measure specific aspects of code and analyze the profiler's results. Remember that the specific results shown in this chapter are particular to the machine on which the test was performed, but we'll try multiple approaches, measuring each attempt so that we can identify some common, repeatable patterns in the results.

To demonstrate how this works, next we'll examine how simply changing a field's type can dramatically affect the performance of code that relies on using Equals.

Measuring Basic Performance with Equals

The Equals method is an often neglected aspect of code optimization in C#. This method is a good candidate for performance measurement because it's always available (since every type inherits it from the object base class) but also customizable (as a virtual member of object). In this section, we measure the default behavior of Equals for a simple value type so that we can compare the profiler's results with the results from overriding Equals with our own implementation.

Struct types inherit a value-based equality comparison from the ValueType class, overriding the default implementation defined by the object universal base class. This ensures that when we copy an instance of a struct, the copy compares equal to the original by comparing the fields of each instance. We might be tempted to rely on this behavior, rather than implementing our own override of the Equals method, because it keeps our type definitions shorter and simpler, like the Color struct in Listing 8-2.

```
public readonly struct Color
{
    public Color(int r, int g, int b)
        => (Red, Green, Blue) = (r, g, b);

    public int Red { get; }
    public int Green { get; }
    public int Blue { get; }
}
```

Listing 8-2: Defining a simple struct type

Two instances of `Color` that have the same property values will compare equal. Furthermore, like all structs, `Color` inherits a value-based implementation of `GetHashCode` from `ValueType`, ensuring that two equal `Color` values always produce the same hash code. Additionally, `Color` is an immutable type, making it suitable for use as a key in a data structure that relies on hash codes for efficiency. In Listing 8-3, we create many random `Color` instances and then add them to a `HashSet` in a simple test that we can use to measure how well the `Color` struct performs.

```
var rng = new Random(1);
var items = Enumerable.Range(0, 25000)
    .Select(_ => rng.Next())
    .Select(r => new Color(r >> 16 & 0xFF, r >> 8 & 0xFF, r & 0xFF))
    .ToHashSet();
```

Listing 8-3: Generating a hashing collection

This `Random` class is the Standard Library's *pseudorandom number generator*, the name for an algorithm that uses a deterministic process to produce a sequence of numbers that *appear* random. Notably, the `Random` class will produce the same sequence if it's initialized with the same *seed*—that is, the value used to calculate the first number of the sequence.

NOTE   *Different versions of .NET (or .NET Core) may produce different sequences for a given seed.*

In Listing 8-3, we use 1 as the seed and create new `Color` instances using the numbers generated by calling `Next` on the random-number generator. Since we use the same seed each time, we'll get the same sequence of `Color` instances each time the code runs. This characteristic is most often considered a downside of pseudorandom numbers, but it suits our purpose perfectly because we can run this code multiple times, and the same values for the `Color` instances will be generated for each run. In turn, comparing the performance of different runs is fair in that each run will be comparing identical sequences of `Color` values. We're using a randomly generated sequence to ensure that the final `HashSet` contains a reasonably realistic population of `Color` values.

In Listing 8-3, we create each `Color` instance by masking off the `Red`, `Green`, and `Blue` values from each random number. The profiler output in Table 8-1 shows the performance of the hash table's constructor. For this test, we're simply measuring elapsed time, also called *CPU sampling*, for each method.

Table 8-1: Profile Report of Creating the HashSet

Method	Time (ms)	Signature
87.9% HashSet`1..ctor	50	System.Collections.Generic.HashSet`1..ctor (IEnumerable, IEqualityComparer)
87.9% UnionWith	50	System.Collections.Generic.HashSet`1.UnionWith (IEnumerable)
87.9% AddIfNotPresent	50	System.Collections.Generic.HashSet`1.AddIfNotPresent(T, out Int32)
36.5% Equals	21	System.ValueType.Equals(Object)
14.0% [Garbage collection]	7.9	

We're focusing on the creation of the HashSet and ignoring everything else, including the random-number generation and creation of individual Color objects. Different profilers represent their reports differently, but the information presented is generally similar.

The indentation in the first column of this report shows the call stack being measured. The HashSet constructor on the first line calls a method named UnionWith, which in turn calls AddIfNotPresent. This last method eventually calls the Equals method. The leftmost value in the output shows the time spent by that method as a percentage of the test's total time. In our test, creating the initial sequence of Color values takes up the remainder of the time but isn't really relevant to testing Equals. The next field is the simple name of the method, followed by the absolute time in milliseconds spent in that method.

Finally, the fully qualified name of the method indicates which specific method is being reported. Since our simple Color struct doesn't provide its own implementation of Equals, the output shows that ValueType.Equals is used to add unique keys to the hash table.

As noted earlier, the actual times in milliseconds reported here could change based on a combination of many factors, so they shouldn't be taken literally. However, they establish a baseline we can use to compare the results of other tests.

Hidden Costs of Simplicity

Our Color type uses three values for the RGB components. Although they're being stored in int properties, each one 4 bytes wide, we use only 1 byte for each value by masking off the lowest 8 bits of each argument to Color's constructor. We might infer that we can save on storage space by storing the properties as byte fields rather than int. Listing 8-4 shows the changed Color struct.

```
public readonly struct Color
{
    public Color(int r, int g, int b)
        => (Red, Green, Blue) = ((byte)r, (byte)g, (byte)b);
```

```
    public byte Red { get; }
    public byte Green { get; }
    public byte Blue { get; }
}
```

Listing 8-4: Storing byte fields for color components

We still allow int arguments to the Color constructor so that our users won't have to explicitly cast the arguments to byte when creating Color values. Casting the int values explicitly to byte has the same effect as the masking operations we used in Listing 8-3: the value is truncated to just the lowest 8 bits. If we use this version of Color in the test to produce a HashSet from Listing 8-3, the results are quite different. Table 8-2 shows just the call tree for AddIfNotPresent.

Table 8-2: Profile Report of Adding Objects with byte Fields to the HashSet

Method	Time (ms)	Signature
99.9% AddIfNotPresent	7,494	System.Collections.Generic.HashSet`1 .AddIfNotPresent(T, out Int32)
39.6% Equals	2,967	System.ValueType.Equals(Object)
8.66% [Garbage collection]	650	
0.16% [Thread suspended]	12	

We see a dramatic change in the execution profile of the code, with the AddIfNotPresent method taking well over seven full seconds to complete. Comparing this report to Table 8-1, we can see clearly that the main reason for the extra time is the Equals method inherited by Color from the ValueType base class.

In some instances, ValueType.Equals can perform a *very* fast bitwise comparison, but with several caveats: this comparison can't be used if any field is a reference, a floating-point number, or a type that itself overrides Equals. Two different reference values could refer to objects of a type with its own Equals method, and a bitwise comparison would compare them as not equal, even if Equals would return true. For the same reason, any value type with its own Equals method could use that method to compare some values with different bit patterns as equal. Two floating-point numbers with matching bit patterns aren't necessarily equal; in particular, if both values are NaN, they shouldn't compare equal.

Another condition for the fast comparison to be used is that a struct must be *tightly packed*, meaning its fields don't require any padding to be properly aligned in memory. The three int fields in the original implementation of Color would automatically be aligned in memory. However, using byte instead means the fields aren't tightly packed, so we must use another, much slower comparison, with the substantial performance penalty shown in Table 8-2.

The ValueType.Equals Method

When the fast bitwise comparison isn't applicable, the implementation of Equals in ValueType is necessarily very general, because it must work for any struct type, regardless of the number of fields the struct has or their type. In addition to having fields of built-in primitive types, a struct can contain references to class instances and instances of other user-defined values, any of which may have its own custom Equals implementation.

The implementation of ValueType.Equals first must determine which fields need to be compared. It does this by using *reflection*—programmatically inspecting (or changing) the run-time structure of the program—to discover all the instance fields, which immediately comes with a quite significant run-time cost. Reflection isn't usually associated with high-performance algorithms, and this certainly accounts for the reduction in performance caused by altering our struct's int fields to use byte instead.

After determining the array of fields, ValueType.Equals obtains each field's value. If the field value isn't a null reference, its Equals method is called with the value from the corresponding field in the struct being compared. As a result, every value type field in both structs will be boxed in order to perform the comparison, because using reflection to obtain the values means each value is accessed via an object reference, adding further cost.

The root cause of our performance problem is that the change from using int properties to byte values means that the underlying backing fields of Color are no longer tightly packed. Consequently, ValueType.Equals can't use the fast bitwise comparison and instead employs reflection to discover the values to be compared. To address this issue, in Listing 8-5 we override the Equals method and provide our own implementation to compare the property values.

```
public readonly struct Color
{
    public Color(int r, int g, int b)
        => (Red, Green, Blue) = ((byte)r, (byte)g, (byte)b);

    public byte Red { get; }
    public byte Green { get; }
    public byte Blue { get; }

    public override bool Equals(object? obj)
        => obj is Color other &&
            Red == other.Red && Green == other.Green && Blue == other.Blue;
}
```

Listing 8-5: Overriding the Equals method

The report in Table 8-3 from rerunning the test shows that while we've substantially improved its speed, we still have work to do.

Table 8-3: How the Overridden Equals Method Performs

Method	Time (ms)	Signature
100% AddIfNotPresent	2,889	System.Collections.Generic.HashSet`1 .AddIfNotPresent(T, out Int32)
20.4% Equals	588	Color.Equals(Object)
8.15% [Garbage collection]	236	

Notice that our override of Equals is consuming a much smaller percentage of the overall time in AddIfNotPresent, although this approach is still much slower than the test using our original version of Color that had int properties.

This report tells us that the majority of the time was spent in the code of AddIfNotPresent as opposed to any methods called by it. To discover why, we'll use a different kind of profiling, sometimes known as *instrumentation profiling*, or *tracing*, which records the number of times each method is called in a program. Because this requires the profiler to intrusively measure a running program, the time measurements are often much higher; however, knowing which methods are being called most often is valuable information. Table 8-4 shows the tracing report for AddIfNotPresent and the methods called within it, including the number of times each method was called.

Table 8-4: Tracing Report for Equals

Method	Time (ms)	Number of calls	Signature
99.9% AddIfNotPresent	16,681	25,000	[...]
40.3% Equals	6,724	312,222,485	Color.Equals(Object)
1.76% [Garbage collection]	293	1,593	

This report has an extra column that shows the number of times each method was called during the program's execution. The tracing report took significantly longer to run, but more importantly, it shows the Equals method being invoked a huge number of times. In fact, the number of invocations of Equals is suspiciously close to the triangular number of 25,000— the number of elements in the original sequence. The *triangular number* of some number n is the sum of the whole numbers from 1 to n. When n is 25,000, the triangular number is 312,512,500.

While we've customized Equals for the Color struct, the HashSet class also uses GetHashCode when adding or searching for a key, and our Color type relies on the default GetHashCode implementation inherited from ValueType. Let's look at how this relates to the number of times Equals is called in our test.

The ValueType.GetHashCode Method

As Chapter 5 explained, the elements in a HashSet are unique; every key in the table exists only once. A new object is added to a HashSet only if it doesn't already exist in the table; otherwise, it's ignored.

When we add an item to the HashSet in this example, the implementation uses GetHashCode to identify existing keys with the same hash code. The fact that the hash codes are the same doesn't necessarily mean any of the existing keys have the same value as the new item. If no existing key has the same hash code as the new item, the new object is added to the table. If one or more existing keys have hash codes that match the new item's hash code, the Equals method is used to determine whether the item should be added. Each key with the same hash code is compared with the new item in turn, and if no match is found, the new item is added to the table as a new key.

Having Equals being called so often in our test indicates that GetHashCode for our Color type is producing hash codes that aren't well distributed. When the first element is added to the hash table, Equals isn't called at all, because there's nothing to compare with. If the second element has an identical hash code to the first, Equals is called to determine if they're identical keys. This process will repeat for each subsequent element that has the same hash code as an existing key.

If all of the Color objects in the initial sequence of 25,000 elements produce identical hash codes but have different values, adding the final new element will require a call to Equals for all of the existing 24,999 keys.

In fact, the default implementation of ValueType.GetHashCode inherited by the Color struct will likely produce many identical hash codes, regardless of whether the Color instances have different values. The reason is related to the poor performance of the implementation of Equals provided by ValueType, and it explains why the number of calls to Equals is so close to the triangular number of the sequence length.

If instances of a struct can be compared using the fast bitwise comparison for Equals, the ValueType.GetHashCode method produces hash codes based on the bit pattern of the instance in memory. If, on the other hand, the struct isn't eligible for the fast bitwise comparison, the default GetHashCode implementation considers only the first non-null instance field of the struct—the Red property in our Color type—with the result that we can get a maximum of only 256 unique hash codes. We solve that problem by implementing our own GetHashCode method to produce more unique hash codes, preferably so that each distinct Color value produces a unique hash code.

The HashCode.Combine Method

In Listing 8-6, we add our own override of GetHashCode for the Color struct to complement our overridden Equals method, and implement the new GetHashCode by using the HashCode.Combine method from the Standard Library.

```
public override bool Equals(object? obj)
    => obj is Color other &&
       Red == other.Red && Green == other.Green && Blue == other.Blue;

public override int GetHashCode()
    => HashCode.Combine(Red, Green, Blue);
```

Listing 8-6: Overriding a GetHashCode method

The `Combine` method produces well-distributed hash codes based on its inputs, and while we might be able to write our own carefully optimized replacement, doing so is far from trivial. Now when we run the test, we see that the combined effect of overriding both `Equals` and `GetHashCode` reduces the number of calls to the `Equals` method by a considerable amount, as shown in Table 8-5.

Table 8-5: Tracing Report for the Overridden `GetHashCode`

Method	Time (ms)	Number of calls	Signature
48.8% AddIfNotPresent	16	25,000	[...]
38.1% Combine	12	25,000	System.HashCode.Combine(T1, T2, T3)
1.42% Resize	0.5	12	System.Collections.Generic.HashSet`1 .Resize(Int32, Boolean)
0.27% Equals	0.09	18	Color.Equals(Object)

Even accounting for the overhead of counting the method calls, this report shows a vast improvement in speed compared with our previous results and demonstrates the close relationship between `Equals` and `GetHashCode`. We pay a high cost in efficiency if we accept the default behavior of `Equals` and `GetHashCode` provided by `ValueType` rather than implementing those methods ourselves in our custom struct types.

If we revisit the profile of our original struct that had `int` fields but no method overrides, we can see that even though that struct could be packed efficiently, the `Equals` method is still invoked much more frequently than in our latest version (see Table 8-6).

Table 8-6: Tracing Report for a Packed Struct with No Overrides

Method	Time (ms)	Number of calls	Signature
85.6% AddIfNotPresent	101	25,000	[...]
30.1% Equals	36	1,219,104	System.ValueType.Equals(Object)
7.54% [Garbage collection]	8.9	17	
0.42% Resize	0.5	12	System.Collections.Generic.HashSet`1 .Resize(Int32, Boolean)

We'd certainly notice a performance problem if we were to scale up the number of elements being added to the `HashSet`.

Besides `HashSet`, several other collection types rely on hash codes for efficiency, including `Dictionary` and `Lookup` types. Therefore, it's essential that we override both `Equals` and `GetHashCode` methods for any type that could be used as a key for hashing collections.

Optimizing Equality

While overriding both `Equals` and `GetHashCode` produces the most impressive performance improvements, we can do more to fine-tune equality comparisons. After all, the `Equals` method is used in circumstances other than when we're creating data structures that rely on hash codes.

Our `Color` struct is a relatively simple data type, and its `Equals` method is already quite efficient. To probe the characteristics of `Equals`, we'll make a much more complex `Purchase` value type, shown in Listing 8-7. The `Purchase` struct overrides both `Equals` and `GetHashCode` with custom implementations but doesn't yet implement the `IEquatable<Purchase>` interface. We'll implement that interface for `Purchase` later to see how that affects the performance of `Equals`.

```
public readonly struct Purchase
{
    public Purchase(Product item, DateTime ordered, int quantity)
        => (Item, Ordered, Quantity) = (item, ordered, quantity);

    public Product   Item { get; }
    public DateTime  Ordered { get; }
    public int       Quantity { get; }

    public override bool Equals(object? obj)
        => obj is Purchase other &&
           Item.Equals(other.Item) &&
           Ordered == other.Ordered && Quantity == other.Quantity;

    public override int GetHashCode()
        => HashCode.Combine(Item, Ordered, Quantity);
}
```

Listing 8-7: Defining a more complex data type, `Purchase`

The `Purchase` type has three fields, one of which is another nontrivial type named `Product`, shown here:

```
public readonly struct Product
{
    public Product(int id, decimal price, string name)
        => (Id, Price, Name) = (id, price, name);

    public int      Id { get; }
    public decimal  Price { get; }
    public string   Name { get; }
```

```
public override bool Equals(object? obj)
    => obj is Product other &&
        Id == other.Id && Price == other.Price && Name == other.Name;

public override int GetHashCode()
    => HashCode.Combine(Id, Price, Name);
}
```

The Equals method of Purchase needs to do a little more work than the Equals method for the Color type back in Listing 8-5. When we compare two Purchase instances for equality, the Equals method must also ensure that the Item properties match, which involves a method call to Product.Equals.

NOTE *The Purchase type is quite large—40 bytes plus padding, assuming a 64-bit architecture—so we should expect copying instances around to be less efficient than for the smaller Color type. That won't affect our profiling, though, as we'll still be comparing reports for the same types. We'll return to the cost of copying large struct instances in "Copying Large Instances" on page 272.*

Instead of a HashSet, we'll use the SequenceEqual method to compare two very large lists of Purchase objects, as shown in Listing 8-8. This process will exercise the Equals method, allowing us to measure its efficiency. To magnify the performance of Equals compared to the cost of the surrounding code, we increase the number of elements to 10 million.

```
var items = Enumerable.Range(0, 10_000_000)
    .Select(id => new Purchase(new Product(id, id, "Some Description"),
                                DateTime.MinValue, id))
    .ToList();

Assert.That(items.SequenceEqual(items), Is.True);
```

Listing 8-8: Testing to exercise equality

In the Enumerable.Range method, we use digit separators, available since C# v7.0, to make the large literal number easy for human readers to parse. Digit separators make no difference to the compiler: the number we use for the length of the initial sequence is still a plain int value.

The SequenceEqual method compares two sequences and returns true if they have the same elements in the same order. The algorithm obtains an element from each sequence and compares those elements by using the Equals method. SequenceEqual doesn't try to optimize its result by checking if the two sequences are in fact the *same* sequence, so here we create only one sequence of 10 million elements and compare it with itself. Table 8-7 shows the profiler report for the call to SequenceEqual.

Table 8-7: Exercising the Equals Method

Method	Time (ms)	Signature
77.5% SequenceEqual	1,227	System.Linq.Enumerable .SequenceEqual(IEnumerable, IEnumerable)
49.3% Equals	781	Purchase.Equals(Object)
24.3% [Garbage collection]	384	
10.6% Equals	168	Product.Equals(Object)
0.75% get_Item	12	Purchase.get_Item()
0.38% Unbox	6.0	System.Runtime.CompilerServices .CastHelpers.Unbox(Void*, Object)

We can see that garbage collection contributes a significant portion of the time required by Equals. Each call to Equals with a Purchase instance results in the argument being boxed, as Purchase is a struct and the parameter type of the Equals override is object, a reference type. Furthermore, the Purchase.Equals method calls Product.Equals, which also requires its argument to be boxed. The consequence is that we're allocating many boxed objects on the heap, placing the garbage collector under fairly significant pressure to keep memory usage under control.

In each Equals method, the parameter needs to be unboxed back to its original type so that its properties can be compared; the cost of unboxing the object parameter for each of the Equals methods is tiny but has a measurable impact. We can avoid the costs of boxing, and much of the associated cost of garbage collection, by implementing IEquatable<T> for both Purchase and Product types.

The Effect of IEquatable<T>

The SequenceEqual method automatically selects the best (the most efficient) implementation of Equals available to perform the comparisons. Internally, SequenceEqual uses the EqualityComparer helper class from Chapter 5 to determine how to compare elements. If the element type T implements IEquatable<T>, it's guaranteed to implement a type-safe overload of Equals, and that overload will be called by SequenceEqual.

If we implement the IEquatable<Purchase> interface and provide our own type-safe overload of Equals, the SequenceEqual method will use the IEquatable<Purchase> interface method by default, avoiding the need for boxing and then unboxing the argument to Equals. In turn, this reduces memory pressure because the arguments aren't copied to the heap, resulting in fewer objects for the garbage collector to inspect. In our example, those reductions are considerable, so implementing the IEquatable<Purchase> interface should produce a measurable benefit. Listing 8-9 shows the changes required in Purchase.

```
public readonly struct Purchase : IEquatable<Purchase>
{
    --snip--

    public bool Equals(Purchase other)
        => Item.Equals(other.Item) &&
            Ordered == other.Ordered && Quantity == other.Quantity;

    public override bool Equals(object? obj)
        => obj is Purchase other && Equals(other);
}
```

Listing 8-9: The IEquatable<Purchase> implementation

We've added an `Equals(Purchase other)` overload to perform the comparisons between each of the property values. The original `Equals` override still needs to unbox its `object` parameter in order to call the type-safe `Equals` overload, but the `SequenceEqual` method won't call `Equals(object?)` because we've also changed the `Purchase` declaration to implement the `IEquatable<Purchase>` interface. In Listing 8-10, we make similar changes in `Product` so that calling `Product.Equals` from the `Purchase.Equals` method won't require boxing the `Product` instance.

```
public readonly struct Product : IEquatable<Product>
{
    --snip--

    public bool Equals(Product other)
        => Id == other.Id && Price == other.Price && Name == other.Name;

    public override bool Equals(object? obj)
        => obj is Product other && Equals(other);
}
```

Listing 8-10: Implementing IEquatable<Product>

The results of the test from Listing 8-8, incorporating the changes from Listings 8-9 and 8-10, still with 10 million `Purchase` elements, are shown in Table 8-8.

Table 8-8: Measuring the Type-Safe Equals Method

Method	Time (ms)	Signature
62.6% SequenceEqual	546	System.Linq.Enumerable .SequenceEqual(IEnumerable, IEnumerable)
13.0% Equals	114	Purchase.Equals(Purchase)
5.48% Equals	48	Product.Equals(Product)
2.05% op_Equality	18	System.DateTime.op_Equality(DateTime, DateTime)
1.37% get_Ordered	12	Purchase.get_Ordered()
1.37% get_Item	12	Purchase.get_Item()

Comparing this report with Table 8-7, we can see that the total time for SequenceEqual has been greatly reduced, but also that our new Equals method is significantly faster than the original Purchase type's version without the type-safe implementation of IEquatable<Purchase>. Much of the difference is thanks to the lack of garbage collection, but we're also benefiting from removing the need to box and unbox the Purchase and Product values.

Property Accesses

Our Equals(Purchase) method spends a measurable portion of its time accessing properties to compare them. All of the properties of both Purchase and Product are automatic properties, and every access to those properties is a method call—for example, the calls to get_Item and get_Ordered shown in Table 8-8. While the JIT compiler may often be able to optimize such calls away by inlining the underlying method, there's no guarantee that it will. In Listing 8-11, we change Purchase to introduce our own private fields and alter Equals to compare the fields directly rather than accessing the property values for comparison.

```
public readonly struct Purchase : IEquatable<Purchase>
{
    public Purchase(Product item, DateTime ordered, int quantity)
        => (this.item, this.ordered, this.quantity) = (item, ordered, quantity);

    public Product  Item => item;
    public DateTime Ordered => ordered;
    public int      Quantity => quantity;

    public bool Equals(Purchase other)
        => item.Equals(other.item) &&
           ordered == other.ordered && quantity == other.quantity;

    public override bool Equals(object? obj)
        => obj is Purchase other && Equals(other);

    public override int GetHashCode()
        => HashCode.Combine(item, ordered, quantity);

    private readonly Product item;
    private readonly DateTime ordered;
    private readonly int quantity;
}
```

Listing 8-11: Comparing fields rather than properties

Although not shown here, we also change Product to replace its automatic properties with private fields. Table 8-9 shows the results of comparing 10 million elements the same way we have previously.

Table 8-9: Comparing the Performance of Fields vs. Properties

Method	Time (ms)	Signature
51.2% SequenceEqual	442	System.Linq.Enumerable .SequenceEqual(IEnumerable, IEnumerable)
9.73% Equals	84	Purchase.Equals(Purchase)
3.47% Equals	30	Product.Equals(Product)
1.41% op_Equality	12	System.DateTime.op_Equality(DateTime, DateTime)

Although replacing automatic properties with fields shows a small improvement, it's an example of a micro-optimization. We've cut the time needed for SequenceEqual by more than half compared to the version that didn't implement IEquatable<Purchase>, but we're still talking about only a few hundred milliseconds in absolute time. We had to dramatically increase the size of the sequence to amplify the results enough to be observable, and most applications don't routinely need to compare lists of 10 million elements.

Implementing the IEquatable<T> interface is a much more important step. Not only do we benefit from an increase in speed, but our type makes much more efficient use of memory by not needing to box the argument to Equals. Implementing IEquatable<T> for value types is more than a performance optimization; it establishes that our type follows that protocol, enabling certain library features to operate more efficiently and signaling efficiency to human readers too.

The Equality Operators

The final part of implementing a full set of equality comparisons for a type is to write our own operator== with its companion operator!=. Listing 8-12 shows those operators implemented for Purchase.

```
public readonly struct Purchase : IEquatable<Purchase>
{
    --snip--

    public bool Equals(Purchase other)
        => item == other.item &&
           ordered == other.ordered && quantity == other.quantity;

    public static bool operator==(Purchase left, Purchase right)
        => left.Equals(right);

    public static bool operator!=(Purchase left, Purchase right)
        => !left.Equals(right);
}
```

Listing 8-12: Implementing equality operators for Purchase

Again, we also add equality operators to the Product type (not shown), allowing us to compare the item field in Purchase by using == instead of calling its Equals method. Each operator implementation simply forwards to our type-safe Equals method, where the comparison is performed.

While we can write a test to call operator== in order to measure its performance characteristics, we can also arrange for the SequenceEqual method to call the operator rather than Equals by providing our own equality comparer.

The Generic IEqualityComparer<T> Interface

The SequenceEqual method doesn't invoke Equals directly on the sequence elements to compare them. Instead, it relies on an implementation of IEqualityComparer<T>, which is part of the Standard Library and declared in the System.Collections.Generic namespace.

An implementation of IEqualityComparer<T> requires an Equals method taking two parameters of type T, and a GetHashCode method with a single T parameter. The Standard Library provides some default implementations of IEqualityComparer<T>, including one for instances of T that implement the IEquatable<T> interface, which is what our uses of SequenceEqual have relied upon thus far.

The SequenceEqual method has an overload that takes a second parameter whose type is IEqualityComparer<T>, so we can provide our own implementation to be used instead of the default comparer. In Listing 8-13, we create our own implementation of the IEqualityComparer<T> interface, substituting Purchase as the generic parameter, and pass an instance of our custom comparer to SequenceEqual.

```
public sealed class EqualsOperatorComparer : IEqualityComparer<Purchase>
{
    public bool Equals(Purchase x, Purchase y)
        => x == y;

    public int GetHashCode(Purchase obj)
        => obj.GetHashCode();
}

var items = Enumerable.Range(0, 10_000_000)
    .Select(MakePurchase)
    .ToList();

Assert.That(items.SequenceEqual(items, new EqualsOperatorComparer()));
```

Listing 8-13: Creating a custom IEqualityComparer<T> implementation

Our implementation of IEqualityComparer<Purchase> defines its Equals method to compare its two parameter values with == instead of the parameter type's Equals method. We don't need a separate implementation for Product because the Equals member method in Purchase uses == directly to compare the Product values. Now, when we use SequenceEqual to compare two sequences of `Purchase` items, the algorithm will use `operator==` for the comparisons. Table 8-10 shows the profiler report for comparing 10 million `Purchase` items.

Table 8-10: How `operator==` Performs

Method	Time (ms)	Signature
48.8% SequenceEqual	475	`System.Linq.Enumerable.SequenceEqual [...]`
22.2% Equals	216	`EqualsOperatorComparer .Equals(Purchase, Purchase)`
9.28% op_Equality	90	`Purchase.op_Equality(Purchase, Purchase)`
9.28% Equals	90	`Purchase.Equals(Purchase)`
5.53% op_Equality	54	`Product.op_Equality(Product, Product)`
3.69% Equals	36	`Product.Equals(Product)`

When we define `operator==` for any type, the compiler translates it to a static method named `op_Equality`, shown in this profiler report. That method takes both of its parameters by value, so we're making a lot of copies of both `Purchase` and `Product` instances. We can reduce the number of copies needed by changing the `operator==` methods to take their parameters by reference instead.

Read-Only in Parameters

To reap the benefits of altering our `operator==` methods to take their parameters by reference rather than by value, we can use read-only in parameters. They are specifically intended for avoiding copies of large value type instances and are appropriate when we don't need to mutate the parameter variables.

We shouldn't expect a huge improvement, however, because we can't avoid all the copies being made when comparing the `Purchase` elements in our sequence. In particular, the `EqualsOperatorComparer.Equals` method must take its parameters by value to match the signature defined in the `IEqualityComparer<T>` interface.

Similarly, as shown in Listing 8-14, the type-safe `Equals` method defined in `Purchase` itself takes its parameter by value according to the `IEquatable<T>` interface, but we can add a new overload of `Equals` that uses an in parameter and use the same mechanism to alter the equality operators to take all their parameters by reference.

```
public readonly struct Purchase : IEquatable<Purchase>
{
    --snip--

    public bool Equals(in Purchase other)
        => item == other.item &&
```

```
        ordered == other.ordered && quantity == other.quantity;

    public bool Equals(Purchase other)
        => Equals(in other);

    public static bool operator==(in Purchase left, in Purchase right)
        => left.Equals(in right);

    public static bool operator!=(in Purchase left, in Purchase right)
        => !left.Equals(in right);
}
```

Listing 8-14: Overloading using in parameters

We make the Equals method with an in parameter the main implementation and forward to it from the equality operators and the implementation of IEquatable<Purchase>. Although in parameters are transparent to calling code, the rules for overloading will give preference to the method with no parameter modifiers, unless we add an in modifier to the argument when calling the method. Therefore, we explicitly select the overload with in parameters by adding the in keyword to the argument we pass wherever we call Equals.

NOTE   *Replacing value parameters with in parameters is a version-breaking change, requiring extra care if binary compatibility is a consideration.*

We don't need to change the implementation of our EqualsOperatorComparer to pass the arguments by reference, since our operator== method doesn't have an overload taking parameters by value. We can reuse the EqualsOperatorComparer from Listing 8-13 to run the test, with the results shown in Table 8-11.

Table 8-11: Results of Passing by Reference to operator==

Method	Time (ms)	Signature
45.1% SequenceEqual	437	System.Linq.Enumerable.SequenceEqual [...]
20.9% Equals	203	EqualsOperatorComparer.Equals(Purchase, Purchase)
10.5% op_Equality	102	Purchase.op_Equality(in Purchase, in Purchase)
9.23% Equals	90	Purchase.Equals(in Purchase)
7.38% op_Equality	72	Product.op_Equality(in Product, in Product)
7.38% Equals	72	Product.Equals(in Product)

Comparing these results to Table 8-10, we can see the improvement is quite modest. While we certainly get some benefit from avoiding copying Purchase objects, that benefit is limited to operator== actually being called. Table 8-12 shows a tracing report with counts of the number of method

calls, showing that the JIT compiler is inlining all but a very few calls to
operator==.

Table 8-12: Tracing Report for Comparing in Parameter Values

Method	Time (ms)	Number of calls	Signature
1.88% SequenceEqual	2,013	1 call	System.Linq.Enumerable.SequenceEqual [...]
0.69% Equals	735	10,000,000 calls	EqualsOperatorComparer.Equals(Purchase, Purchase)
[...]			
0.08% op_Equality	82	126,402 calls	Purchase.op_Equality(in Purchase, in Purchase)

While using in parameters in our definition of operator== is free in that
it requires no changes to calling code, we shouldn't expect too much from
it. We also shouldn't simply apply in parameters routinely, even when using
them wouldn't detract from a method's readability. Passing small value
types by reference may incur a penalty due to the extra level of indirection
required to access the value itself via a by-reference variable. As with any
optimization feature in the code, we should introduce in parameters only
where our measurements show that they're warranted.

How Type Affects Performance

Our choice of types in an application can affect its overall performance in
various ways. The types we use to represent values in an application are the
most important part of that choice because the other types will usually be
classes in any case. Values, on the other hand, can be represented as structs,
classes, records, or record structs. In this section, we'll examine some of
the factors that can help us decide between using struct types and class
types to implement those value types, and how much those factors affect
performance.

We often hear that structs, and therefore record structs, should be
small because it's expensive to copy large instances around in memory.
With that in mind, we'll start by attempting to isolate the cost of copying
instances from the other factors affecting performance.

Measuring the Cost of Copying

As with our previous performance measurements, we need to establish
a simple baseline against which we can compare further performance
reports. Since we want to measure the cost of copying a large value type,
first we have to measure the cost of copying a small, simple type, like the
IntField struct we create in Listing 8-15.

```
public readonly struct IntField : IEquatable<IntField>
{
    public IntField(int value)
        => this.value = value;

    public bool Equals(IntField other)
        => value == other.value;

    private readonly int value;
}
```

Listing 8-15: Creating a simple struct with a single `int` field

To exercise copying, we'll again use the `SequenceEqual` method, which copies elements from the sequences to compare them and will copy them again to call the `IEqualityComparer<T>.Equals` method. Here, we return to using the default equality comparer, which will call our type-safe `Equals` method, passing its argument by value. Listing 8-16 shows the code we'll use to produce our benchmark performance profile.

```
var items = Enumerable.Range(0, 10_000_000)
    .Select(i => new IntField(i))
    .ToList();

Assert.That(items.SequenceEqual(items));
```

Listing 8-16: Testing simple copies

For this test, we'll profile a debug build of this code to try to minimize the effects of the method inlining performed by the JIT compiler. Method arguments are copied only if the method is invoked normally, and inlining would make measuring the cost of those copies unreliable; two different runs of the code could easily make a different number of copies. Table 8-13 shows the CPU sampling report for comparing two sequences of 10 million `IntField` items in a debug build, which inhibits the JIT compiler from inlining method calls.

Table 8-13: Measuring the Cost of Copying a Simple Struct

Method	Time (ms)	Signature
57.0% SequenceEqual	90	System.Linq.Enumerable .SequenceEqual(IEnumerable, IEnumerable)
7.60% Equals	12	IntField.Equals(IntField)

The `SequenceEqual` algorithm does little other than obtain an element from each sequence and compare one to the other with `Equals`. The difference between the time taken by `Equals` and the total time spent in `SequenceEqual` here is all overhead, representing the time taken to obtain each pair of elements from the sequences and copy the arguments for `Equals`.

Copying Large Instances

Copying a simple struct type such as the `IntField` struct in Listing 8-15 is no more expensive than copying a plain `int` value; a simple test (not shown here) that compares two sequences of `int` values will confirm it. The `IntPlus3x16` struct in Listing 8-17, which adds three entirely redundant `Guid` fields, is significantly larger than the `IntField` struct. Each `Guid` is 16 bytes, making this struct somewhat larger than even the most generous recommended limit for the size of a value type.

```
public readonly struct IntPlus3x16 : IEquatable<IntPlus3x16>
{
    public IntPlus3x16(int value)
        => this.value = value;

    public bool Equals(IntPlus3x16 other)
        => value == other.value;

    private readonly int value;

    private readonly Guid _padding1 = Guid.Empty;
    private readonly Guid _padding2 = Guid.Empty;
    private readonly Guid _padding3 = Guid.Empty;
}
```

Listing 8-17: Creating an extremely large struct

Note one subtlety in the `IntPlus3x16` struct: the `Equals` method doesn't consider any of the `Guid` fields of the type, because they're always all identical in any case. The reason is that we're trying to measure just the cost of copying, so this `Equals` method performs precisely the same operations as the `IntField` type in Listing 8-15. While the padding fields play no part in the `Equals` method or any other operation, the `IntPlus3x16` type is a struct and therefore copied by value, so *every* field will be copied. We run the same test from Listing 8-16, with the results shown in Table 8-14.

Table 8-14: Measuring the Cost of Copying an Extra-Large Struct

Method	Time (ms)	Signature
52.5% SequenceEqual	228	System.Linq.Enumerable .SequenceEqual(IEnumerable, IEnumerable)
2.71% Equals	12	IntPlus3x16.Equals(IntPlus3x16)

Compare Table 8-14 with Table 8-13: the time spent in the `Equals` method is identical in both reports, although the `SequenceEqual` method has taken over twice as long to complete because of the extra overhead of copying the instances of the larger `IntPlus3x16` type. The `Equals` method in both tests is performing the same operation, so the increase in time must be entirely due to the cost of copying instances.

Weighing Object Construction Costs

The cost of copying a large struct is not the only aspect to consider when using a type with several fields. For one thing, equality comparisons will usually take every field or property into account, making those comparisons more costly than for a type with only one or two fields. Initializing an instance of a type with several fields also comes with a cost.

The Purchase and Product types in Listing 8-18 are the positional record struct equivalents of the Purchase and Product structs we defined earlier in Listing 8-7. Because they're record struct types, the compiler generates all the equality comparisons, making them much simpler to define than their struct counterparts.

```
public readonly record struct Product
    (int Id, decimal Price, string Name);

public readonly record struct Purchase
    (Product Item, DateTime Ordered, int Quantity);
```

Listing 8-18: Defining Product and Purchase as record structs

We'll use the CompareSequences method shown in Listing 8-19 to create a sequence of Purchase instances and record the performance. We return here to profiling a release build so that the results account for any optimizations afforded by the JIT (or AOT) compiler.

```
private static Purchase MakePurchase(int id)
    => new Purchase(new Product(id, id, "Some Description"),
        DateTime.MinValue, id);

public static void CompareSequences(int count)
{
    var items = Enumerable.Range(0, count)
        .Select(MakePurchase)
        .ToList();

    Assert.That(items.SequenceEqual(items));
}
```

Listing 8-19: Creating a sequence of randomly generated objects

The CompareSequences method follows a pattern similar to that we've used previously to create a sequence and then call SequenceEqual to compare the elements. For the purposes of making the performance report clear, we use MakePurchase as a method group argument for the Select expression. That way, we can measure its performance directly, without introducing any overhead by using a lambda expression—something we'll return to in "How Common Idioms and Practices Affect Performance" on page 279. Table 8-15 shows the profiler report for creating 10 million Purchase objects using the MakePurchase method.

Table 8-15: Performance Report for Creating the Purchase Sequence

Method	Time (ms)	Signature
29.4% MakePurchase	294	MakePurchase(Int32)
2.45% op_Implicit	25	System.Decimal.op_Implicit(Int32)
2.03% Purchase..ctor	20	Purchase..ctor(Product, DateTime, Int32)
1.41% Product..ctor	14	Product..ctor(Int32, Decimal, String)

While the nested constructor for the Product type increases the time taken to create Purchase objects, the majority of the time is spent within the implementation of MakePurchase, suggesting that initializing the instances and copying them around is the costlier factor. In particular, creating a new Product and then copying the instance to the Purchase constructor is one copy we can avoid by making Product a reference type.

Reference Type Performance

When we copy a reference variable, the object instance isn't copied at all, making the copy inexpensive. Here we make Product a sealed record instead of a read-only record struct:

```
public sealed record Product
    (int Id, decimal Price, string Name);
```

Records using this positional syntax are immutable reference types by default. For the Product type, the compiler inserts init-only properties for the Id, Price, and Name properties, meaning that one instance can be safely and efficiently referenced by several containing objects. Since none of the properties has a set accessor, there's no risk of inadvertent changes being made via aliasing references. More pertinently for our test, once the Product instance is created, only the reference to it needs to be passed to the Purchase constructor.

For this test, we leave the Purchase type as a record struct, since we're trying to avoid having to copy its nested Product. However, using a reference type for Product introduces other overhead, as we can see in the profiler report in Table 8-16 for creating 10 million Purchase objects.

Table 8-16: Performance Report for Creating Reference Type Values

Method	Time (ms)	Signature
77.8% MakePurchase	1,409	MakePurchase(Int32)
34.9% [Garbage collection]	632	
0.33% Product..ctor	6.0	Product..ctor(Int32, Decimal, String)
0.33% Purchase..ctor	6.0	Purchase..ctor(Product, DateTime, Int32)

The MakePurchase method is significantly slower than in Table 8-15, with the main culprit being garbage collection. Changing Product to be a record rather than a record struct has put considerable pressure on the garbage collector, which takes time even if it can't collect any objects.

The lesson here is that the common advice to use value types for objects that are short-lived is at least partly related to memory pressure and the cost of garbage collection. Value type instances, because they aren't allocated on the heap, don't incur those costs. Copying even huge object instances isn't always the most significant expense, so changing large value types to be reference types to avoid copying can, as in this example, have a detrimental effect on a program's overall performance.

We have other factors to consider. If, for instance, we expect many of the Purchase objects in an application to have identical Product values, we may benefit considerably by having all those Purchase instances sharing the same Product instance, making a reference type implementation much more attractive.

Benefits of Reference Equality

The MakePurchase method from Listing 8-19 that we've been using to create Purchase instances creates a new Product object for each Purchase object. In Listing 8-20, we change MakePurchase so that rather than creating a new Product each time, we assign one of a small number of shared Product instances to each new Purchase. Since Product is a record and therefore a reference type, each Product will be shared by many Purchase objects.

```
private static readonly List<Product> SharedProducts = new()
{
    new Product(0, 0, "Some Description"),
    new Product(1, 1, "Some Description"),
    new Product(2, 2, "Some Description"),
    new Product(3, 3, "Some Description"),
    new Product(4, 4, "Some Description"),
};

private static Purchase MakePurchase(int id)
{
    var component = SharedProducts[id % SharedProducts.Count];
    return new Purchase(component, DateTime.MinValue, id);
}
```

Listing 8-20: Sharing references among objects

We initialize a short list of Product instances before creating any Purchase objects. A Product reference is selected from this list according to the id value used to create a Purchase. Now that the MakePurchase method isn't creating any new Product instances, we'd expect it to run much more quickly, which the report in Table 8-17 confirms.

Table 8-17: Assigning Preallocated Product Objects

Method	Time (ms)	Signature
17.1% MakePurchase	86	MakePurchase(Int32)
2.38% Purchase..ctor	12	Purchase..ctor(Product, DateTime, Int32)
1.18% get_Item	5.9	System.Collections.Generic.List`1 .get_Item(Int32)

More significantly, comparing Purchase instances for equality will now be much faster because so many of them share a Product instance. The implementation of Equals for record types includes the simple optimization of starting with an identity comparison of the two references. When two Product variables that are being compared both refer to the same instance in memory, there's no need to continue checking the individual fields, since they must be identical. Table 8-18 shows the report for comparing sequence elements for 10 million Purchase objects.

Table 8-18: Comparing Sequences with Shared References

Method	Time (ms)	Signature
68.3% SequenceEqual	350	System.Linq.Enumerable .SequenceEqual(IEnumerable, IEnumerable)
27.1% Equals	139	Purchase.Equals(Purchase)
11.7% get_Default	60	System.Collections.Generic .EqualityComparer`1.get_Default()
9.36% Equals	48	System.Collections.Generic .GenericEqualityComparer`1.Equals(T, T)
3.52% Equals	18	Product.Equals(Product)

If we run the same test by using a record struct for Product—that is, assigning one of a few precreated instances of Product to each Purchase—we can compare the performance of sharing references versus copying each Product. Table 8-19 shows the report for SequenceEqual for 10 million Purchase objects when Product is a record struct.

Table 8-19: Comparing Sequences with Copied Instances

Method	Time (ms)	Signature
59.5% SequenceEqual	591	System.Linq.Enumerable .SequenceEqual(IEnumerable, IEnumerable)
13.3% Equals	132	Purchase.Equals(Purchase)
12.7% Equals	126	System.Collections.Generic .GenericEqualityComparer`1.Equals(T, T)
9.01% Equals	89	Product.Equals(Product)
1.22% Equals	12	System.DateTime.Equals(DateTime)
0.60% get_Default	6.0	System.Collections.Generic .EqualityComparer`1.get_Default()

Although the headline time for the `Purchase.Equals` method is almost identical in each case, the `SequenceEqual` method using the record struct in Table 8-19 is considerably slower than for the record in Table 8-18. Record structs can't take advantage of the simple reference identity optimization available to records, although many of the calls to `Product.Equals` will have been inlined by the JIT compiler. The result is that we see the extra cost of having to copy the record struct values and compare their fields in `SequenceEqual`, rather than `Purchase.Equals`.

Measuring the Compiler-Generated Equals Method

The positional record struct syntax used in Listing 8-18 for the `Purchase` and `Product` types makes their definition compact, but that comes with minor, although measurable, efficiency compromises. The type-safe `Equals` method implementing the `IEquatable<T>` interface for records and record structs is generated by the compiler, whether or not they use the positional syntax. While convenient, that's not necessarily the most efficient implementation. When we're working with many objects, it can be worth our while to write our own `Equals` method for record and record struct types, in which case the compiler won't generate one for us.

You saw in Chapter 5 that the compiler inserts code to obtain the default `EqualityComparer` object for each field. For example, Listing 8-21 shows roughly the `Equals` method created by the compiler for the `Purchase` record struct in Listing 8-18.

```
public bool Equals(Purchase other)
    => EqualityComparer<Product>.Default.Equals(_Item_field, other._Item_field) &&
       EqualityComparer<DateTime>.Default.Equals(_Ordered_field, other._Ordered_field) &&
       EqualityComparer<int>.Default.Equals(_Quantity_field, other._Quantity_field);
```

Listing 8-21: A record struct's Equals method

The real names of the backing fields assigned by the compiler are invalid in regular C#, so there's no chance they could clash with any of our own identifiers; the names used here merely illustrate the idea. Despite using the backing fields directly rather than accessing the properties to perform the comparisons, obtaining the default `EqualityComparer` implementation for each field on *every call* to `Equals` could impair efficiency. Table 8-20 shows the profiler output when using the `SequenceEqual` method to compare two lists of 10 million `Purchase` record struct objects.

Table 8-20: Comparing Sequences with Record Struct Instances

Method	Time (ms)	Signature
55.7% SequenceEqual	558	System.Linq.Enumerable .SequenceEqual(IEnumerable, IEnumerable)
13.7% Equals	138	Purchase.Equals(Purchase)
10.2% Equals	102	System.Collections.Generic .GenericEqualityComparer`1.Equals(T, T)
3.58% Equals	36	Product.Equals(Product)
1.80% Equals	18	System.Decimal.Equals(Decimal)
0.60% Equals	6.0	System.Int32.Equals(Int32)
0.60% get_Default	6.0	System.Collections.Generic .EqualityComparer`1.get_Default()

While the JIT compiler may inline some or all of the uses of the `EqualityComparer<T>.Default` property and the calls to its `Equals` method, there's no guarantee that it will be able to do so. As we did earlier when replacing property accesses with fields, we can define our own `Equals` method to directly compare the values without needing to use `EqualityComparer<T>`. However, we can't access the compiler-generated backing fields for the properties generated for a positional record struct. Instead, in Listing 8-22 we use a simple record struct for `Purchase`, where we define our own private fields and a constructor to initialize them.

```
public readonly record struct Purchase
{
    public Purchase(Product item, DateTime ordered, int quantity)
        => (this.item, this.ordered, this.quantity) =
            (item, ordered, quantity);

    --snip--

    public bool Equals(Purchase other)
        => item.Equals(other.item) &&
            ordered.Equals(other.ordered) && quantity == other.quantity;

    private readonly Product item;
    private readonly DateTime ordered;
    private readonly int quantity;
}
```

Listing 8-22: Constructing a private field for the Purchase struct

We also add our own implementation of `Equals` to directly compare the fields we've defined. This custom `Equals` replaces the implementation that the compiler would have introduced had we not defined our own. We'd also need to add properties to expose the field values, although neither that nor the `Product` type, which changes in a similar way, is shown here. Rerunning the code to compare two sequences of 10 million `Purchase` items produces the report shown in Table 8-21.

Table 8-21: A Comparison Using Customized Equals

Method	Time (ms)	Signature
100% SequenceEqual	440	System.Linq.Enumerable .SequenceEqual(IEnumerable, IEnumerable)
12.3% Equals	54	Purchase.Equals(Purchase)
8.18% Equals	36	Product.Equals(Product)
1.36% Equals	6.0	System.DateTime.Equals(DateTime)

By providing our own Equals method, we've improved the performance of SequenceEqual by around 20 percent compared with the results in Table 8-20, partly because our implementation may be giving the JIT compiler more effective opportunities for inlining code. Comparing larger sequences produces similar results, so if we're particularly sensitive to performance and frequently compare many items, this kind of optimization may be beneficial.

The performance improvement we see here occurs primarily because Purchase is a relatively complex type. A much simpler positional record struct—for example, one with a single int field—most likely wouldn't benefit from the optimizations we made in Purchase and Product. The principal benefit of the positional record syntax is its simplicity, which makes it clear to any reader what the type represents. We sacrificed that simplicity for a small gain in raw performance, an improvement that was visible only with the help of a profiler. This example highlights the importance of measuring performance before trying to hand-optimize our code by second-guessing the compiler.

How Common Idioms and Practices Affect Performance

Some common practices in C# draw undue criticism regarding performance. It's natural and common to believe that a higher level of abstraction in source code comes with a cost in performance, and that's true to some extent: C# is a *high-level* programming language, and our programs are ultimately translated to native machine code over multiple steps. We could handcraft our own machine code to perform the same task, but C# code is more portable, more easily maintained, considerably less error-prone, and much easier to read and write than machine code. Those benefits usually far outweigh any cost in performance.

It's not, however, universally true that high-level code results in performance penalties. In this section, we'll investigate looping and pattern matching, two common C# features that enable us to succinctly express complex ideas in C# while providing performance comparable or even superior to their lower-level counterparts.

Looping and Iteration

In this chapter, we've used LINQ in its *fluent syntax* form several times for the purposes of creating sequences of objects. LINQ, which has been part of C# for many years, will be recognizable to most programmers with more than a passing familiarity for the language and its idioms. Listing 8-23 shows an example of using the fluent syntax to create a list of Purchase objects.

```
private static Purchase MakePurchase(int id)
    => new Purchase(new Product(id, id, "Some Description"),
        DateTime.MinValue, id);

var items = Enumerable.Range(0, count)
    .Select(i => MakePurchase(i))
    .ToList();
```

Listing 8-23: LINQ fluent syntax

LINQ has an alternative *query syntax* that some C# programmers find more agreeable. Listing 8-24 shows the equivalent query syntax for creating the items sequence in Listing 8-23.

```
var query = from i in Enumerable.Range(0, count)
            select MakePurchase(i);

var items = query.ToList();
```

Listing 8-24: LINQ query syntax

The compiler generates identical CIL for both Listings 8-23 and 8-24, so the choice between them is primarily driven by which we find clearer to read. One optimization is possible, although it can be applied only to the fluent version: avoiding the lambda as an argument to the Select method. That lambda needs to capture the i variable so the compiler will generate a closure object, which results in an extra level of indirection to call the MakePurchase method. To avoid the closure, we can instead pass MakePurchase as a method group argument, as shown in Listing 8-25.

```
var items = Enumerable.Range(0, count)
    .Select(MakePurchase)
    .ToList();
```

Listing 8-25: Optimizing LINQ by using a method group

To compare the efficiency of each approach, first we profile the version from Listing 8-23, which uses a lambda. Table 8-22 shows the report for creating a list of 10 million items.

Table 8-22: Performance of Creating a Sequence Using LINQ with a Lambda

Method	Time (ms)	Signature
98.1% ToList	415	System.Linq.Enumerable .ToList(IEnumerable)
36.0% MakePurchase	152	MakePurchase(Int32)
31.3% <Closure> b__3_0	132	<> c. <Closure> b__3_0(Int32)
31.3% MakePurchase	132	MakePurchase(Int32)

The identifier name <>c is the closure object the compiler generates to capture the i variable, and one example of the compiler introducing names that would be illegal in our own code. The closure has an instance method, <Closure> b__3_0, which in turn calls our MakePurchase method. The MakePurchase method makes two appearances in this report—both inside and outside the closure method—as a result of the JIT compiler inlining some calls to the <Closure> b__3_0 method and calling MakePurchase directly.

The report in Table 8-23 shows the performance when using the method group approach to create 10 million items.

Table 8-23: Performance of Creating a Sequence Using LINQ with a Method Group

Method	Time (ms)	Signature
100% ToList	430	System.Linq.Enumerable.ToList(IEnumerable)
71.9% MakePurchase	309	MakePurchase(Int32)

Somewhat counterintuitively, the version with the closure object was just slightly faster than that with the method group. We shouldn't read too much into that, as the difference is well within the margin for error when comparing runs. However, it does tell us that no matter the absolute difference, using a lambda carries no significant performance penalty.

The closure object representing the lambda is created only once for the whole expression, not for every element produced for the Select method. Even though the closure object represents an extra level of indirection for each call to MakePurchase, the JIT compiler inlines many of the calls to the closure's <Closure> b__3_0 method and either calls MakePurchase directly or inlines its contents too.

We could create a similar sequence in a few other ways. Let's investigate two common approaches to see how their performance compares with using LINQ.

The Iterator Approach

Iterators are a fundamental part of C# and underpin other higher-level features, including LINQ. In fact, LINQ has become so ubiquitous in modern C# that it can be easy to forget that it's based on two system interfaces: the IEnumerable<T> interface, which is an abstract view of a sequence of elements of type T, and the IEnumerator<T> interface, which represents an iterator that can get each element of an IEnumerable<T> one at a time. The basic mechanics are that the IEnumerable<T> interface has a single method named GetEnumerator that returns an implementation of IEnumerator<T>.

Both interfaces are largely hidden in modern code, although IEnumerable<T> remains important as the protocol for types that represent sequences and as the home of the extension methods, such as Select and Where, that make up most of the LINQ system.

The IEnumerator<T> interface also forms the basis for the foreach loop, which is one way of enumerating the elements of a sequence that implements `IEnumerable<T>`. In Listing 8-26, we write our own simple `ToList` method, which allows us to record its performance for comparison with the LINQ equivalents. Our `ToList` uses foreach to populate a list of `Purchase` objects and therefore depends on the iterator provided by the `Enumerable` `.Range` method.

```
public static List<Purchase> ToList(int count)
{
    var items = new List<Purchase>();
    foreach(var i in Enumerable.Range(0, count))
    {
        items.Add(MakePurchase(i));
    }

    return items;
}
```

Listing 8-26: Populating a list using foreach

Comparing our `ToList` method with the LINQ version in Listing 8-23, the first thing to notice is that we need to declare the target list of `Purchase` objects before the loop. The foreach loop obtains an `IEnumerator<int>` from `Enumerable.Range`, and the body of the foreach block is run for each element in the iterator. We can see the basic mechanics when we look at the profiler's report for the `ToList` method in Table 8-24.

Table 8-24: Profiling the Iterator Approach

Method	Time (ms)	Signature
100% ToList	638	ToList(Int32)
41.2% AddWithResize	263	System.Collections.Generic.List`1 .AddWithResize(T)
38.1% MakePurchase	243	MakePurchase(Int32)
0.95% MoveNext	6.1	System.Linq.Enumerable+ RangeIterator .MoveNext()
0.95% get_Current	6.0	System.Linq.Enumerable+ Iterator`1 .get_Current()

This profile report shows the workings of the foreach construct; the get_Current and MoveNext methods belong to the `IEnumerator<T>` interface and, as their names suggest, allow us to obtain the current element and move the iterator to the next item in the sequence.

This report also shows that our handcrafted `ToList` is considerably slower than the LINQ version reported in Table 8-22, but we haven't made optimal use of the `List<Purchase>` facilities. Since we know in advance the number of items we need, we can avoid most of the expense of the `AddWithResize` method and specify the list's capacity in the constructor call like this:

```
var items = new List<Purchase>(count);
```

By explicitly requesting a capacity, we allocate enough memory for count items before adding new elements so that the list won't need resizing when it runs out of space. If we rerun our profile test, as Table 8-25 shows, it's much more in line with the previous tests.

Table 8-25: Preallocating a List's Capacity

Method	Time (ms)	Signature
100% ToList	426	ToList(Int32)
63.0% MakePurchase	268	MakePurchase(Int32)
4.28% MoveNext	18	System.Linq.Enumerable+ RangeIterator .MoveNext()
1.41% get_Current	6.0	System.Linq.Enumerable+ Iterator`1 .get_Current()

Our tests demonstrate that using LINQ, at least for the reasonably simple task of generating a sequence of elements, is at least as efficient as using the foreach loop. We can try one other approach, however: the for loop.

The Loop Approach

Our method of creating a list of Purchase objects is based on creating a sequence of int values and translating them with the Select method into a new sequence of Purchase objects. Listing 8-27 shows how we achieve the same result with a basic for loop, which doesn't rely on iterators and merely runs the body of the loop the number of times specified in the loop condition.

```
public static List<Purchase> ToList(int count)
{
    var items = new List<Purchase>(count);
    for(int i = 0; i != count; ++i)
    {
        items.Add(MakePurchase(i));
    }
    return items;
}
```

Listing 8-27: Using a simple for loop

As we did for the foreach loop, we must create the target List<Purchase> before entering the loop, and we use the constructor to set its capacity. In the loop's body, we use the MakePurchase method to add a new Purchase as we have previously. Table 8-26 shows the profiler report for creating a list of 10 million Purchase objects with the for loop.

Table 8-26: The Direct for Loop Performance

Method	Time (ms)	Signature
100% ToList	417	ToList(Int32)
67.3% MakePurchase	281	MakePurchase(Int32)
5.70% op_Implicit	24	System.Decimal.op_Implicit(Int32)

Once again, there's no significant difference between the performance of the for loop approach and that of the other approaches we've tried. The main difference between using LINQ and using either the foreach or for loop is one of style: the LINQ code is more direct and allows us to express our intent declaratively, whereas the for and foreach loops are more procedural. The LINQ expression allows us to focus on the outcome we require, whereas both looping approaches focus on the steps or instructions to follow.

Pattern Matching and Selection

One common benefit of a declarative rather than procedural style is that we write less code to achieve the same result. While this saves on the amount of typing we do, that is just a side effect. The real benefit comes from having less syntax for a human reader to comprehend. Replacing explicit loops with LINQ-style functional expressions is one example. Many of the LINQ expressions are based on loops internally, but the loop constructs themselves are hidden from user code. Manually iterating sequences with loops and explicit conditions can be prone to errors, and complex loop constructs are generally harder for a human reader to follow than a call to a method like Select or ToList.

The other common application of declarative techniques is in selection code: replacing if and switch statements with pattern-matching expressions.

Consider the constructor in Listing 8-28, which validates the parameter value by matching it against the rules specified by some patterns.

```
private const double ZeroKelvin = -273.15;

private Temperature(double celsius)
    => amount = celsius switch
    {
        double.NaN
            => throw new ArgumentException(--snip--),

        < ZeroKelvin or double.PositiveInfinity
            => throw new ArgumentOutOfRangeException(--snip--),

        _ => celsius
    };
```

Listing 8-28: Pattern matching for validation

The Temperature constructor throws an exception if the argument given is double.NaN and also prohibits values that are less than ZeroKelvin or equal to PositiveInfinity. Values for the celsius parameter that don't match either of those rules are assigned to the amount field by the discard pattern, which is the final pattern in the switch expression.

Compare Listing 8-28 with Listing 8-29, which achieves exactly the same outcome but uses if...else statements to test the incoming parameter value.

```
private Temperature(double celsius)
{
    if(celsius is double.NaN)
    {
        throw new ArgumentException(--snip--);
    }
    else if(celsius < ZeroKelvin || celsius is double.PositiveInfinity)
    {
        throw new ArgumentOutOfRangeException(--snip--);
    }
    else
    {
        this.amount = celsius;
    }
}
```

Listing 8-29: Chaining if and else for validation

We could make this code less syntax-heavy by removing the redundant else statements and allowing the if blocks to fall through if the value doesn't meet the if condition. While doing so would make the code shorter, it's more error-prone if new conditions are added.

Another alternative is to use a switch statement, as shown in Listing 8-30.

```
switch (celsius)
{
    case double.NaN:
        throw new ArgumentException(--snip--);

    case < ZeroKelvin:
    case double.PositiveInfinity:
        throw new ArgumentOutOfRangeException(--snip--);

    default:
        this.amount = celsius;
        break;
}
```

Listing 8-30: Using a switch statement for validation

This version is closer to the switch expression in Listing 8-28, and the two forms of switch can be easily confused. The principal difference is that here we assign the amount field as part of the default leg, whereas in the switch expression, the amount field is assigned the value of the whole expression.

In a departure from the rest of this chapter, we don't need to run a performance profile to compare Listings 8-28 through 8-30 because the compiler produces almost identical code for each—broadly, the same code as shown in Listing 8-29. The compiler may change the order of the conditions in the CIL, but that doesn't change the logic in any way.

Summary

We do not consider it as good engineering practice to consume a resource lavishly just because it happens to be cheap.
—Niklaus Wirth, *Project Oberon: The Design of an Operating System, a Compiler, and a Computer*

Code optimized by hand is often harder for a human reader to follow, usually because it frequently involves replacing simple idioms, such as loops and pattern matching, with lower-level constructs. When a program runs more slowly than we think it should, it can be tempting to dive straight in and change the parts of the code we suspect are bottlenecks. Programmers' optimization instincts are, however, notoriously unreliable. We're likely to make our code more difficult to read while failing to improve performance in any meaningful way.

Optimizing code by hand is almost always an exercise in exchanging clarity and simplicity for performance. We can judge whether this is a reasonable trade only by measuring the performance before and after the change. Even when we improve performance in a section of code, we must still decide whether we've made the code less clear and, if so, whether the change is justified. We must also be certain that our optimizations haven't changed the program's behavior in any way. Slow, correct code is always preferable to incorrect code, however good its performance. That's not to say that good enough can't be correct—frequently a compromise is necessary between performance and accuracy or precision—but we need to know the point at which inaccurate really does mean incorrect.

The use of well-known idioms and patterns helps human readers easily understand code. Correspondingly, when we depart from those common designs, we make our code harder to follow. Therefore, we must be selective in applying optimizations to the areas of code that will bring the greatest benefits.

Overriding the behavior of Equals isn't difficult for the vast majority of types, but it adds an implementation detail that represents extra cognitive overhead for anyone who needs to *understand* our code.

Using records to represent value-like types removes much of that added complexity because the compiler generates the correct implementations for us. However, even accepting that default behavior won't necessarily yield the most efficient code.

Careful code optimization, supported by evidence from a profiler, can yield better performance in both speed *and* memory use. Modern computers are fast and usually have more than enough memory, but that doesn't mean we should waste either resource.

AFTERWORD

*There are two ways of constructing a software design: One way is to make it so simple
that there are obviously no deficiencies, and the other way is to make it so complicated
that there are no obvious deficiencies. The first method is far more difficult.*
—Tony (C.A.R.) Hoare, 1980 Turing Award Lecture

Computer programming is a subtle art. A successful programmer needs more than knowledge of a programming language's syntax. Getting the most out of any programming language requires a deep understanding of its *mechanics* (how the syntax elements fit together) and its *semantics* (how those elements define and control the resulting program's behavior).

Semantics can be low level, such as the effects of copy-by-value behavior on equality comparisons between objects, or more conceptual, such as the application of different kinds of polymorphism. Semantics also plays a part in application design: carefully designed objects can express different concepts in a system, giving the code structure and meaning.

Understanding the mechanics and semantics of C# allows us to write code that makes better use of the language constructs. This comes with several potential benefits: more efficient use of memory and processor resources; simpler, easier-to-understand code (by other programmers as well as ourselves); and an enhanced capability to add new features and diagnose errors.

When designing a system, whatever its size and purpose, it's easy to focus on the big architectural components that form the application's overall shape. Even when a design is emergent—that is, it takes shape organically as we start creating features—the fine-grained values are easily forgotten or dismissed as the small, passive bits of data passed between the more interesting system interfaces. In this book, we've explored the relationship between those values and other application elements because recognizing value types as the *currency* of information in a system gives us opportunities not only to better express the overall design, but also to clarify the purpose of the code that uses them. Rich custom value types help us establish a ubiquitous language in an application that plays an important part in conveying a design and its overall purpose. They also enable the compiler to catch more errors before run time.

Addressing every feature of a complex language like C# in a book like this is not practical, partly because C# is an evolving language. Its features expand constantly to meet the needs of programmers in all domains. This is a Good Thing™ because the software development landscape is also continually evolving, but C# programming practitioners are responsible for keeping up with that progress. In this book, I've presented numerous techniques and features to help you better understand C# as it is today, and I hope I've also inspired you to explore the characteristics, performance, and semantics of features that the C# language designers add in the future.

Understanding the intricacies of C# semantics for value and value-like types can be challenging, but your effort will be rewarded with richer, clearer designs that are easier to maintain and extend. I hope this book has given you a deeper appreciation for and knowledge of the diverse facilities that C# provides for creating these types, and, most importantly, I hope it has made you a better programmer.

APPENDIX

FURTHER READING

Chapter 1

- The simplified equations for projectile motion used in the examples are explained on Wikipedia at *https://en.wikipedia.org/wiki/Projectile_motion*.

- Frances Buontempo's *Genetic Algorithms and Machine Learning for Programmers* (Pragmatic Bookshelf, 2019) has a whole section on ballistics. This chapter's initial example was taken from that book and then abused for didactic reasons.

- You can find out more about the problem of primitive obsession, and its antidotes, here:

  - "Primitive Obsession" wiki page, *https://wiki.c2.com/?PrimitiveObsession*
  - Refactoring Guru website, *https://refactoring.guru/smells/primitive-obsession*
  - Fit wiki page, *http://fit.c2.com/wiki.cgi?WholeValue*
  - "The CHECKS Pattern Language of Information Integrity," by Ward Cunningham, *http://c2.com/ppr/checks.html*

- The Quantity pattern is described in Martin Fowler's *Analysis Patterns: Reusable Object Models* (Addison-Wesley Professional, 1996). The Primitive Obsession code smell is identified in his book *Refactoring: Improving the Design of Existing Code* (Addison-Wesley Professional, 2018).

- Mixing up the units of values in calculations can have serious consequences; see "When NASA Lost a Spacecraft Due to a Metric Math Mistake" by Ajay Harish: *https://www.simscale.com/blog/2017/12/nasa-mars-climate-orbiter-metric/*.

- Kevlin Henney's book *97 Things Every Programmer Should Know* (O'Reilly, 2010) has lots of good advice on this general subject and many others. Representing domain concepts in the code is nicely captured by Dan North in Chapter 11, and by Einar Landre in Chapter 65.

- Henney also looks at Value Object, Whole Value, Class Factory Method, and other patterns for values in "Patterns in Java," which applies equally well to C#: *https://www.slideshare.net/Kevlin/value-added-43542768*. Also see his paper "Factory and Disposal Methods: A Complementary and Symmetric Pair of Patterns," from the 2003 VikingPLoP (Pattern Languages of Programs) conference, at *https://www.researchgate.net/publication/238075361*.

- It has long been recognized that keeping objects simple helps in creating programs that are understandable. The single responsibility principle—the *S* in SOLID—is perhaps the most well-known guidance on this: *https://en.wikipedia.org/wiki/SOLID*.

- However, the benefits of separate responsibilities were recognized in the 1970s, if not earlier, when Edsger Dijkstra wrote about separating concerns:

  - "The Effective Arrangement of Logical Systems," *https://www.cs.utexas.edu/users/EWD/transcriptions/EWD05xx/EWD562.html*

  - "On the Role of Scientific Thought," *https://www.cs.utexas.edu/users/EWD/transcriptions/EWD04xx/EWD447.html*

Chapter 2

- The Common Type System is summarized in the following Microsoft documentation:

  - *https://docs.microsoft.com/en-us/dotnet/csharp/programming-guide/types/#the-common-type-system*

  - *https://docs.microsoft.com/en-us/dotnet/standard/base-types/common-type-system*

- The Microsoft documentation for the language rules around struct types is at *https://docs.microsoft.com/en-us/dotnet/csharp/language-reference/language-specification/structs*.

- More information on the behavior of System.Threading.Monitor with respect to lock objects can be found at *https://docs.microsoft.com/en-us/dotnet/api/system.threading.monitor?view=net-6.0#Lock*.

- The specific overload resolution rules regarding optional parameters are explained at *https://docs.microsoft.com/en-us/dotnet/csharp/programming-guide/classes-and-structs/named-and-optional-arguments#overload-resolution*.

- Eric Lippert explains *why* initializers for read-only fields and constructors run in the order they do at *https://docs.microsoft.com/en-gb/archive/blogs/ericlippert/why-do-initializers-run-in-the-opposite-order-as-constructors-part-one*.

- Lippert has written extensively on the subject of value types in C#, including the following:

    - "The Truth About Value Types," *https://docs.microsoft.com/en-gb/archive/blogs/ericlippert/the-truth-about-value-types*

    - "The Stack Is an Implementation Detail, Part One," *https://docs.microsoft.com/en-gb/archive/blogs/ericlippert/the-stack-is-an-implementation-detail-part-one*

    - "The Stack Is an Implementation Detail, Part Two," *https://docs.microsoft.com/en-gb/archive/blogs/ericlippert/the-stack-is-an-implementation-detail-part-two*

- Nullable reference types are documented by Microsoft at *https://docs.microsoft.com/en-us/dotnet/csharp/nullable-references*.

- Additionally, Jon Skeet blogs about his early experiences with nullable reference types at *https://codeblog.jonskeet.uk/2018/04/21/first-steps-with-nullable-reference-types/*.

- Tony Hoare made his famous apology for the `null` reference at the QCon conference in 2009. The abstract is available at *https://qconlondon.com/london-2009/qconlondon.com/london-2009/presentation/Null%2bReferences_%2bThe%2bBillion%2bDollar%2bMistake.html*.

Chapter 3

- The C# Language Specification describes the variable categories at *https://docs.microsoft.com/en-us/dotnet/csharp/language-reference/language-specification/variables*.

- The rules regarding definite assignment are also described in the C# Language Reference at *https://docs.microsoft.com/en-us/dotnet/csharp/language-reference/language-specification/variables#94-definite-assignment*.

- Jon Skeet looks at parameter passing by reference and by value in his blog at *https://jonskeet.uk/csharp/parameters.html*.

- The third edition of *C# in Depth* by Jon Skeet (Manning, 2014) has a detailed analysis of closures in Chapters 5 and 16.

- Closures are not new to C#, but their behavior has changed in some ways; capturing a loop variable is one example. Eric Lippert's blog has a good article on the rationale behind the *old* (pre–C# v5) behavior of capturing loop variables in function objects: *https://ericlippert.com/2009/11/12/closing-over-the-loop-variable-considered-harmful-part-one/*.

- An overview of several C# features for efficient code, including read-only structs and `in` parameters, is at *https://docs.microsoft.com/en-us/dotnet/csharp/write-safe-efficient-code*.

- The C# Programming Guide describes ref returns and ref locals at *https://docs.microsoft.com/en-us/dotnet/csharp/programming-guide/classes-and -structs/ref-returns.*

- Although ref returns and ref locals weren't introduced until C# v7.0, the idea has been around much longer, as Eric Lippert explains at *https://ericlippert.com/2011/06/23/ref-returns-and-ref-locals/.*

- Vladimir Sadov examines the rules around whether a ref local is safe to return at *http://mustoverride.com/safe-to-return/.*

- The operation of the garbage collector is a complex topic, but a good starting point is the Microsoft documentation at *https://docs.microsoft .com/en-us/dotnet/standard/garbage-collection/fundamentals.*

- Andrew Hunter also describes garbage collection in his blog at *https:// www.red-gate.com/simple-talk/development/dotnet-development/understanding -garbage-collection-in-net/.*

- The Microsoft documentation on value tuple support from C# v7.0 onward is at *https://docs.microsoft.com/en-us/dotnet/csharp/language -reference/builtin-types/value-tuples.*

Chapter 4

- Eric Lippert has written extensively about value types and touches on modifying returned values at *https://ericlippert.com/2008/05/14/ mutating-readonly-structs/.*

- Lippert examines the construction of value types and the use of an intermediate temporary instance in this post: *https://ericlippert.com/ 2010/10/11/debunking-another-myth-about-value-types/.*

- The C# Language Specification on object creation can be read online at *https://docs.microsoft.com/en-us/dotnet/csharp/language-reference/ language-specification/expressions#117152-object-creation-expressions.* Object initializers are covered at *https://docs.microsoft.com/en-us/dotnet/csharp/ language-reference/language-specification/expressions#117153-object-initializers.*

- The Microsoft documentation on casts, including a link to user-defined conversion methods, is at *https://docs.microsoft.com/en-us/dotnet/csharp/ programming-guide/types/casting-and-type-conversions#implicit-conversions.*

- Jon Skeet investigates read-only fields in his blog at *https://codeblog .jonskeet.uk/2014/07/16/micro-optimization-the-surprising-inefficiency-of -readonly-fields/.*

- The Microsoft documentation for in parameters (*https://docs.microsoft .com/en-us/dotnet/csharp/language-reference/keywords/in-parameter-modifier*) and ref readonly return values and locals (*https://docs.microsoft.com/en-us/ dotnet/csharp/language-reference/keywords/ref#reference-return-values*) has good information on the caveats and rules for correctly using them.

- Sergey Tepliakov's blog has some enlightening articles on in and ref readonly performance too, at *https://devblogs.microsoft.com/premier-developer/*

the-in-modifier-and-the-readonly-structs-in-c/ and *https://devblogs.microsoft .com/premier-developer/performance-traps-of-ref-locals-and-ref-returns-in-c/.*

- The quote from Donald Knuth is from his ACM Turing Award lecture in 1974. He went on to say—much more famously—that "premature optimization is the root of all evil." The full text is available at *https:// dl.acm.org/doi/10.1145/1283920.1283929.*

Chapter 5

- Eric Lippert's blog post on the subject of null is enlightening: *https:// ericlippert.com/2013/07/25/what-is-the-type-of-the-null-literal/.*

- String interning is documented by Microsoft at *https://docs.microsoft.com/ en-us/dotnet/api/system.string.intern?view=net-5.0.*

- A variety of articles address floating-point representation and the pitfalls that can arise. Frances Buontempo gives an overview with examples and further references for those who want to dig deeper in her *Overload* article "Floating Point Fun and Frolics" at *https://accu.org/ journals/overload/17/91/buontempo_1558.*

- Richard Harris has written extensively about floating-point comparisons and arithmetic. This series of *Overload* articles examines the common alternatives to IEEE-754 floating-point:

    - "You're Going To Have To Think!," *https://accu.org/journals/ overload/18/99/harris_1702*

    - "Why Fixed Point Won't Cure Your Floating Point Blues," *https:// accu.org/journals/overload/18/100/harris_1717*

    - "Why Rationals Won't Cure Your Floating Point Blues," *https://accu .org/journals/overload/19/101/harris_1986*

    - "Why Computer Algebra Won't Cure Your Floating Point Blues," *https://accu.org/journals/overload/19/102/harris_1979*

    - "Why Interval Arithmetic Won't Cure Your Floating Point Blues," *https://accu.org/journals/overload/19/103/harris_1974*

- A comparison of C#'s floating-point types can be found in the Microsoft documentation at *https://docs.microsoft.com/en-us/dotnet/csharp/language -reference/language-specification/types#floating-point-types.*

- The Microsoft documentation gives an overview of the constant pattern at *https://docs.microsoft.com/en-us/dotnet/csharp/language-reference/operators/ patterns#constant-pattern.*

- The declaration pattern is described in the Microsoft documentation at *https://docs.microsoft.com/en-us/dotnet/csharp/language-reference/operators/ patterns#declaration-and-type-patterns.*

- Nullable value type operator overloads are described in the C# Language Specification, which has a short remark about operator==, at *https://docs.microsoft.com/en-us/dotnet/csharp/language-reference/builtin-types/ nullable-value-types#lifted-operators.*

- The C# Language Specification also has a section on nullable reference types at *https://docs.microsoft.com/en-us/dotnet/csharp/language-reference/builtin-types/nullable-reference-types*.

- Lippert has a great series of blogs about nullable value types starting here: *https://ericlippert.com/2012/12/20/nullable-micro-optimizations-part-one/*.

- Lippert examines the concept of lifted operators at *https://docs.microsoft.com/en-us/archive/blogs/ericlippert/what-exactly-does-lifted-mean*.

- *MSDN Magazine* looks at why value tuples aren't immutable at *https://docs.microsoft.com/en-us/archive/msdn-magazine/2018/june/csharp-tuple-trouble-why-csharp-tuples-get-to-break-the-guidelines*.

Chapter 6

- For an in-depth look at value types in modeling complex systems, see Dirk Bäumer et al., "Values in Object Systems," *Ubilab Technical Report*, *https://riehle.org/computer-science/research/1998/ubilab-tr-1998-10-1.pdf*.

- Kevlin Henney covers the taxonomy of object types and offers other valuable insights regarding object comparisons in C++ and C# at *https://www.slideshare.net/Kevlin/objects-of-value*.

- Martin Fowler describes the anemic domain model at *https://www.martinfowler.com/bliki/AnemicDomainModel.html*.

- Fowler describes aliasing an object causing bugs at *https://www.martinfowler.com/bliki/AliasingBug.html*.

- Aliasing is not a new idea, either, as you can see in Eric S. Raymond's The Jargon File: *http://www.catb.org/jargon/html/A/aliasing-bug.html*.

- Scott Stanchfield's article on the perils of using a language that has no concept of pass-by value is quite old and focused on the Java of the era, but still enlightening: *http://www.javadude.com/articles/passbyvalue.htm*.

- The contract for IComparable implementations is described in the Microsoft documentation at *https://docs.microsoft.com/en-us/dotnet/api/system.icomparable-1.compareto?view=net-5.0#notes-to-implementers*.

- Henney looks at some patterns for value types, including symmetry, in this conference paper: *https://www.researchgate.net/publication/244405850_The_Good_the_Bad_and_the_Koyaanisqatsi_Consideration_of_Some_Patterns_for_Value_Objects*.

- Scott Meyers wrote seminal books that will be recognized instantly by C++ programmers everywhere, but he has much to say that's relevant to programmers in any language. In particular, *Effective C++*, 3rd edition (Addison-Wesley, 2005), and *More Effective C++* (Addison-Wesley, 1996) look at making interfaces easy to use correctly and hard to use incorrectly, as well as the benefits of moving functions outside of the class.

- Intransitive or non-transitive dice are a fun way to explore and challenge the idea of less-than and intrinsic ordering; see the Rosetta Code site at *https://rosettacode.org/wiki/Non-transitive_dice*.

Chapter 7

- For the Microsoft Developer Network (MSDN) advice on overriding the `Equals` method for values, see *https://docs.microsoft.com/en-us/dotnet/ csharp/programming-guide/statements-expressions-operators/how-to-define-value -equality-for-a-type*.

- This 2005 *MSDN Magazine* article on the internals of how the CLR manages object instances, although clearly out-of-date now, is still enlightening: *https://docs.microsoft.com/en-us/archive/msdn-magazine/2005/may/ net-framework-internals-how-the-clr-creates-runtime-objects*. For a more recent analysis by Adam Sitnik, see *https://adamsitnik.com/Value-Types-vs-Reference- Types/*.

- For a detailed analysis of the kinds of polymorphism, see "On Understanding Types, Data Abstraction, and Polymorphism" by Luca Cardelli and Peter Wegner in *Computing Surveys, http://lucacardelli.name/Papers/ OnUnderstanding.A4.pdf*.

- For a formal definition of subtyping, see "A Behavioral Notion of Subtyping" by Barbara H. Liskov and Jeannette M. Wing, *ACM Transactions on Programming Languages and Systems, https://dl.acm.org/ doi/10.1145/197320.197383*.

- Eric Lippert discusses the Liskov substitutability principle more generally in a series of articles starting here: *https://ericlippert.com/2015/04/27/ wizards-and-warriors-part-one/*.

- Lippert argues that all equality can be derived simply from a conforming implementation of `CompareTo` at *https://www.informit.com/articles/article .aspx?p=2425867*.

- This article by Kevlin Henney on strings and value types is based on the C++ string, but many of the observations are relevant to C#: *https://www .slideshare.net/Kevlin/highly-strung*.

- The term *seam* is usually attributed to Michael Feathers from his book *Working Effectively with Legacy Code* (Pearson, 2004). The relevant chapter is available online at *https://www.informit.com/articles/article.aspx?p =359417&seqNum=2*.

- Mock objects have been a feature of object-oriented unit testing for a long time, and Wikipedia has a good overview at *https://en.wikipedia.org/ wiki/Mock_object*.

- Gerard Meszaros describes the more general concept of a test double in his book *xUnit Test Patterns* (Addison-Wesley, 2007) and online at *http:// xunitpatterns.com/Test%20Double.html*.

- Henney makes a case against the term *reuse* at *https://kevlinhenney .medium.com/simplicity-before-generality-use-before-reuse-722a8f967eb9*.

- For a summary of C# v8.0 ranges that includes the related specification for a generalized `index` operator, see the Microsoft documentation at *https://docs.microsoft.com/en-us/dotnet/csharp/language-reference/proposals/ csharp-8.0/ranges*.

- The calculation for relative luminance was lifted approximately from the International Telecommunication Union Radiocommunication Sector (ITU-R) recommendation on Wikipedia at *https://en.wikipedia .org/wiki/Luma_(video)*, but it's used in this chapter only to demonstrate implicit conversions.

- C# has a few ways to represent conversions between types. Lippert's description of is and as is at *https://docs.microsoft.com/en-us/archive/ blogs/ericlippert/is-is-as-or-is-as-is* and *https://ericlippert.com/2013/05/30/ what-the-meaning-of-is-is/*.

- These articles by Henney are targeted at C++ programmers, but the principles are broadly applicable in any object-oriented language, including C#: *https://www.slideshare.net/Kevlin/promoting-polymorphism* and *https://www.slideshare.net/Kevlin/substitutability*.

- The rules for overload resolution can be found in the C# Language Specification at *https://docs.microsoft.com/en-us/dotnet/csharp/language -reference/language-specification/expressions#1164-overload-resolution*.

- Jon Skeet has blogged about overloading at *https://csharpindepth.com/ articles/Overloading*.

- Lippert looks at some interesting gotchas with respect to overload resolution at *https://ericlippert.com/2006/04/05/odious-ambiguous-overloads -part-one/* and *https://ericlippert.com/2006/04/06/odious-ambiguous-overloads -part-two/*.

- For a high-level description of record types in C# v9.0, see the Microsoft documentation: *https://docs.microsoft.com/en-us/dotnet/csharp/whats-new/ csharp-9#record-types*.

- Type builders are a variation on the Factory pattern. See Erich Gamma et al., *Design Patterns: Elements of Reusable Object-Oriented Software* (Addison-Wesley, 1995).

- Henney describes mutable companions and other value object patterns in his paper "The Good, the Bad, and the Koyaanisqatsi: Consideration of Some Patterns for Value Objects," from the 2003 VikingPLoP (Pattern Languages of Programs) conference, at *https://www.researchgate.net/ publication/244405850*.

Chapter 8

- One example of an intentionally slow algorithm is the bogosort, which is sometimes used as a simple way to deliberately keep a CPU busy; Wikipedia has details at *https://en.wikipedia.org/wiki/Bogosort*.

- One popular library to benchmark code for performance measurement is BenchmarkDotNet, described at *https://benchmarkdotnet.org*.

- Joe Duffy's blog about performance and optimization is now more than a decade old but still thought-provoking, and the principles remain relevant: *http://joeduffyblog.com/2010/09/06/the-premature-optimization-is -evil-myth/*.

- The Microsoft documentation for the `ValueType` override of `Equals` is at *https://docs.microsoft.com/en-us/dotnet/api/system.valuetype.equals?view =net-6.0.*

- Sergey Tepliakov's blog has a wealth of information on why overriding `Equals` is so important, and some good advice and interesting background on `ValueType.GetHashCode`: *https://devblogs.microsoft.com/premier-developer/ performance-implications-of-default-struct-equality-in-c/.*

- For the .NET 6 implementation of the default `GetHashCode` method, see *https://github.com/dotnet/runtime/blob/release/6.0/src/coreclr/vm/comutilnative .cpp#L1878.*

- The default equality for structs is defined in `ValueType` at *https://github .com/dotnet/runtime/blob/release/6.0/src/coreclr/System.Private.CoreLib/src/ System/ValueType.cs#L21.*

- Niklaus Wirth's documentation for Project Oberon can be found at *https://people.inf.ethz.ch/wirth/ProjectOberon/PO.System.pdf.*

INDEX

passing values by reference, 78–79

reference types vs., 70–71

reference type variables vs., 76–77

side effects and direct effects, 88–92

by-reference returns, 97, 99

by-reference variables (ref locals), 84, 94, 97–102, 104, 123, 133, 270

    defined, 95

    keeping within scope, 97–101

    performance vs. simplicity, 101–102

C

callback delegate, mutating arguments for read-only parameters and, 93–94

cancellation

    defined, 142

    mitigating limitations of, 142–144

ceq instruction, 141, 145–147, 151

    bne instruction vs., 171–172

    efficiency of, 216

Character class, default object hash codes and, 153–154

CI (continuous integration) services, 251

classes, xx, xxiii

    abstract, 36

    records vs., 33, 200–201

    default constructors, 52

    defining, 33

    embedded references, 42

    embedded values, 40

    equality behavior in derived classes, 218–219

    equality comparisons, 149–156

    field assignment, 53

    field initializers, 58

    generics and null, 61, 63

    immutability, 33, 35

    inheritance, 34–35

    iterator blocks, 85–86

    memory allocation, 50

    object initializers, 58–59

    parameterless constructors, 54, 57, 59

    protected members, 35

    sealed, 35

    value equality, 48, 214–218

class factory methods, 22–25, 57

    custom vs. generated behavior, 201–202

    returning types implied by units, 27

    symmetry, 23–24, 196

class invariants

    defined, 9

    discarded, 13–14

    establishing, 194–195

    testing, 9

class keyword, 33, 45

Clone method

    boxing, 115

    of record types, 114, 165

clones (deep copies), 200

Close method, reference semantics and, 75

closures

    by-reference parameters and, 84–85

    defined, 84–85

    looping and iteration, 280–281

code craft, 3

coercion polymorphism, 242–247

    conversions for purpose, 245–247

    conversions for representation, 244–245

    widening vs. narrowing conversions, 244

cohesion, 192–196, 198

    clarifying with symmetry, 196

    eliminating duplication, 193–194

    establishing class invariants, 194–195

collisions of hash table elements, 153

ColorBuilder type, as mutable companion type, 246–247

ColorParser type, generic type constraints and, 235–238

Color type

    ad hoc polymorphism, 239–242

    array elements, 41–42

    boxed values, 44

    classes, 33

    coercion polymorphism, 243–247

Displacement method *(continued)*
　　importance and value of good
　　　names, 2–3
　　named arguments, 4–5
　　refactoring implementation, 9–18
　　value validation, 8–9
DistanceInKm method
　　read-only reference parameters,
　　　92–93
　　user-defined conversions, 122–123
Distance type, refactoring and, 16–18
domain-specific types, 9
double argument, 12, 25
double values
　　custom types vs., 4–5
　　equality comparisons, 141–142,
　　　145, 155, 229

E

embedded values, 40–43
　　array elements, 41–42
　　embedded references, 42–43
　　field and property layout, 43
encapsulation, 6–7, 25–26, 28, 192–196
　　abstracting types, 29
　　clarifying with symmetry, 196
　　cohesion and, 192
　　eliminating duplication, 193–194
　　establishing class invariants,
　　　194–195
　　public interface and, 196–199
　　testing, 9
entities
　　characteristics of, 188–189
　　defined, 184–185
Enumerable class, 262, 282
enum (enumerated types)
　　Common Type System, 45
　　defined, 19
　　itemizing units with, 19–22
EqualityComparer class, 263
　　IEquatable interface and, 164–166
　　performance of, 277–278
equality comparisons, 139–172
　　boxing, 158–161, 163
　　built-in, 140–149
　　classes, 149–156
　　compiler-generated, 165–172

contract, 217
equality behavior in derived
　　classes, 218–219
equivalence vs., 203–205
floating-point numbers, 141–142,
　　144–145
generics, 162–165
records, 165–168
reference-based, 47–48, 146–152,
　　177–178
strings, 148–149
structs, 156–162
transitivity, 155
type safe, 152
type substitution, 220–221
value-based equality for classes,
　　214–218
value semantics vs. reference
　　semantics, 177–181
EqualityContract property, 226–228,
　　247
equals-equals operator. *See* == operator
Equals method, 33, 44, 46, 64, 139–140,
　　150–151
　　boxing values and identity
　　　comparison, 158–159, 161
　　canonical form of, 215–217
　　class equality, 151–152, 155–156
　　compiler-generated equality,
　　　165–166, 172, 277–279
　　copying large instances, 272
　　custom vs. generated behavior, 201
　　equality behavior in derived
　　　classes, 219, 221
　　floating-point values, 145
　　generic variable comparison,
　　　163–164
　　GetHashCode method and, 152–156,
　　　259–261
　　IEquatable interface, 164–165
　　inheriting classes, 218–221
　　inheriting record types, 225–228
　　input and output types of virtual
　　　methods, 223, 225
　　measuring basic performance
　　　with, 253–261
　　measuring cost of copying, 271
　　method overloading, 238–239

generics *(continued)*
    base-class constraint, 162–163
    deduced type parameters, 236–238
    default values, 62–63
    equality comparisons, 162–165
    generic delegates for
        polymorphism, 241–242
    interface constraint, 116–117
    null values, 61–62
    parametric polymorphism, 233–238
    partial deduction of generic
        parameters, 237
get accessor, 32–34, 128
    automatic vs. nonautomatic,
        130–131
    methods for, 120–121
    read-only, 134–135
    symmetry with set accessor, 209
GetAddress method, 99
    returning by reference, 99
get_Current method, 282
GetEnumerator method, 281
GetHashCode method
    collision, 152–153
    defining, 154, 157
    performance, 259–261
    ValueType definition, 156, 259
    where used, 152
get_Speed method, 120–121
GetType method, 118, 166, 216, 227
GetValueOrDefault method, 169
Gravity.Earth constant, replacing
        magic numbers with, 11

H

HashCode class, 154, 259–261
hash codes, 152–156
    collision, 152–153
    creating suitable keys, 154
    distribution, 152–153, 259
    Equals and ValueType.GetHashCode
        methods, 259
    using floating-point numbers as
        keys, 154–15
heap, xxiii–xxiv, 37, 40, 50, 73–74,
        107–108
    boxing, 158–161
    identity, 180

hidden copies, 130, 137
    boxes, 118
    parameter passing, 128
    return values, 124–126
    value type construction, 118

I

IComparable interface, 116–117,
        204–208, 228–229, 231
IComparer interface, 206–207
IEEE-754, 141
identifiers for variables, 37
identity comparison, 145, 148, 276
    boxed values, 158–162
    identity equality vs. value equality,
        47–48, 158–159
identity conversions, 150
IEnumerable interface, 85, 241, 281–282
IEnumerator interface, 281–282
IEqualityComparer interface, 165,
        206–207, 267–268, 271
IEquatable interface
    avoiding boxing, 164
    contract for, 217
    IComparable interface vs., 203–205
    implementing, 164, 215–216
    performance effects, 263–265
if...else statements, 81, 285
IFormattable interface, 161
if statements, 284–285
immutability. *See* mutation and
        immutability
imperative code, 89
implementation inheritance, 213–214
    avoiding, 230–232
    containing instead of inheriting
        types, 231–232
    interface inheritance vs., 213
    upholding a type's contract, 224
implicit conversions, 47, 97, 117, 150
    boxing, 117–118
    by-reference variables, 95–97
    coercion polymorphism, 242–247
    defining, 12–13
    discarded invariants, 13–14
    implicit reference conversion, 150,
        220–221
    primitive obsession, 5

read-only properties vs. immutable types, 109–110

record structs, 34

return type instance modification and mutability, 126–127

structs, 32–33

value semantics vs. reference semantics, 181–182

N

NaN (not a number), 8, 144–145, 195, 256, 285

narrowing conversions, 244

NegativeInfinity method, 145

new keyword and expression, 14, 50–51, 56–57, 110

newobj instruction, 146

NextAppointment method, capturing by-reference parameters and, 85

nonautomatic properties (expression-bodied properties), 130

non-destructive mutation, 60

not a number (NaN), 8, 144–145, 195, 256, 285

not constant pattern, 216

nullable reference types, 52, 64–67, 151, 224

Nullable type, 64, 168–172

nullable value types, 60, 63–64, 168–170

null-coalescing (??) operator, 51, 151–152

null-conditional (?) operator, 52, 151

null-forgiving (!; dammit) operator, 66–67

Nullify method, by-reference parameters for extension methods and, 87

NullReferenceException error, 56

null references, 51–52, 56, 65–67, 146–147, 151, 206, 233–234

comparing reference types with null, 61

comparing value types with null, 61

equality comparisons with classes, 151–152

generics and, 61–62

nullable reference types, 52, 64–67, 151, 224

nullable value types, 60, 63–64, 168–170

null-forgiving operator, 66–67

parameterless constructors, 54

O

object address, 180

object base class

Common Type System, 33, 44–46

default equality, 48, 139, 163, 215–216, 253

generic type parameters, 233

object construction and initialization, 49–60

constructors, 51–57

copying value type instances, 110–115

default initialization, 50–51

field and property initializers, 58

measuring cost of, 273–277

memory allocation, 49–50

object initializers, 7, 58–60

init-only properties, 59

non-destructive mutation, 60

object deconstruction, 102–103

object identity, 180, 185–191

and boxing, 158, 161

hash codes, 153

object-oriented programming (OOP), 183–184, 211

object relationships, 183–191

characteristics of, 185–191

design refinement to model object roles, 191

kinds of objects, 184–185

object roots, 99

OOP. *See* object-oriented programming

op_Equality method, 167, 171–172, 268

operators

arithmetic, 14–15, 121–122, 208–209

lifting, 168–170

nonstandard behavior, 209

operators *(continued)*
    symbolic polymorphism with
        overloaded operators,
        240–241
    using expressions with, 121–123
optimization, 101, 142, 250
    boxing, 118
    mutable by-reference parameters,
        91–92
ordering, comparison for, 203–207
    contract for comparisons, 205–206
    equivalence vs. equality, 204–205
    lexicographical ordering, 206
    ordinal comparisons, 206
output parameters, 79–82, 93, 102
    deconstruction, 102–103
    defined, 70
    definite assignment, 80–81
    object deconstruction, 102
    reference parameters vs., 79
    returning by reference, 100
    selecting operations, 81–82
    Try*XXX* idiom, 79–82
overloading, 16, 152, 238–241
    by-reference parameters, 83–84
    constructors, 53–55
    operators, 14–15, 208–209
    overriding vs., 221
override keyword, 149

P

parameterized types, 237–238
parameterless constructors, 54–59,
    62–63
parameters, 69–103
    aliasing, 74–75
    arguments, 38, 118–120
    boxed, 160–161
    by-reference, 70–71, 76–92, 99,
        102–103
    custom types as, 6
    defining interfaces, 223–224
    formal vs. actual, 38
    generic, 61–62, 162–163, 233–238
    input, 70, 92–93, 127–128, 268–270
    kinds of, 70
    modifiers, 70
    naming, 2–5

non-nullable, 52, 66–67
output, 70, 79–82, 93, 102
overloading constructors, 53
overloading methods, 16
passing, defined, 69–70
read-only, 92–102, 127–128,
    268–270
reference, 70–71, 73–74
ref returns, 92–102
value, 70–73
parametric polymorphism, 233–238
    generic constraints and protocol
        interfaces, 233–236
    generic method parameters and
        type deduction, 236–237
    parameterized types, 237–238
Parse method, TryParse vs., 80
passing arguments
    defined, 69–70
    by reference, 70–71, 77–79
    by value, 70–71, 119–120
pattern matching and selection
    conjunctive pattern, 195
    disjunctive pattern, 195
    is constant pattern, 61, 145,
        194–195
    performance of, 284-286
    relational pattern, 195
    switch expression, 20–21,
        284–286
performance, 249–286
    effect of common idioms and
        practices on, 279–286
    effect of types on, 270–279
    measuring and optimizing,
        250–253
    measuring with Equals, 253–261
    optimizing equality, 261–270
    profilers, 252–253
pessimization, 250
Playlist class
    field initializers, 58
    generic type parameter
        comparisons, 162
    parameterless constructors, 54–55
pointers
    managed, 99
    reference types vs., 74

polymorphism, 211–247
ad hoc, with overloading, 238–242
coercion, using conversions,
242–247
inclusion and subtyping, 222–232
inheritance vs., 211–212
parametric, with generics, 233–238
sealed value types, 212–221
positional records and record structs,
33, 53, 55, 131, 201–203, 273
copying, 114
equality, 165–168, 277–279
inheritance, 225–227
PositiveInfinity method, 145, 285
precision, 142–144
Primitive Obsession code smell, 5
private constructors, 23, 57
procedural code
declarative code vs., 89, 284
defined, 89
Product type
copying large value types, 273–279
optimizing equality comparisons,
261–268
read-only vs. immutable, 107–110
value object role, 186–187
profilers, 252–253
Projectile type, returning by
reference, 131–133
properties
abstract, 36
accessing, 120–121, 265–266
as arguments for read-only
parameters, 127–128
automatic
initializers, 58
memory layout, 43
nonautomatic vs., 130–134
performance of fields vs.,
265–266
by-reference parameters and
property values, 82–83
circular dependency, 43
expression-bodied, 130–131
init-only, 59, 112, 114, 274
mutable immutable, 101
property forwarding, 24
property initializers, 58

read-only. *See* read-only properties
returned reference type instance
modification, 125–126
simplifying, 11–14
value of, 82
protocol interfaces, 231, 233–238
pseudorandom number generator, 254
public interface, encapsulation and,
196–199
composing abstractions, 199
extending interface, 197–198
reducing internal interface,
198–199
Purchase type
copying large value types,
273–280, 282–283
optimizing equality comparisons,
261–269
read-only vs. immutable, 107–112
value object role, 186–187

Q

query syntax form of LINQ (Language-
Integrated Query), 280–281

R

race conditions, 96
Random class, 254
ranges (slices), 235
reachable objects, 99
readonly keyword, 32–34
ref locals, 96
structs, 135–136
read-only properties, 7
as arguments for read-only
parameters, 130
avoiding defensive copies, 135
immutability vs., 109–110
and ref returns, 104
read-only reference parameters, 88,
92–95, 129, 131–132
mutable immutable properties, 101
performance vs. simplicity, 101–102
preventing modifications to data,
95–97
read-only type, 135–136
real number, 144
record keyword, 33, 45

records
    abstract, 36
    copying like value types, 114–115
    defining, 33–34
    equality comparisons, 165–168
    inheritance, 34
    inheriting record types, 225–230
    protected, 35
    sealed, 35
    value semantics, 48
`record struct` keywords, 34
record structs
    defining, 34
    equality comparisons, 165–168
    immutability, 34
    inheritance, 34
    value semantics, 49
refactoring, 9–10, 191
reference equality, 145–148, 178–180,
        275–277
`ReferenceEquals` method, 148–149,
        160–161, 216
reference parameters, 65, 70–71, 73–74,
        79, 239
reference return values. *See* ref returns
reference semantics, 45–48, 176–183,
        199–203
    avoiding pitfalls of default
        variables, 200–201
    Common Type System, 45–46
    copying and equality comparison
        behavior, 177–181
    copying variables, 46–48
    implementing custom vs.
        generated behavior, 201–202
    mechanics vs. semantics, 182–183
    mutability, 181–182
    overriding generated methods,
        202–203
reference types
    array elements, 42
    by-reference parameters vs., 70–71
    classes, 33
    default initialization, 52–53
    identity comparison, 47
    inheritance, 34, 36
    instance lifetime, 37
    instance storage, 40

locks and semantics, 46–47, 180
nullable, 64–66
performance, 274–275
pointers vs., 74
records, 33
return type instance modification,
        123, 125–126
value of, 73–74
value-like performance, 274–277
value types vs., xx, 31, 70–71, 123–126,
        176–181, 212–213, 273–277
reference variables
    aliasing and, 74–75, 88, 96,
        107–110, 125, 178–180
    boxing and unboxing, 44
    by-reference parameters vs., 76–77
    defensive copies, 131–132
    equality comparisons, 145–148, 177
    fields of value types, 107–110
    instance storage, 42
    non-nullable reference variables,
        64–65
    passing by reference, 77–78
    reference storage, 37
    scope, 37
    value of, 39
referential transparency, 180
reflection, 49, 156, 257–258
ref locals, 95–96, 132–134. *See also*
        by-reference variables
`ref` parameter modifier, 76–78, 80,
        82–88
    defined, 70–71
    passing by reference, 77
    property value arguments for,
        127–128
    returning by reference, 94–97
`ref readonly` locals (local read-only
        reference variables), 96,
        132–134
ref returns (reference return values), 92
    keeping by-reference variables
        within scope, 97–101
    performance vs. simplicity,
        101–102
    preventing modifications to data,
        95–97
    returning values by reference, 94–95

ValueTuple type, 170, 172
ValueType class
    Common Type System, 45–46, 211
    copying and identity, 48–49, 177–8
    default equality, 156–159, 163, 165,
        253–260
value types
    advantages of, xxiii–xxiv
    arithmetic, 14–15
    avoiding defensive copies, 135–136
    construction, 52–53, 112–113
    copying, 110–115
    defensive copies, 129–130
    embedded fields, 43
    identity comparison, 47
    inheritance, 36
    initialization, 56–57
    instance fields of, 98
    instance lifetime, 36–37
    instance storage, 39
    nullable, 63–64
    parameters and, 71–73
    passing variables by reference,
        78–79
    polymorphism, 211–247
    record structs, 34
    reference types vs., xx, 31, 70–71,
        123–126, 176–181, 212–213,
        273–277
    return type instance modification,
        123–124
    sealed, 35, 212–221
    semantics, 45–48
    size of instances, 91–92, 136,
        270–274
    structs, 33
variables, 37–39. *See also* array variables;
        by-reference variables; local
        variables; parameters;
        reference variables
    associated types, 38

avoiding pitfalls of default
        variables, 200–201
    capturing, 84–85
    copy-by-value semantics, 73–74
    copying, 46–48
    defined, 37
    definite assignment, 39
    embedded, 40–43
    identifiers, 37
    kinds of, 37–38
    lifetime of, 36–37, 131–132
    read-only, 134–136
    values vs., 38–39, 82, 123–127
Velocity type
    abstraction, 17, 28–29, 199
    by-reference parameter
        limitations, 82
    non-destructive mutation, 90–91
    perils of mutable value types,
        126–127
    property methods, 120–123
virtual dispatch, 212, 228
virtual methods, 34, 36, 118
vocabulary, 191–192, 199
Volume type, implementation
        inheritance and, 228–230

W

Where method, 85, 281
whole numbers, 140–141
widening conversions, 244
with keyword, 60, 90–91, 114–115
WithPercentAdded method, 197–198
WriteLine method, 118

Y

yield statement, 85–86

Z

ZeroKelvin constant, using for
        validation, 285

The C# Type System is set in New Baskerville, Futura, Dogma, TheSansMono Condensed, and Architect's Daughter.

RESOURCES

Visit *https://nostarch.com/c-type-system* for errata and more information.

Never before has the world relied so heavily on the Internet to stay connected and informed. That makes the Electronic Frontier Foundation's mission—to ensure that technology supports freedom, justice, and innovation for all people—more urgent than ever.

For over 30 years, EFF has fought for tech users through activism, in the courts, and by developing software to overcome obstacles to your privacy, security, and free expression. This dedication empowers all of us through darkness. With your help we can navigate toward a brighter digital future.